An Invasion of (corporate) Locust

Critical Dangers in the Lack of Consumer Information Privacy

What We All Need To Know and Understand About
The Secrets of Computer Systems Automation, Information, and
Privacy

First Edition

Written By
Darlene R. Miles

First Edition

Library of Congress Cataloging in Publication Data
LCCN 2007938159
ISBN 978-0-9799788-0-7 0-9799788-0-7

Darlene R. Miles

An Invasion of (corporate) Locust

Mondar Media and Publishing LLC

'An Invasion of (corporate) Locust' by Darlene R. Miles

This page intentionally left blank

*For **Monique,***
You are the air that I breathe.
Love Mom

Acknowledgements

First and most important, I would like to thank my daughter Monique A. Miles for your support and patience during my writing project. I truly thank you for listening to my details, over and over, and over again - as though it was new information each time☺. I also thank you for your talents in marketing and graphics. Not only are you my daughter but your business intuition is impeccable.

I love you and I appreciate you – mom.

To Angelo S. Pullen of SUREFire Communication, you have the patience of *Job*. Thank you for your contributions in web design and to my book cover. I look forwarded to working with you into the future.

A Special Thank you to my family who has supported me throughout my writing project; Terry, Darnelle, and Craig – I thank you all for your prayers and continued positive words and encouragement.

Darlene

Content

'An Invasion of (corporate) Locust' by Darlene R. Miles

'An Invasion of (corporate) Locust' by Darlene R. Miles

'An Invasion of (corporate) Locust' by Darlene R. Miles

'An Invasion of (corporate) Locust' by Darlene R. Miles

'An Invasion of (corporate) Locust' by Darlene R. Miles

'An Invasion of (corporate) Locust' by Darlene R. Miles

'An Invasion of (corporate) Locust' by Darlene R. Miles

xiv

'This great book will become an essential tool for 21st Century living.'

Samuel E. Tidmore IV
President/CEO
The Village TV

'This book is very detailed on its subject matter, and should serve as a reference book in every home. The book is written to guide the layperson against corporate intrusion into their personal and financial information. Every consumer will find this book to be extremely beneficial as a reference guide for life. There is information for everyone. I heartily recommend **'An Invasion of (corporate) Locust'** to all.'

Kwaku Obosu-Mensa Ph.D.

'An Invasion of (corporate) Locust' by Darlene R. Miles

An Invasion of (corporate) Locust

Chapter I – Introduction

Just as Americans move to become more 'Green' in hopes of preserving the quality of life here on earth, the impact of consumer information theft is as dangerous. Everyone loses due to these invasions on consumer privacy, both consumers and corporations. However, the impact is felt most greatly by the average consumer trying to live, work and save for a future, while corporations continue to map out 'hidden' ways to capture and resell consumer information. These invasions are not limited to just the capture and resell of consumer information it also includes ill-developed automated systems and business practices that steal millions from consumers.

The impact of consumer information theft by way of the various forms that I have detailed in my book has created a negative impact to the financial well-being of everyone. From banking systems failures to background information integrity, to financial information theft, to the loss of consumer information privacy - the invasions continue and the cost of privacy increases. Corporations and their behaviors help to fuel this flame of increased cost of privacy and the greatest cost falls on the consumer. The cost to consumers to regain and restore their loss of privacy when corporate systems are hacked and consumer personal information is stolen and sold to data brokers is extreme.

What is now of greatest cost to consumers is the loss of personal information that is caused by our day-to-day 'business relationships' with corporate America. Consumer information continues to be captured, passed on, or sold by way of these so-called 'corporate developed relationships' to a point that when consumer information is stolen the consumer has no idea how these 'so-called' developed relationships ever occurred.
What has happened to this world that we live in? For those who may have lived long enough to have experienced a time in life where we as humans and (now identified as 'consumers') could live in a town, go to bed at night and not worry if the doors to your

homes were locked. To worry about identity theft was unconceivable. Now we have to worry about who is capturing or stealing our personal information, when is it being captured or stolen, and where is our information being transferred after this capture or theft. Yes, theft.

As a Consultant and Consumer, I have become quite concerned with the level of consumer personal and financial information invasions. Invasions occurring by way of consumer systems automation, consumer information sharing, the true lack of consumer information protection, and other business practices that are dangerous to the personal and financial lives of consumers. Because of these concerns, I have chosen to share my fifteen plus years of knowledge, expertise, and experiences with these systems, business practices and the impact to the lives of consumers.

In 2006, the Fair Trade Commission's (FTC), Consumer Sentinel, the database developed by the FTC, received over 670,000 consumer complaints of Identity Theft. The percentage breakdown was 36% identity theft complaints, which equates to 246,035 consumer complaints and 64% of the remaining complaints, were related to other forms consumer fraud. These consumer losses totaled more than *$1.1 billion*.

Since 2004 consumer information misuse and (corporate) identity theft has increased to epidemic proportion. The consumer financial losses are reaching into the billions of dollars. The FTC launched this database in 1997, and has recorded over 3.5 million consumer complaints through the year 2006.

The invasion of (corporate) locust has become dangerous to the lives of consumers. This invasion of locust does not come from the sky, or from the ground, nor the trees, and it's not after your fall harvest. This invasion comes from your computer, your bank, your finance company, your grocer, your retail stores, your courtroom, your insurance companies, and at times, your employer – and it's after that most priceless crop of all: your personal, medical and financial information.

'An Invasion of (corporate) Locust' by Darlene R. Miles

2

These locusts are not bugs or aliens or even strangers. These locusts are unauthorized access to your personal information (invasions), made without your consent or knowledge. Corporations are invading, storing, and reselling critically dangerous levels of consumer information everyday. Our personal information is being captured, traded, and sold, or simply given away by unscrupulous companies, who we conduct business with each day.

Information used that consumers are not aware of regarding; consumer's credit, medical records information, background information, spending habits, internet behaviors, and family personal and historical information among other factors.

With high levels of documented consumer identity theft in the areas of personal, financial, and medical records information, which also included internet and home computer information theft, I have compiled a 'first-of-its-kind' consumer definitive reference guide of critical identity theft 'prevention and protection' information. Critical information that will provide the systematic process that we can implement, to begin protecting our information from corporate invasion.

What consumer do not know or understand is the process in which personal, financial, and medical records information is being invaded and utilized by corporations nearly every minute of the day. The process of unauthorized invasions, the capture, storing and re-selling of consumer information by corporations has resulted in an increase of consumer information and identity theft.

The invasions onto a consumer's personal and financial information has reached epidemic proportion, and these invasions must stop. Invasions from corporations that we consumers chose to conduct business with each day. These invasions also include the consumer reporting agencies that continue to provide and report unauthorized consumer information to their clients. These corporate invasions are out of control.

'An Invasion of (corporate) Locust' by Darlene R. Miles

There was a time in history where a person could trust a handshake when conducting business or rely on information produced from a computer system; well that time no longer exists. Most consumer-automated systems are not reliable and at times flawed and 'self-help' consumer information is not always readily available. As for the 'handshake' to complete a business deal, it just does not have the same meaning as it did with our parents.

Unfortunately, there is currently so much 'corporate' consumer deception. Deception occurring when consumers are seeking financing, insurance or employment and promotion, or simply when attempting to obtain a mortgage interest rate that will not drive them into a future foreclosure. Deception by insurance companies when consumers are attempting to obtain insurance and do not understand the factors or information that is being used against them. Continued deception by corporations when a consumer is informed that they have negative information in a background check - when they truly do not, and no one is willing to provide the guidance or assistance in the removal or repair of that negative information.

Deception continues when consumers cannot rely on the courts to effectively remove, expunge, or seal negative information when the removal or Expungement is granted by the courts.

Most consumers encounter these types of situations and have nowhere to turn for help or understand what factors were used against them that resulted in a negative outcome. Most of these (corporate) deceptions begin with the unauthorized invasions into a consumer's personal, financial, and medical information. The authorizations that are now being used by corporations go beyond any 'stated written' authorizations granted by a consumer. These invasions affect us all, from top executives to college students, and are not publicly known to consumers.

Consumers are not aware of the *use* of these additional factors that corporations are now utilizing to determine consumer-worthiness, such factors as 'consumer risk-based analysis and what this means to a consumer. *As a consumer advocate, I find this use of consumer information to be the most dangerous use of unauthorized information in the history of humankind.*

What is most important to consumers is that your personal, financial, and medical information does not have to be at risk any longer.

What I have compiled in my book is a definitive 'self-help' reference of critical consumer information on these corporate 'secrets' and much more in my book, *'An Invasion of (corporate) Locust'*.

I not only detail for the consumer, what these factors consist of, I also document which industries are now utilizing this approach to consumer analysis. With 20 years of expertise in consumer systems automation and consumer data acquisitions, I also discuss the qualities of the consumer information that corporations are compiling and the dangers of its use. Corporations and consumers will find this information to be quite riveting.

In my role as an Information Systems Consultant and former Director of Operations, I have had experience working on various project teams in the development of several consumer-automated systems. This exposure is not limited to the development of these various systems but also includes the business practices and privacy laws surrounding these systems. While not all systems negatively affect the lives of consumers there are many automated systems that do. These negative affects are sometimes the results of poor system design while other automated systems are designed to invade the privacy of consumers. The 'invasive' systems and 'invasive' corporate business practices are the systems and practices that I am addressing throughout my book.

My exposure to consumer systems information and consumer privacy laws is not limited to the field of Information Systems Technology, but includes the development of web-based Consumer

Information and Background Reporting Systems, also known as CRA's. Additional systems and business practices addressed are in the insurance industry and various insurance automated systems, court automated systems, computer automated patient records systems, banking systems, mortgage systems and of course the privacy laws that surround these systems.

My book is designed to provide information *'in plain English'* to consumers about some of the most critical dangers in the lack of consumer information privacy. In addition I provide consumers with information on how to identify these affects, report violators and when moving forward, how to protect your personal information. While addressing various automated systems of concern, I am also addressing some positive corporate consumer business processes that will be guaranteed to save consumer time and money.

I have also included documented processes that will allow consumers, through several systematic processes to take control of various areas of their lives. I am addressing several life situations where consumers may have had a feeling of hopelessness, or just ran into a brick wall while attempting to gain resolution. Such topics as:

- ***How to Prevent (corporate) Consumer Identity Theft***
- ***How to Remove Negative Background Information***
- ***What You Need To Know About Your Insurance Company and Insurance Policy Writing***
- ***Banking Systems Automation and What You Should Know About Your Check Transaction, Credit and Debit Card Usage***
- ***What your Financial Institutions Know about You, Your Family and Associates***
- ***Automated Billing Systems and What You Should Know***
- ***Protecting Your Medical Information and What Is Shared About Consumers***
- ***How to Utilize Privacy Laws and Acts to Repair Your***

Own Credit Information
- *College Students – Protecting Your Information, What You Should Know*

As a former Director or Operations of a consumer reporting agency and background checking company, I had an opportunity to experience the true definition of the consumer's lack of privacy. I became appalled by the levels of consumer information that exist out in the *ozone* and how that information is so freely bought and sold, be it accurate or inaccurate. The experience increased my passion to help protect consumer information. While 'mastering' the industry I grew to understand the privacy laws that surround consumer privacy and web-based automated exchange of information. In addition, I had an opportunity to experience the various levels of consumer (background) information that companies and corporations request for employment purposes, financial investigations, residential and commercial leasing and for a host of other purposes.

In my book, I also address the various privacy laws and government regulations that I have had exposure to while working as a consultant on the development of various software application. Regulations or Acts such as; SOX (Sarbanes Oxley Act) resulting from various corporate debacles such as WorldCom, Enron and Adelphia. The U.S. Patriot Act resulting from the various attempts on the lives of Americans, HIPAA (Health Information Portability Act) was implemented to provide privacy of consumer's health and claims information, and DPPA (Drivers Privacy Protection Act) among others. I address how those Acts or Laws have influenced the development of consumer-automated systems and the sharing and accessing of consumer information. In addition, most importantly, I address how these Laws and Acts are now being used against consumers.

In addressing the various systems, I also address the various industries that utilize these sometime ill systems and their unscrupulous business behaviors. I not only provide consumers with pertinent information on consumer automated systems, information and privacy - and their affects on the lives of consumers, I also share some of my personal (consumer) and professional experiences that will help consumers with one of the most critical financial impacts to your life – mortgage financing and buying a home!

I am confident that my book will help consumers avoid some of the pit-falls of life that result from an 'automated' and 'lack of privacy' world.

Chapter 2 - About the Author

As a Consumer Advocate, Technology Manager, and Information Technology Systems Consultant with twenty years of experience, I have tried to be a perpetual student. I have never passed an opportunity to learn. I have always worked to gain as much knowledge that I could about every aspect of software development and the various systems that affect the lives of consumers. This pursuit of knowledge includes gaining a sound understanding of the qualities, now known in the Information Technology world as 'Best Practices'. These 'Best Practices' should always be implemented to assure software application developments accuracy, and they are sometimes not.

I have always tried to be pragmatic in my approach, having the ability to question and probe deeper to resolve a problem, to search for the facts while concentrating on a good solution and making the right decisions objectively. As a Technology Manager and Consultant, engaged by my clients to implement software developments process improvement, I have always had to look outside of the scope of my respective areas of responsibility to gain knowledge and understanding of the true impact of any software application change. What I have seen over the years, and as time has progressed from the late 1980's to now, is that - not much have changed. There are still 'bad practices' in place where software development is involved resulting in most cases, in poor systems coding of consumer software applications. Yes, technology has progressed but the habits of most IT Project teams have not. Most businesses are still in a hurry to develop and deploy new applications or application enhancements; most developers are still not effective in developing and testing applications quickly before moving through additional code testing phases. Software application testing does not always have the importance that it should and 'software development' project requirements are consistently changing during development, and so on.

Just imagine trying to assemble a model car and someone continues to send you new parts as you have nearly completed the gluing of several critical pieces…it is the same concept when developing software applications. At some point, you have to stop changing what is to be built and build what you have. This is a major problem in the software development world. Changing pieces, not enough time to validate those changes (in most cases), resulting in defective systems being forced into the lives of consumers. Have you ever wonder why you could not access your on-line banking information or why your telephone or cable bill amounts changed so drastically, or why your email or calendar stored to a wireless handheld 'synced' device was deleted in error from the company's server? One reason is those poorly *designed consumer application systems changes, and lack of structured controls in place as these code changes are being implemented and released for use.*

One of my greatest concerns as a consumer and IT Consultant has also been the lack of consumer privacy in systems automation and the use of our 'personal and private', and what corporations call 'public' information. I do not feel that any consumer's personal, financial or medical information should ever be considered as public information. Unfortunately, corporations are now sharing and brokering consumer information as though it is public information, and this invasive practice is wrong. There is no other way to put it…It's wrong.

My industry experience consists of various business disciplines, disciplines that include the development, implementation, and process improvement of banking systems, mortgage systems, and web-based consumer background information systems. I am licensed in insurance (property, casualty and life and health) and has years of experience in insurance systems automation and insurance sales and marketing systems. As an IT consultant, I have years of experience in insurance health claims and billing systems, mortgage financing systems, and various court automated systems. The expertise in court systems includes the development and court implementations of traffic-criminal and civil court case processing systems. Additional expertise includes computer-based patient and provider medical records systems, driving records systems – (DMV or BMV) Bureau of Motor Vehicles Reporting, and State Superior and Supreme Court Reporting. As a former Director of Operations, I developed relationships with most states throughout the United States, Canada, and Mexico for consumer data acquisition and access to consumer information for a consumer-reporting agency. This relationship included the access and acquisition of consumer credit information, driving records information, and nearly every level of the courts, within a state for access to their consumer court case information. In addition, and as a consultant I have had consulting, project management and software quality assurance management, and client implementations of a host of non-consumer systems. Automated systems such as, manufacturing (Metal Stamping and Screw Machine Industry), distribution, raw steel manufacturing, automotive parts manufacturing, and various automated accounting systems, amongst others.

Being licensed in insurance and a former agent, I address the automated systems that were utilized for insurance quoting, and how those systems affect the lives of consumers (both negative and positive affects). With several years experience with mortgage financing systems and the mortgage industry, I share some of the 'secrets' of the mortgage financing industry. These secrets include how consumers can obtain the best mortgage finance rates.

As a Director of Operations of a consumer-reporting agency, our company developed web-based automated systems that provided consumer background information to clients. I feel the information surrounding consumer reporting agencies is extremely important information and must be shared with consumers. Information provided to our clients consisted of consumer (background) information, criminal and traffic court records checks, credit information, and driving records information for all fifty states including Canada and Mexico. In addition, we supplied arrest and civil court information for all fifty states. Other consumer information included, credit bureau reporting, employment verification, education verifications, social security information validations (SSN Fraud Usage), and comprehensive background checks *(which included more consumer information than anyone should ever need or have access to).*

The client base consisted of residential and property management clients (rentals and leasing), banking (consumer financing, new account opening and fraud prevention), media representatives, investigators, employers, employment recruiters, data-brokers and other data-resellers along with various 'other' types of clients. With additional expertise and experience in the development of 'computer based (patient) medical records' systems, I provide riveting consumer information about the quality of automated patient medical records systems, medical coding, and medical billing systems.

I have had many consumers ask questions about the various business systems applications that I have had exposure to over the years. Various consumers with a need to understand how these systems actually work, can they be trusted, *and if not, how would they affect our lives?* Since I have had some of the same consumer experiences (negative and positive) with some of these systems, I provide those answers in this book.

Being involved in systems automation since the 1980's, I have had a wealth of experience working with systems automation at all levels. In the role of Director of Operations for the consumer background checking company (also known as a consumer reporting agency), I managed teams of researchers, and client service representatives who supported our clients in obtaining consumer background information. I also managed the testing of newly developed web-based applications, documented user and employee training documentation, and more. Your observation is correct; I wore many hats in this position since the company was (initially) a small privately owned consumer information reporting company.

My research staff had the primary responsibility of performing research of new consumer background information, and to validate (when required) existing background information obtained by our company. The consumer information was released via a web-based application to clients, in most cases, instantly unless data was not stored on our servers. Some of the consumer information was retrieved directly from the supplier, data-broker or vendor site, while other consumer information was historically stored with very little updates applied. Since some form or new data was received almost on a daily basis, my client service and research representatives were tasked with the responsibility of checking our internal database for new or updated information. Additional responsibility involved the continued contact with various sources or suppliers of consumer information throughout the United States, Mexico, and Canada. What was most interesting about this process was the quality of consumer information that bounces back and forth from supplier to reseller, and then to the client - I will talk about this process in more detail in later chapters on Background Information and its quality.

Our services were not limited to just supplying consumer background information on driving records, convictions (criminal), civil judgments, consumer credit reports, employment and education verification, it also included social security number verification and comprehensive background checks on anyone that the 'contractual client' provided a *fiduciary* reason for their request. Our clients were located in all fifty states.

My staff became very good at consumer information research. The company became so good at research, that we could find anyone, anywhere in the United States and within minutes. In addition, when required, we could utilize a vendor supplied consumer comprehensive report for a broader scope of consumer historical and current information. This report was widely used to locate consumers for clients who leased million-dollar heavy equipment but 'forgot' to return the equipment. The comprehensive report was an excellent 'skip tracing' tool. Due to the comprehensive level of information contained in this report, the report was also used by some investigative agencies. This report is currently being used by, and sold to almost anyone by the same vendor (data-broker) and supplier of consumer information.

A comprehensive background report would include a consumers 'extremely' detailed level of personal and financial information. Information such as, the consumers name or alias names, employment history, social security number history, and date issued. Additional information consisted of the consumers residence history, and property/parcel detail of all property owned. The detail goes further to include the spouses detailed information, any alias names, other family members and their alias names, which also includes their dates of birth and SSN numbers. This report also included anyone else living at the consumers residence and their personal and financial information. This report also includes all vehicles owned, and when or where the vehicle(s) were licensed by anyone of that residence. The report also lists property owned anywhere in the United States, and any professional licensing granted. For consumer drivers' license information, the report includes the driver's license number history and driver's record history for everyone located at the residence. The report also includes criminal and civil records check information. Now this is where the report becomes even stranger and more ridiculously invasive, the report also includes the consumers' neighbors' information. Neighbors located on both sides of their primary residence, the family members of those neighbors (and why exactly was this information supplied in such detail or required as part of this report?). In addition, the report also provided the dates of birth of each neighbor's household members, their social security numbers, family spouses and children, and much more.

Sadly, and from a consumer privacy prospective - all you had to do was connect to this vendor's site to obtain this information in one solid report in minutes, *unbelievable*. This report was also resold to our clients by our office. This report was to me the most invasive report in the world into the life of a consumer. *This type of background report is currently being used by several companies and employers, and in most cases scrupulously.* I will talk more about this 'comprehensive background' report in later chapters.

My Approach to Writing This Book

My approach is to provide information for consumers *'In Plain English'* and definitively. My objective is to share my knowledge and experiences, and provide information that will help consumers understand the level of information invasions that exist in the various consumer (systems) and business practices that I address throughout my book. I identify how these various systems and business practices are being utilized to invade consumer information and what the ill affects are to the lives of consumers. I also address how consumers can identify these invasive behaviors, report violations and how to protect personal information into the future.

My book is written and structured so that each topic or issue, along with the solution, or cost-saving strategy will be addressed on a per chapter basis.

Why Write about Consumer Automated Systems, Consumer Information and Consumer Privacy

As a consumer and IT Consultant, I have become appalled with the levels of privacy invasion, privacy violations, identity theft, and corporate lack of concern about consumer information protection that exist today. As systems technology progresses the ability for consumer information theft is increasing, and this theft is costing millions each year. Why would you say it has increased? The increase is due to the lack of concern in protecting consumer information, and the world of consumer information brokering, sharing, and reselling. Consumer information is being sold as fast as water flows over the Niagara Falls and that is quite rapid. In addition, consumer information is being captured in every form possible but not protected after that capture. When I say 'captured', I refer to every bank check written, every credit or debit card used, every phone call to a customer service representative, every time we access the Internet and more.

Over the years I have had clients, colleagues, staff, family and friends ask questions about most, if not all of the areas I have now written about in my book. Be it a client, professional, executive, stay-at-home mom or dad, college student or an individual just seeking employment, we have all been impacted at one point or another in our lives by these various topics that I have chosen to write about.

What I have tried to accomplish in my book is to address some of the most critical areas of our lives that are impacted by corporate intrusion and systems automation. Systems automation that can at times be flawed, or designed to negatively affect us all as consumers.

My hope is that my book will educate consumers about these systems while providing the systematic steps for consumers to implement in protecting their personal, financial and medical records information into the future. In addition, my hope is that my book will trigger some form of revisions to consumer privacy laws, and increase the penalties for consumer information abuse and unauthorized invasions. Unfortunately, the abuse of consumer information by corporations does continue to increase and at all levels. *What is most important is that you will find that your information does not have to be at risk anymore.*

What I have chosen to do is to share information that I know will make a difference in the lives of consumers and will not only be informative, but will definitely make a positive impact. I know that my book will save consumers time, money and lessen some of life's aggravation.

I have gained a wealth of knowledge over the years with these goals in mind; I never forget in difficult times to put God first, to project Excellence and Perfection in what ever I have touched, and to be Humble, and Thankful...

I am confident that consumers will find this book to be one of your best investments. Knowledge is truly Power!

Chapter 3 - The System Automated Process

I have had a multitude of roles over the years on software development projects, from Director of Operations to Project Manager overseeing all aspects of a project, to Project and Software Quality Assurance Manager. In all of these roles your challenges are generally the same - not enough time, money (budget), resources or the Business Lines (project sponsors) do not have the understanding that the software specifications should be baselined at one point in the project. Like, before coding begins??? (Just a little humor here.) *(Baseline; to make a decision and stick to it on what is to be created or developed, not continue to change ideas, or concepts, during software development, etc.)*

What I have always enjoyed is the process of driving out the requirements for a software development project. Documenting the process or steps and tasks, on what needs to be performed, the impact of the system change to other areas or infrastructures, the estimated timelines to completion, and the user or customer impact of what is to be design. I have never strayed too far from the drafting of the test strategies either. Where there appears to be constant failure, is in the change in design during development with little time increased on the development phase of the project. *This failure is generally when problems begin with the quality of software applications.*

In no way am I indicating that all automated systems are all poorly designed or written (developed), Ahhhh No? Software project teams can only work with what they are given in specifications and designs (what is to be built), time (what is the estimated time required to build this application), budgets (what is the estimated cost to complete the application) and resources (do I have a qualified team to build the application). What I am indicating throughout my book is that humans and corporations make mistakes during system development. Some mistakes deliberate and some mistakes not. I am also indicating that any consumer information or documentation received from an automated system should be validated for its accuracy, in some way. As a Consultant, in whatever capacity or role that I played on a project team it would be said that I was very detailed and accurate in my delivery of information. It would also be said that I cared about the quality of the developed 'end product' - but I am only one person.

A major concern that I have had is an issue with the handling and lack of security of consumer information within the life of these automated systems. I found that consumer's information was at most times, at risk. The government enacts and passes laws to protect consumer information but consumer information is not being protected. I have seen the use of private medical records used for testing and development of a new computer based patient records systems when those medical records should not have been utilized for that purpose. There are laws that govern how a patient's medical information can be used, or viewed, with or without authorization. Sadly, most IT vendors do not care how consumers personal information is used, handled, protected, viewed, and or printed on hard copy during the development of new automated software system. And keep in mind, a vendor can not have access to any consumer information for the use of development or testing software applications without obtaining it directly from the client, be it a hospital, bank or any other type of client, the practice of using 'live' un-sanitized consumer information for development and testing of new systems applications continues today. Right now, today in 2007 you can purchase a consumer medical records from a supplier of background and consumer information. This is reckless and ridiculous behavior. No one should ever have access to consumer's medical records without the consumer's direct written authorization.

What project teams and corporations fail to realize is, just as development and project teams have access to a client's database of consumer personal, medical and financial information, someone, somewhere has access to theirs?

'An Invasion of (corporate) Locust' by Darlene R. Miles

Chapter 4 - Consumer Privacy Laws – Personal, Credit, Health and Online Information…Understanding Your Legal Rights and How to Protect Your Information

There are no true Laws or Acts to protect all consumer information and consumer privacy. Even though the various National Laws and Privacy Acts were enacted over the last ten or so years, companies still continue to invade, share, resell and store (house) consumers information in a multitude of databases or automated systems that are used to broker consumers information everyday.

Due to one newly enforced Consumer Privacy Acts, companies are required each year to mail consumers a document outlining their internal and external privacy practices. Generally we consumers by-pass that document, not read it, file it or throw it away. The document is a yearly document and generally requires that you either Opt-Out' of the companies 'sharing, trading or selling' of your personal information' (since this is truly what it is), or authorize the company to sell, trade and share your information when we consumers do not respond by mailing back the 'Opt-Out' document.

Most companies hide their practices of sharing and selling of consumer information by stating that they only share your information with other divisions of their corporation or only with corporate partnerships of their company. What the heck does that mean? We grant that 'open-end' selling authorization to companies when we do not 'Opt-Out' by completing and returning that yearly document. After all, why allow companies to make money on your personal and or purchasing (consumer habits) information. Why allow your personal information to be placed out into the 'ozone of information Hell'. Don't do it. Complete and mail those 'Opt-Out' statements, back to the respective companies. Mailing the 'Opt-Out' statements back will also decrease the number of junk mail items sent to your home.

Currently the Gramm-Leach-Billery Act is designed to protect a consumer's financial information that is collected, used, and shared online. The Children's Online Privacy Act was enacted to protect the online privacy of children when online. Federal and State laws do offer some form of protection for various kinds of consumer personal information that is collected about consumers. However, online companies continue through their 'systems automation' processes to collect, and compile, and share consumer's online information. Now in an age of computer technology and a greater use of the Internet by consumers, companies now capture and store whatever types of information they chose on all consumers.

Since the Fair Trade Commission has moved to educate companies and consumers on privacy laws and the assessment of penalties when infractions occur, we as consumers must be more diligent in our reporting of violations. In addition, and at the national level, Congress has enacted some privacy laws. Therefore, you can see from the list to follow that you have privacy rights for specific kinds of information, information maintained about you in the Health Care System, your Credit Information, and your Driving Records information. However, as you will see throughout my book and chapters to come, companies abuse these laws every day. What I feel needs to occur is consumers must begin to report all incidents of violations, and the assessment of penalties for violations should be much greater.

In the chapters to come I will help consumers understand how to immediately recognize violations when they occur and how to apply these consumer laws when reporting violations. I will also help you to understand how penalties are assessed when violations against consumer information occur, *but most important* – I will identify various steps for consumers to put in place to protect your information into the future.

Here are some important Privacy Acts and Laws that consumers should gain a better understand:

'An Invasion of (corporate) Locust' by Darlene R. Miles

- The Fair Credit Reporting Act (1970)
- Credit Repair Organization Act
- Financial Modernization Act (Gramm-Leach-Bliley Act) (2000)
- Privacy Act of 1974
- Health Insurance Portability and Accountability Act of 1996
- Driver's Privacy Protection Act of 1994
- Right to Financial Privacy Act (1978)
- Family Education Rights and Privacy Act (1974)
- Children's Online Privacy Protection Act (COPPA) of 1998
- Privacy Protection Act of 1980
- Cable Communications Policy Act of 1984
- Electronic Communications Privacy Act (1986)
- Video Privacy Protection Act of 1988
- Telephone Consumer Protection Act of 1991
- Communications Assistance for Law Enforcement Act of 1994
- Telecommunications Act of 1996

Legal protection for privacy does vary from state to state. While Congress may have enacted National laws, some states are taking it upon themselves to enact their own laws to protect consumers. For your states consumer protection laws, you should contact your states Attorney Generals office or website.

Necessary Steps to Increase Your Online Privacy

In a world of increased systems automation, various corporations, hackers and the federal government is constantly capturing consumer information while consumers are logged on the Internet.

Obviously, there is nothing we consumers can do about information that is being captured by the federal government while on the Internet. We can however put the necessary steps in place to block some Internet hackers and the various invasions by online marketing companies and individuals, who capture (steal) our personal or financial information while on the Internet. The corporate capture or stealing of consumer information for the purpose of analyzing consumer habits, the sharing of consumer information, or the re-selling to other companies. All of this is occurring every time a consumer logs on to the Internet. A very important step to implement with your personal computer is to first remove, by deleting - all *Temporary (Internet) Files* and *Cookies* that have already been placed on your computer when you accessed the Internet in the past. And believe me, if you have never removed these Temporary 'Internet' Files from your computers hard-drive, you will have thousands now stored. Before you begin to delete these files, take a look at some of the expiration dates of the files that random companies or individuals have stored on your computer. The dates will blow your mind. The following are some suggestions to help you protect your information while online into the future.

- *Block Cookies,* this can be done via your Web Browser. Some Cookies may be required in order to access some websites so you may chose to set to 'Prompt for Third-Party Cookies', or a 'Prompt for all Cookies", if you chose. Without this control, anyone who wishes can plant crap on, and in your computer. *Cookies are messages that web servers pass to your web browser and are stored on your computer.* Cookies (text files) generally holds the time and date that you visited a website, your on-line purchase information, your passwords to member sites such as your banks online user ids and more. Most Cookies do not originate from the web site that you are visiting but instead from Marketing companies who may be managing the banner ads that display on a particular site. The Marketing companies use their Cookies to create detailed profiles on consumers who select ads on their client's sites. Then there are those companies who are just fishing and planting Cookies as you surf the web. You will be quite surprised at who is trying to plant Cookies on your computer when you are visiting a website and chose to block or manage Cookies.

- *Block Pop-ups*, they can not only capture your information when you click to open a Pop-up, *they can also plant viruses.*

- *Clear your Temporary Internet Folder regularly,* this folder stores Cookies that some times are dated for years out and resides on your computer. This folder also stores your visited sites, your passwords and much more. Delete the contents of this temporary folder regularly. Moreover, it has the nerve to be entitled 'temporary'....hummmm?

- *Clear your Internet History*, you may want to set your number of days to store 'search' history - to the number (0) zero days. If you need to remember a web address, add it to your 'Favorites' list.

- *Clear your 'Google' Search History regularly.* I found this step to be quite interesting since Google does not provide clear instruction on performing this task. What you can do is place your mouse in the first (left) position of the 'search' box and click the left side of your mouse once to display your list of searches. All websites that you have searched in the past should appear. You can delete the displayed list by pressing the delete button on your keyboard. If this does not work effectively for you, you can type each letter of the alphabet, starting with the letter 'A' to display the searches or sites previously searched, then press and held down the 'Delete' button to delete the displayed list. You can continue this alpha selection through the alphabet to the letter 'Z'.

- *Turn File and Printer Sharing OFF* on your Desktop or Laptop. Especially the 'file' sharing?

- *Limit the level of information you share* online.

- *Make sure the website is Secure when purchasing* by checking the web browser for a secured website. Check for the letters 'https://' rather then just 'http://'. The letter 'S' indicates a secured site. Understand that the site may still capture your information via a 'Cookie' but at least the site should be secured where others cannot see or access your personal information.

- *Password protect any important documents* that you email. You should also password protect important documents on your desktop. You can perform this task in Microsoft Word by having your document open, then click on 'File' then click to 'Save As', click 'Tools' to view and display the dropdown list, then select 'Security Option' to add a 'Password' to Open, and of course, click the OK button to Save the Password. *When attaching the document to your email DO NOT include the password in the email???* Pick up the phone and call the person with the password or use some other means to relay the password.

- *Do not use office email for personal information.* Unfortunately, the government has enacted a law **that permits companies to review deleted** company email. So what did that just indicate you?

- *Have multiple email addresses,* one for business that may consist of your complete name, and one encrypted for foolishness such as Message Boards and Chatting.

- *Do not reveal personal information to anyone while online.* If you are contacted online by someone requesting your personal information, or making a request online to update your account information randomly, pick up the phone and call the company to complete or validate their request.

- Last, when possible *use a Re-loadable Credit Card* for online purchases when possible. You can purchase re-loadable credit cards from most banks Visa or American Express gift cards and use those for online purchases. This will help to protect your personal credit card information. This may also help you with your budget. When the card is empty, you have to re-load it with cash not credit.

(FCRA)Fair Credit Reporting Act – A Very Important Act for Consumers

The Fair Credit Reporting Act covers a multitude of consumer regulations on privacy, however, companies continue to disseminate (sell and distribute) consumer's information without regards to consumer privacy laws.

The Fair Credit Reporting Act, in summary, covers regulations to protect the following areas of consumer information:

- Consumer Credit Information and Credit Reporting Agencies
- Medical Information Privacy
- Consumer Background Information Limitations

One great use of the (FCRA) Fair Credit Reporting Act is the use of the guideline to '*repair your own credit information*'. This Act provides the clear guidelines for any consumer to begin and end the process to clear up their negative, incorrect, and aged credit information from your credit file. The next chapter will provide consumers with the necessary steps to take, to repair your own credit.

How to Repair Your Credit and Avoid Using a Credit Repair Company

The following (FCRA) Fair Credit Reporting Acts information will arm consumers with information to _repair your own credit_. The following information is presented to provide you with a step-by-step process to begin repairing your credit information. Not only will this chapter help consumers with the Credit Repair process, it will also help consumers understand how to correct, challenge, monitor and maintain a good consumer credit file.

My goal with this chapter is to successfully get consumers on their way to a clean credit file and to provide the information that will help consumer's understand this simple process - were most companies who provide credit repair may present as a difficult process. As a consumer with improved credit you can save money by obtaining lower interest rates on loans, lower insurance premiums and get the financing you need when you need it.

It is important to remove derogatory (bad or negative) information from your credit file when it should not be there due to age or incorrect information. It is important to have items reported as 'paid' when they are paid in full. It is important to have items reported as 'Closed by Consumer' when you chose to close an account. All of the statements that appear on most credit report formats can affect your credit scores and definitely are viewed by potential creditors and employers, this is why the task of credit clean up is so important. Do not leave incorrect information on your credit file. As a consumer, you can perform the task of credit file clean up on your own without having to pay someone a fee to do this for you. Since I will only address parts of this FCRA Act, that addresses consumer credit - I ask that consumers visit the (FCRA) Fair Credit Reporting Act website for the complete details of this Act.

In the information to follow I will address some of the credit information reporting periods or 'time guidelines' for reporting and retaining information on a consumers credit file. I will address the timelines that are imposed on credit reporting agencies to investigate consumers inquires and to remove or correct consumer information, this includes Background Reporting companies who are referred to as (CRA) Consumer Reporting Agencies within the Fair Credit Reporting Act.

Most consumers are not aware that credit-reporting agencies must verify and validate credit file information when a consumer states that the information is incorrect. When a consumer reports to a CRA, be it a credit reporting agency or a background checking company, the clock starts ticking upon receipt of the consumer notification or inquiry request. Make sure that you make your request regarding an incorrect background check in writing and of course (without saying) retain a copy of that notification – this will be your only proof if a fine for violating consumer laws is later imposed upon the violator. For notification to credit reporting agencies, generally your inquiry will be submitted via their individual websites, so print a copy of your 'request to investigate submission', which can be obtained directly from their respective websites. Your copy may only be the printing of a hardcopy of the Internet webpage (page) that shows your request, or the completed form that is generally provided upon completion of your online review of your credit information. I will talk more about this process in the next chapters.

Be prepared to spend some time at your computer or at least the necessary time reviewing (with a fine-tooth-comb) your credit report information once you obtain it. You can choose to access your reports and print them to have a working hardcopy or view directly from the credit reporting agencies website. To save trees ☺ I would view the entire report first, and then type your notes regarding incorrect information directly onto the website, then print the entire report with your comments and corrections. When you print from the website, you will create a 'time stamped' document with your submitted request for corrections and possibly have a reference number from the credit-reporting agency appearing on your document. I personally suggest that you only request the *free* credit report and not pay any company for your credit information. I would also recommend that you not spend any money purchasing your credit score unless you need it for mortgage or auto financing. To begin the 'clean-up' process a credit score is not necessary. Besides, once you have corrected any incorrect information your score will improve, so why pay for a credit score in the initial request.

For consumers without access to the Internet, you can call the credit reporting agencies toll free numbers and request your free report. Generally you will reach an automated system that will require that you enter or speak certain personal information such as your social security number, date of birth, address and possibly answer a couple of questions regarding some or your account balances or account descriptions to validate your identity. The report will be mailed to you, generally within 7 to 10 business days. In most cases, you will receive it in less time than that.

Once the hard copy report is received, review it carefully and do not hesitate to call the credit-reporting agency with any questions that you may have. Remember, people are people – good and bad we do encounter, so be patient and kind since this person has your credit file at hand and can (I have seen) drag out this process. More times then not you will reach someone ready to assist you in the clean-up process. Keep in mind, and in some cases for paid accounts you may be asked to provide proof of payment, etc., if the credit agency cannot validate the information. Your (copy) of the proof of any 'paid-in-full' accounts' will only help to get your issues resolved quicker. When you receive a credit report by mail you have to 'generally' respond in writing, by mail with your written inquires or corrections. Keep a copy of the report with your comments and corrections. You may be able to fax your inquires (back) to the credit reporting agency rather than to mail the documentation, phone the agency to ask if the fax option is available to you. Once the credit-reporting agency receives any information, they have to act on it by law. Stay strong and patient and keep all of your original documents, only send copies, if

'An Invasion of (corporate) Locust' by Darlene R. Miles

required.

Remember to create and keep an on-going file. Keep the corrected credit report indefinitely once you receive it since items removed from your credit file (report) should not re-appear on your credit report without written notification to you by the credit-reporting agency. The credit-reporting agency must receive certification from the creditor, if an item is to be placed back on a credit report once the information is removed.

The Credit Repair Process

To begin the review process I recommend that you load your printer with lots of paper since there is nothing like a 'working hard copy' document (credit report). Be prepared to print out your report. You should also be prepared to respond on line to challenge incorrect or aged information at the time you initially view your reports. If you feel, you will need time to review the report off-line, then print the initial report and take your time reviewing. You will be able to go back and forth for a specified period of time to make corrections. Make sure that you work to respond to incorrect information within the credit reporting agencies stated timeline, generally 30 days. After the stated 30 day deadline to correct your information, and if you want to request another copy of your credit report, you may be asked to pay for that copy of the report. However, you have a legal right to request corrections whenever they are found, and you should always be sent a corrected report after corrections are made to your report by the credit-reporting agency.

- Request your combined 'free' credit reports from all three reporting agencies. You may obtain a free credit report from the top three credit reporting agencies by logging onto the 'annualcreditreport.com' website. I have chosen to use this site since it is supported by all three credit-reporting agencies. There is another site that uses the words *free credit...*' It appears that this site is only supported by one credit-reporting agency, even though they state that they will return all three credit bureau reports to you. In addition, they all try to sell you something else along with your free credit report, such as your credit score. Keep the report *free* and keep your credit card in your pocket unless there is a need to obtain your credit score for mortgage or auto financing.

- Review the detail of each report including your name, address, employer, time on the job and creditors. *A Special Note:* Do not hurry to provide corrected information on your employment or personal change of address if you have current collections activity in process. Sorry for that comment, for those who may have issue with it? I feel consumers have lost enough privacy and my goal is to provide help and not hinder consumers. If you have active collections activity or unpaid accounts appearing on your credit report, changing your address or listing your current employer may expose you to scrupulous collection companies. I would prefer that you are able to make the contact with your unpaid accounts without having some crazed collector contacting your employer or filing a legal garnishment of your wages, or attaching your bank account, and so on. (I will talk more about the collection process later.) So again, do not change your address or employer information if you chose not to.

- Pay special attention to your Inquires by creditors. Make sure that all accounts appearing on your credit report, open or closed are your accounts. Make sure that all inquiries into your credit report or credit history was initiated by you. Also, check for any Inquires that appear with strange company names. *Any inquires into your credit file without your authorization is a (FTC) Federal Trade Commission and (FCRA) Fair Credit Reporting Act violation.* Make a special note of any violations BUT make sure that you print your hard copy as proof of these violations since the credit reporting company can possibly be liable along with the company or individual(s) who fraudulently requested your credit file without your authorization.

- Respond immediately and in writing or via the credit reporting agencies website to report inaccurate information. Be aware that the clock starts clicking when they receive your notification of inaccurate information. The FCRA Section 611 states, in summary, and regarding deletions - the furnisher of the report has 30 days to remove the inaccurate information (please read that section for any exceptions). Make sure to record the Incident or Investigation number provided by the credit reporting company as the investigation tracking number. Print a hard copy of all of your requests for correction.

- Print out all information from the website and file it in your personal file to monitor changes. These dates will be important if the credit bureaus do not comply with the stated deadlines, (i.e. 30 days to remove or correct information or remove old information that is over 7 years old, for negative information, etc.).

- Pay close attention to any reinvestigation dates per the FCRA and Fair Trade Commission guidelines. It may take some time for you to 'completely' review your report. The credit-reporting agency will give you generally 30 days from the date that the report is requested to submit your requests for correction, so work quickly. You do not have to submit all of your requests at once. Keep in mind that the clock starts clicking for each individual correction request.

- Keep in mind that your request to remove an inaccurate item from your credit report *must be verified* by the credit-reporting agency; this includes incorrect background information resulting from a background check. If the information cannot be verified by the credit reporting agency or background checking company who supplied the report within the 30 days (refer to FCRA for exclusion) then the *information must be removed*.

- You should be provided with a toll free number to speak with a representative to discuss any concerns. Keep in mind that humans are humans, some good, and some bad, so be patient and hope that you do not reach an unkind individual. Generally, the credit reporting agencies will work quickly to remove any old accounts that are older then 7 years including most collection account (excluding some government college loans). The removal includes aged accounts when included in a bankruptcy; however, the bankruptcy will remain either the seven or 10-year period dependent upon the type of bankruptcy filed. On accounts included in a bankruptcy, the clock does not start clicking until the Dismissal Date of the Bankruptcy, so keep that in mind. The accounts included in a bankruptcy are eligible for deletion also at the 7-year mark. Please read the FCRA Act for additional exceptions since there may be exceptions based on types of loans and loan amounts, but generally and for everyday consumers, the standards stated here do apply. You still want these items removed and in most cases, the credit reporting agencies are not in a hurry to remove them on your behalf. If you experience unnecessary delays or arguments with an individuals at any of these credit reporting agencies, do not hesitate to quote the FCRA Law when necessary and in writing.

- Print out the status of your credit report *changes* and *corrections* each time you visit the credit reporting agencies website as proof of correction dates. Strangely I have seen where 'Charged-Off' or 'Paid Accounts" reappeared on a consumer's credit report, especially a 'charged-off' aged account that was sold and resold to collection companies. Always keep records of any disputed paid accounts proof

of payment.
- Reinsertion of deleted information can occur after deletion only if the credit-reporting agency receives *Certification of accuracy of information,* per Section 611 of the Fair Credit Reporting Act. The consumer must receive written notification of the reinsertion of deleted information within five business days of the reinsertion.

- Provide a 'Statement of Dispute' of not more then 100 words to your credit report. The dispute can be in reference to an account that cannot be resolved with the creditor, such as co-signed accounts with another primary owner, other then you, a spouse's account that you are left with, etc. You can also generally use these statements to explain why a financial hardship occurred, such as loss of your job or long-term illness what resulted in a bankruptcy or delinquent accounts. Creditors do consider those statements, including mortgage companies.

- If any accounts have been forwarded to outside collection agencies and payment was made directly to them, make sure that you retain the receipts as proof of payment for a couple of years (or longer). *Financial institutions sell their unpaid collection accounts, generally to the highest bidding collection company.* These accounts can sometimes be sold repeatedly for years. Sadly each time these accounts are sold, they are sold (generally) for less then the account balance but once in the possession of a new collections company they charge the consumer the original amount owed plus processing additional fees. This is generally why some collection companies will offer the consumer a settlement balance that will be offered for a specified period of time, making such statements as, 'If you respond and pay within the next 30 days, we will accept this lesser amount'. If this happens to you, re-negotiate to reduce the balance even more and get that arrangement in writing from the collection agency before paying a single dollar.

Keep records of payments for accounts that are paid after 'charge off' and/or placed in collection, or you may find yourself fighting some strange collection company years later.

- *Last and just as important.* Since negative credit information, *excluding government college loans and bankruptcies,* can only remain on your credit report for 7 years, if a seven year anniversary of a 'bad-debt' is approaching, my personal opinion is to *leave it alone* unless you are prepared to see that item restart the seven year cycle of appearance on your credit report again? Most consumers are not aware that when you contact a creditor on an old debt (lets say, years old) the clock is reset for another 7 years of reporting that debt. Now on the other hand, if you are attempting to finance a home, you cannot have charged-off or un-paid accounts appearing on your credit report, the delinquent account should be paid. The only accounts that I have see financing companies not request that they are immediately paid, were medical bills. So again, do not restart a ticking time bomb if not necessary.

Credit Repair Organizations (The "Credit Repair Organization Act") – What Consumers Need To Know About Credit Repair Companies

Sec. 2451. Regulation of Credit Repair Organizations

Section 2451 establishes the *"Credit Repair Organization Act" for the purpose of regulating credit repair organizations,* any entities that states that they can improve a consumer's credit record, credit history, or credit rating, or provide assistance or advice to this end. Section 2451 is intended to ensure that consumers are provided with relevant information regarding credit repair organizations and to protect consumers from unfair or deceptive advertising and business practices by these organizations. Any depository institutions (banks), credit unions, non-profit organizations, and creditors assisting consumers to restructure debts owed to them are specifically excluded from the definition of "credit repair organization" and are not covered by the Credit Repair Organization Act.

To summarize Section 2451:
- Prohibits any person from making a statement, or counseling a consumer to make any statement, to a consumer reporting agency or a current or prospective creditor that is untrue or misleading with respect to the consumer's credit worthiness, rating or standing or that is intended to alter the consumer's identification in order to conceal accurate and relevant adverse information about the consumer

- Prohibits any person from making or using any untrue or misleading representation of the services of the credit repair organization.

- From committing, or attempting to commit any fraud or deception on any person in connection with the offer or sale of the services of a credit repair organization.

- Prohibits credit repair organizations from charging or receiving a fee for the performance of any service for which the credit repair organization has agreed to perform before the service is fully performed.

- Requires credit repair organizations to make specific written disclosures to consumers about their rights under current law to obtain their credit report, dispute inaccuracies without the use of a credit repair organization, and inform the consumer of their right to _sue a credit repair organization for violations of this section,_ and amongst other violations.

- Requires written contracts with specific terms relating to the organization's fees and services, and other information; provides a three-day contract recession period; makes null and void any waiver by a consumer of any rights or protections provided by this section; and authorizes private right of actions and class actions against these organizations for violations of this section.

The FTC is required to enforce compliance with this section under the Federal Trade Commission Act. In addition, States may enforce this section, if no FTC action is pending. The FTC may intervene in any State action.

Section 2451 also provides a summary of information on a few of the civil penalties for companies and credit reporting agencies that do not comply with these laws.

Section 611 and Section 605 of the Fair Credit Reporting Act is of most importance when addressing corrections to your Credit Reports:

Section 611 of the Fair Credit Reporting Act covers the Procedure in case of dispute accuracy. The following is a summary of provisions:

- Reinvestigations of Disputed Information

- Prompt Notice of Dispute to Furnisher of Information

- Extension of period to reinvestigate

- Limitations on Extensions

- Consumers' Notification of Determination or a request to verify accuracy (my interpretation)

- Treatment of Inaccurate or Unverifiable Information (Sec. 611 states, 'promptly delete or promptly modify item')

- Certification of reinsertion of information

- Procedure to prevent reappearance of accurately deleted information

- Responsibility of consumer reporting agency to notify a consumer through *reseller*. This provision is in place when resellers of information such as background checking companies request a consumer report and are notified, by the consumer that the information is inaccurate. The reseller should contact the credit-reporting agency and submit the inquiry; however, the reseller provisions do not require that they communicate with the consumer as required by the credit-reporting agency. So in other words, notify the 'reseller' immediately about the inaccurate information but work directly with the credit-reporting agency on your own correction. I have seen this situation occur when Background information is requested that include a credit report. The reseller has an obligation to report accurate information, but remember that the information is yours so take charge, especially if the incorrect information is tied to new employment.

- Consumers 'Statement of Dispute'. FCRA states that the consumer will have a right to provide a written record of dispute of no more then 100 words, to be added to the consumer's credit report.

Although all provisions are important, I found these provisions to be of most importance in arming consumers when working to correct your credit reports.

Reporting of 'Adverse Information' on your Credit Report

Section 605 of the Fair Credit Reporting Act addresses requirements relating to information contained in your consumer report. (What can appear in your credit report and the timelines that apply?)

The following is my interpretation and a summary of some of the provisions within this section that states credit reporting timelines. Please, please refer to the FCRA website for complete detail of this information.

- Section A covers *'Information excluded from consumer reports'*, Bankruptcies for 10 years Civil Judgments and arrest records not more than 7 years or the governing statue of limitation, whichever is the longer period.

- *Account charged off or placed in collections*, not more than 7 years.

- *Limitation on reporting the names, addresses, and phone number of medical providers unless coded* to avoid identification associated with the type of medical service (my interpretation).

- *Exemptions to the exclusion* that may be tied to a transaction amount of over 150,000 or to a Bankruptcy (please read the provision for additional detail).

- *Report reporting period of 7 years.*

- *Key factors in credit score information*; the credit-reporting agency shall include in the report a clear and conspicuous statement what factors were used to calculate the score, such as number of inquires, high account balances, etc.

'An Invasion of (corporate) Locust' by Darlene R. Miles

- *Indication of closure of account by consumer*; the credit reporting agency must indicate on the report if an account was requested closed by the consumer.

- *Indication of Dispute by Consumer*; if the consumer notifies the credit-reporting agency of a disputed item, the credit reporting agency must indicate on the report that an account is disputed by the consumer.

- *Truncation of Credit Card and Debit Card Numbers*; now this is quite important and some retailers and restaurants are still not complying with this provision. The provision states; *no person that accepts credit cards or debit cards for the transaction of business shall print more than the last 5 digits of the card number or the expiration date upon any receipt provided* to the cardholder at the point of the sale or transaction. The exceptions are if the credit or debit card is copied with an old fashion credit card machine where the entire imprint is ran over (remember those). I probably would not shop there if I saw that type of machine taking an imprint of my entire credit or debit card. The other exceptions would be if the account number were hand-written on a credit card document for processing, again – if I would see that occurring, I would stop the transaction. In addition, the other exception is if a copy of your credit card is taken for the transaction, again... hummm? Therefore, in other words your receipt should only display 4 to 5 digits of your credit card number and not the entire account number when electronically processed.

- Notification of consumer address correction: If a person has requested a consumer report relating to a consumer and the address is different then the address on the report the agency shall notify the requester of the existence of the discrepancy. Keep this in mind and it does occur sometimes.

Consumers Must Receive Written Notice of 'Adverse Action' from an Employer – What does this mean?

Adverse Action Procedures and Consumers Rights

What is an 'Adverse Action Notification'? The document details your rights as a consumer - in the event 'Adverse (negative) Information is found within the context of a consumer's background (check) information. Employers will sometimes consider poor credit, a criminal conviction, or a poor driving history, as 'adverse information', it depends upon the company.

Where companies fail is that most companies do not specify in writing, what information they will request in a background check; credit report, criminal or civil records and possible driving records, if driving is a part of the employment requirement. Along with the request for authorization to access a consumer's background information, the consumer must receive an 'Adverse Action Notification' which details the consumers rights to address any adverse information obtained in their background.

In an age of background checks, employers must request (in writing), the authorization to access a potential or existing employee's background information if a background check is required for employment. Unfortunately most companies or (CRA) Consumer Reporting Agencies do not provide the consumer with a written notice of 'Adverse Action' at the time that the consumer is asked to sign the authorization for a background check and in most cases consumers are not provided their 'rights' after adverse information is obtained.

My opinion is, these consumer 'rights' should appear in a separate section of the authorization (form) and a signature should be obtained from the consumer or employee prior to background information being obtained. For consumers that did not receive your notification of your rights, during or after the company requested access to your background information, the company was in violation of the Fair Credit Reporting Act.

For Employers

If you receive a reply on a Consumer Report of Adverse Information for an 'Adverse Action', that states that Adverse information was found on a consumer or potential employee:

If you rely on a consumer report for an "Adverse Action" - denying a job application, reassigning or terminating an employee, or denying a promotion — be aware that:

Before you can take the adverse action, you *must give the individual a 'Pre-Adverse Action Disclosure'* that includes a copy of the individual's consumer report and a copy of *'A Summary of Your Rights Under the Fair Credit Reporting Act'* — a document prescribed by the Federal Trade Commission. The (CRA) Consumer Reporting Agency that furnishes the individual's report will give you the 'Summary of Consumer Rights', or at least they should.

After you have taken an Adverse Action, you must give the individual notice — orally, in writing, or electronically — that the action has been taken in an adverse action notice. It must include:

- The name, address, and phone number of the (CRA) Consumer Report Agency (credit reporting agency, background checking company, etc.) that supplied the report.
- A statement that the CRA that supplied the report did not make the decision to take the adverse action, and cannot give specific reasons for it.
- A notice of the individual's 'Right to Dispute' the accuracy or completeness of any information the agency furnished.
- In addition, that the consumer was informed of his or her right to an additional free consumer report from the agency

upon request within 60 days.

I have included a sample 'Adverse Action' letter for reference in my book. The sample letter can be found in chapter 6. This is a sample 'Adverse Action' letter *for reference only* and is similar to the letter that I used as a Director of Operation for the CRA.

Protecting Your Credit Information

Did you know that the credit bureaus sell consumer credit file information and allow random inquires at various levels without proof or a fiduciary (legal authorization from you) reason to access your information? I recommend that you check your credit file yearly and challenge any inquires placed on your credit file that did not result from a credit request made by you.

I have seen where mortgage companies have randomly requested credit reports without consumer authorization in order to market their products. This to me is a form of identity theft. Other random (so-called) credit reporting agencies (not the top three) will also randomly access your credit report without authorization. This action is in violation of the FCRA (Fair Credit Report Act), and should be reported to the Fair Trade Commission, your State Attorney General, and to the credit-reporting agency that provide the report. After reporting these types of violations you should also request that the 'inquiry' be removed from your credit file, but first obtain a hard copy of that 'false' inquiry for your records. The consumers request for removal of incorrect information (the inquiry) can be made based on the Fair Credit Reporting Act; the credit-reporting bureau must remove that type of inquiry. Too many credit inquires can affect your credit score.

In addition, be careful when purchasing a vehicle. The auto financing departments within some auto dealerships will sometimes send your information to several financing companies in an attempt to obtain an auto loan for you. This will generally occur when your credit score is a little lower then what is required to obtain the best or lowest interest rate. Request that the dealership submit the hardcopy credit report that they initially generate. Have them forward that original report to any or all-potential financial companies. Do not allow the company to generate more then one credit report on you for that one transaction. If shopping around for a new vehicle it will not hurt to have your credit report with the displayed credit score on it with you. Of course, to obtain your credit score it generally will cost you, but it will save you time, aggravation and a possible decrease to your credit score.

How to Stop the Selling of Your Consumer Credit File and Personal Information by Credit Reporting Agencies and ChexSystems

This is one of those hidden secrets. Most consumers are not aware that Credit Reporting Agencies and ChexSystems sell consumer credit and personal information. This consumer information selling occurs at various levels. Levels such as those 'soft inquires' which are supposedly the consumers credit file header information (which is too much information), or 'hard inquiries' which are those 'inquiries' when you apply for credit or employment and a company or individual obtains your complete and detailed credit file information. Credit-reporting agencies do not restrict access to a consumers credit file unless the consumer has placed a restriction or halted public access of their credit information. What is not made public to consumers is the process that is available to stop the selling of credit file information and inquires at all levels, and to everyone. That process is the process of adding a *Security Freeze* to your credit file. This chapter will cover the procedure in detail to add a Security Freeze to your credit file.

What occurs when a Security Freeze, not an 'Alert', is placed on your credit file with the credit (bureau) reporting agencies – they can no longer sell or allow access to your credit file to anyone. After a Security Freeze is placed on your credit file, if your credit information is made available or sold to the credit bureau's clients (resellers, brokers and background companies), the credit reporting agency is then in violation of federal law.

Why place a Security Freeze on your credit file you ask? One important reason to place a Security Freeze is if your identity has been compromised or personal information is stolen. Another reason may be to regain your privacy. There are so many companies that access a consumer credit information and resell your information without your authorization everyday. This includes the top three credit reporting agencies. In addition, ChexSystems also sells consumer information and this includes your bank information, bank account numbers, driver's license and social security information. However, even with a Security Freeze, ChexSystems states that they will still make your information available (now let me quote their statement correctly), *'Please be advised that security freeze requirements do not apply to pre-screening inquires made by creditors who may want to offer pre-approved credit or demand deposit account information service companies.'*. Therefore, in other words, ChexSystems appears to state that they will continue to sell your consumer file regardless of the *freeze*. This is quite interesting since they are not suppliers of credit information, so how exactly do they supply information to creditors who want to supply pre-approved credit offers…think about that? However, freeze their records in addition to freezing the top three credit bureaus. I would think that privacy laws would still apply here but I am not an attorney.

Blocking Your Credit File from Your Background Check

As a Director of Operations of a background checking company it was a minor process for the supplier of that 'so-called' comprehensive background information to make consumer credit information, header or otherwise available, within the content of their report. In addition, there are scrupulous corporations that purchase consumer information everyday from credit reporting agencies then resell the information, so if you are concerned and want to stop the selling and *random unauthorized access* to your credit file – then place the appropriate *security freeze* on that information. This action will *block* access to your credit file as part of consumer Background Checks. If a company requires access to your credit file, you will have to grant specific access to that company in writing to the credit reporting agency. No one will have random access without your authorization.

When a Security Freeze is placed on your credit file, it can be placed on your file for as long as your chose or with some agencies for one (1) or for seven (7) years.

The process of adding a Security Freeze is somewhat simple however, each credit reporting agency has different requirements and do not readily advertise this feature on their websites, so here's a little help. The addresses displayed are the current mailing addresses for all three of the top credit reporting agencies when requesting a Security Freeze of your credit file. Keep in mind that each credit reporting agencies requires that you submit additional information with your request to freeze your credit file. In addition, if your request to freeze your file is not due to identity theft a fee may be charged to freeze your file, please refer to the state fee structure, which is available at each credit reporting agencies web site. What is interesting here is that we cannot bill the credit reporting agencies when they make profits on the selling of our personal information, but we have to pay to stop them from selling ours? However, the fee is currently quite small and may range from $5.00 to $10.00. Please check with each credit reporting agency for their fee structure since it does vary from state to state.

The current mailing addresses for each credit reporting agency are listed on the next page. Please check with the credit reporting agencies for any address updates or changes before submitting any information to the following addresses.

TransUnion Security Freeze
P.O. Box 6790
Fullerton, CA 92834
FAX: (714) 525-0668

Equifax Security Freeze
P.O. Box 105788
Atlanta, Georgia 30348
Certified Mail

Experian Security Freeze
P.O. Box 9532
Allen, TX. 75013

As you see, TransUnion currently will allow the consumer to fax their request where Equifax currently requires that you mail your request via certified mail. Interesting, certified mail to a post office box. I guess you might not want a 'return receipt'. Just joking – you can request a return receipt and receive proof of delivery for some post office box deliveries. I do suggest that you request the 'proof of delivery', and retain that proof of delivery for your records.

Each credit-reporting agency has different requirements for supporting information. An example of the supporting information is as follows.

1. Name
2. Address
3. Date of Birth
4. Social Security Number
5. Proof of current address such as a current utility bill
6. Payment of applicable fees to request a security freeze of your credit
7. If you are an identity theft victim, and are requesting a security freeze, you must also include a copy of a police

report, Identity Theft report, or other government law enforcement agency report, such as a DMV report with your Security Freeze request.

Now to address ChexSystems. ChexSystems provides consumer information validations to financial institutions when consumers open bank accounts (and more). This company not only validates and retains information regarding every bank account that a consumer opens, the locations of those accounts, the bank account and routing numbers, your social security number and date of issue, your date of birth, and your driver's license number. They also store, reports and sell consumer banking account historical information to their clients. Please refer to the chapter and section on ChexSystems, in my book, for more details – you will be quite surprised.

However, ChexSystems require a Notarized request to freeze your file with their company. The request should be mailed to their Consumer Relations department.

ChexSystems
Consumer Relations
7805 Hudson Road Suite 100
Woodbury, Minnesota 55125
1.800.513.7125

Prior to submitting any documentation to request a Credit Security Freeze, I asked that you contact each of these entities to verify the information that I have provided or visit their websites for updates or changes to these instructions. Also, be aware that the information and instructions on placing a Security Freeze is not readily available on any of their web sites. You will have to *hunt* for the information and I do mean *hunt*.

If Your Personal Information Is Stolen (What To Do) – The 'after-effects' of Identity Theft

Identity theft can occur in so many forms. Theft can occur when a corporation's computer system is hacked and consumer information is stolen by strangers. It can occur when someone begins to apply for credit in another consumers name, or when you receive notification from a company that consumer information has been stolen by an employee of their company, yes – employee of a company. Identity theft can also occur when someone uses your information in the commission of a crime, or in the use of your health insurance information thus creating medical records information that will now be tied to your personal medical history. There are so many forms of consumer identity theft.

Regardless of the form of identity theft, receiving notification that theft of your personal or medical information has occurred, can be devastating to a consumer, it was for me. Over the last five years, I have received several notifications that my personal information was 'hacked' from either a company's system, or that my information was stolen by an employee of a company. The notifications indicated that my information was also sold to a data-broker. Of course, not my information alone but it was my personal and financial information as a part of a massive consumer information theft.

I would say that two of the most scary identity theft notifications were received from the Designer Shoe Warehouse (DSW) and from Certegy Check Services. From DSW I was notified by letter that my checking account, credit card, and drivers license information was stolen (hacked) from their system. From Certegy Check Services I received a worse notification by letter, which stated that one of their employees had stolen and sold consumer information to a data-broker who in turn sold the information to a limited (?) number of direct marketing organizations - and my information was one of those consumers. In addition, Certegy had

'An Invasion of (corporate) Locust' by Darlene R. Miles

49

the audacity to state – limited number? What a joke. For those who may not know these companies, Certegy Check Services processes and approves checks for various retail stores. This was a another very serious invasion of consumer information. A loss, such as this had previously required a lot of my time, energy, and loss of income to try to block the use of my (previously) stolen information - from these system hackings. Now here I go again.

At approximately the same time I received the DSW letter, I also received notice from two banks both reporting thefts of consumer credit card and bank information. The notifications from banks were not at the level of the DSW notification, or the later notification from Certegy - but all were just as harmful to me.

Because of the initial level of information stolen from the Designer Shoe Warehouses system it required that I obtain another bank account. Since my driver's license information was also stolen, it required that I obtain a police report in order to change my driver's license number since that number follows you for life or until you apply for another driver's license in another state. I then had to request new credit card numbers since I do shop for shoes and had no idea which card number was stolen. I also had a 'credit alert' placed on my credit report. A 'credit alert' instructs creditor to watch for unusual or suspicious activity in your accounts, and instructs new creditors to contact you separately before approving or granting credit. In addition to the 'credit alert', I placed a 'Credit Security Freeze' on my credit reports. A security freeze on your consumer credit file prohibits credit agencies from sharing your credit file information with anyone. Once a 'security freeze' is placed on your credit file, access to your credit file can only be granted by you, in writing to the credit agency. No one can obtain your credit file, without your written authorization, so be aware of that. A credit freeze must be submitted in writing to all three credit-reporting agencies. In this chapter of the book I addressed how to place a Security Freeze on your credit file. I no longer use credit cards randomly and keep a lower limit on one card in the event of credit card theft.

All of the steps taken to recover from identity and personal information theft were very time consuming, and little did I know I had not completed the process. I then had to change all auto-debits, bank accounts and much more. This process took nearly a month to complete.

When the letter was received from Certegy Check Services, regrettable I had to start this processes all over again. These companies, their 'so-called' automated systems, their storing of, and their lack of protection of consumer information is ridiculous behavior and continues to place consumer information at risk.

Just a recap of my process; Contact all of the credit reporting companies to place an Alert or Security Freeze on your credit file to prevent further information identity theft. I would then contact the area police department to file a police report. Give a copy of the police report to your bank. Contact your credit card companies to change your credit card numbers. Dependent upon what information is stolen, you may want to obtain a new drivers license number from the driver license bureau. Our license number are generally issued to us as teenagers, that number does not change, if in the hands of thieves, and accompanied with your social security number, name, and address – you are at risk of fraud. If your checking account information is stolen, you will want to close your bank account and open another account.

A final note on this subject, I no longer write checks at stores that require my driver's license information and is now very careful where I use credit or debit cards. What is most scary about this process of 'system' identity theft is the level of information that is captured and stolen from consumers, and the possibilities of where your information can be sold – be it somewhere oversees or to marketing companies within the United States. When does it stop?

Please also refer to the chapter on 'Scam Proofing Your Life' for additional 'consumer-information' protection information.

(FCRA) Fair Credit Reporting Act - The Violations and Penalties for Companies who Access Consumer Credit without Authorization

Several companies have had penalties assessed by the (FTC) Fair Trade Commission due to (FCRA) Fair Credit Reporting Act violations over recent years, companies such as Choice Point, Safeco Insurance and the top three credit reporting agencies. The government takes these violations seriously. The following summary of sections strongly applies to the violations of the Fair Credit Reporting Act.

Section 2412 Civil Liability applies to the FCRA section 616 and section 617; to summarize:

- States that any person who willfully or negligently fails to comply with the Fair Credit Reporting Act can be penalized. Previously, a private right of action for these violations was available only against a (CRA) Consumer Reporting Agency or a user of information. Therefore, furnishers of information (Resellers, or Background Companies), including financial institutions, now may be subject to civil liability in certain cases (Please review Section 2413 for additional information).
- This section also provides a minimum of $100 and maximum of $1000 civil penalty for willful noncompliance of the Fair Credit Reporting Act, as alternative actual damages, in addition to punitive damages and fees and costs.
- If the willful noncompliance is the result of obtaining information under false pretenses or knowingly without a *permissible purpose*, a consumer is entitled to receive actual damages or $1,000, whichever is greater.
- Any person who obtains a consumer report from a (CRA) Consumer Reporting Agency under false pretenses or knowingly without a permissible purpose is liable to the CRA for actual damages or $1,000, whichever is greater.

'An Invasion of (corporate) Locust' by Darlene R. Miles

Section 2412 also provides that, if any filing in connection with an action for civil damages was made in bad faith or for the purpose of harassment, the court must award attorney fees to the prevailing party.

Sec. 2413. Responsibilities of Persons Who Furnish Information to Consumer Reporting Agencies.

Section 2413 adds a new section, to be codified as section 623 of FCRA, which imposes new duties and liability on furnishers of information to CRAs. In addition to their role as *users* of consumer credit reports, financial institutions also frequently serve as 'furnishers' of information to CRAs. *This strongly applies when financial institutions report mortgage payments as late when they are not and does not correct the information within time guidelines as stated in the FCRA.*

Section 2413 continues with the following provisions, (in summary):

- Prohibits furnishers of information from providing any information to a Consumer Reporting Agency when they know, or avoid knowing, that the information is inaccurate.
- Requires that a company or person who furnishes information to a CRA promptly notify the Consumer Reporting Agency of inaccurate or incomplete information when errors or omissions are found.
- Requires that delinquent account display the date of delinquency.
- Requires that if a consumer informs a furnisher (reseller, etc.) of a report, that the information is inaccurate or incomplete, that the furnisher must investigates the disputed information and report back to the CRA promptly. The furnisher must report the results back to the CRA after the investigation is completed and with the results.
- Furnishers of information to Consumer Reporting Agencies may be subject to private right of action for willful violation or negligent noncompliance that requires the reinvestigation procedure for disputed information. (There are additional provisions for this statement. Review this section for additional detail.)

Sec. 2414. Investigative Consumer Reports. (This section amends Section 606 of FCRA)

- Prohibits a Consumer Reporting Agency from furnishing consumers investigative report to a requester unless the requester of the report provides a certification that the required disclosures have been submitted to the consumer.
- Prohibits a Consumer Reporting Agency from obtaining information to prepare an investigative consumer report for employment purposes, if the inquiry by the requesting employer or prospective employer would violate Federal or State equal employment opportunity laws. This includes information in the report relating to arrests, indictments, convictions, civil actions, tax liens or outstanding judgments unless the CRA has verified the accuracy of the information within the last 30 days.
- Prohibits the including of adverse information in the report obtained from a personal interview with a friend, neighbor, or associate of the consumer, among others, unless the CRA has followed procedures to obtain confirmation of the information from an additional source, and the person interviewed is the best possible source of the information. *(Now I personally find this one interesting.)*

Sec. 2415. Increased Criminal Penalties for Obtaining Information Under False Pretenses.

- Increases penalties for anyone found guilty of obtaining information from a Consumer Reporting Agency under false pretenses, this would include Consumer Reporting Agency officers or employees who knowingly provide consumer information to unauthorized persons. These fines are defined under Title 18 of the U.S. Code, can include fines of not more then $5000, and imprisoned for up to two years.

Sec. 2416. Administrative Enforcement.

- Provides the Fair Trade Commission, and other Federal Regulatory agencies with the authority to enforce the Fair Credit Report Act. This includes actions against providers (furnishers, resellers, etc.), and users. (Please review for additional detail)
- Provides the provisions for the Fair Trade Commission to impose Civil Monetary penalties. Penalties up to $2500 for each violation. (Please review the provision for additional detail).

Sec. 2417. State Enforcement of Fair Credit Reporting Act.

- This section requires the State to provide the relevant Federal agency with written notice of an action, a copy of the complaint, and permits the Federal agency to intervene in the action, request removal of the action to Federal district court, and file petitions for appeal. If the appropriate Federal regulator has already instituted a civil or administrative action for a violation of the Fair Credit Reporting Act, this section prohibits States from bringing an action for the same violation during a pending Federal action. (Review the Provision for additional detail and exceptions.)

The following sections are provided in title only. Please review the Provisions for detail:

Section 2417 permits the "chief law enforcement officer" of a State or other designated State official, also to bring certain types of enforcement actions in Federal or State court against persons (including national banks) for violations of FCRA, as well as State laws.

Sec. 2418. Federal Reserve Board Authority.

Section 2418 amends section 621 (15 U.S.C. 1618s) to provide that the Fed, in consultation with the appropriate Federal agencies, may issue an interpretation of any provision of FCRA as it applies to any bank, thrift, or credit union, or their holding companies or affiliates.

Sec. 2419. Preemption of State Law.

- Previously, section 622 of Fair Credit Reporting Act provided that FCRA does not "annul, affect, or exempt any person subject to the FCRA from complying with the laws of any State with respect to the collection, distribution, or use of any information on consumers, except to the extent that those laws are inconsistent with the FCRA, and then only to the extent of the inconsistency.
- This Section modifies this provision (renumbered as section 624) by providing that FCRA expressly preempts State law in discrete areas, including
    - Prescreening;
    - The time by which a CRA must take any action concerning disputed information;
    - The duties of a person who takes any adverse action with respect to a consumer;
    - The duties of persons who use a consumer report in connection with any credit or insurance transaction that is not initiated by the consumer and that consists of a firm offer of credit or insurance;
    - Information contained in consumer reports (except that existing State laws are grandfathered);
    - Responsibilities of persons who furnish information to CRAs (except that certain laws of Massachusetts and California are grandfathered);

- The exchange of information among affiliates (except for certain laws of Vermont); and
- The form and content of the summary of a consumer's rights under FCRA required in any consumer disclosure.

As this is a summarization of information, please review this provision for additional details.

Sec. 2420. Effective Date.

- This section provides that, unless otherwise specified, the amendments made to Fair Credit Reporting Act are effective one year after enactment (September 30, 1997). Any person that is subject to the Fair Credit Reporting Act may comply with the new provisions prior to that date.

Sec. 2421. Relationship to Other Law.

- This section provides that FCRA does not supersede or otherwise affect 18 U.S.Code 3721 with respect to motor vehicle records for surveys, marketing, or solicitations.

Sec. 2422. Federal Reserve Board Study.

- This section requires the Federal Government, in consultation with the other Federal banking agencies and the Fair Trade Commission, to conduct a study and report to Congress in six months on whether organizations which are not subject to FCRA are engaged in the business of making sensitive consumer identification information (including social security numbers, mothers' maiden names, prior addresses, and dates of birth) available to the public; whether these activities create undue potential for fraud and risk of loss to insured depository institutions; and whether Federal law should be amended to address these risks.

Sec. 2452. Credit Worthiness.

*Interesting, this Section should apply to Insurance 'Red-Lining"
but doesn't...Why Not?*

This section provides legislation that assures that individuals
should generally be judged for credit worthiness based on their
own credit worthiness and not based on their zip code or
neighborhood.

Building Your Case for (FCRA) Fair Credit Reporting Act Violations and (FTC) Fair Trade Commission Complaints

Violations committed against consumers, as it applies to the
(FCRA) Fair Credit Reporting Act can cover a multitude of areas.
Some areas of non-compliance can range from a (CRA) Consumer
Reporting Agency, such as a Background Checking Company that
does not act upon a consumers request to verify inaccurate
'Adverse Information', which results in the loss of employment.

Another example could be a Credit Reporting Agency, reporting
inaccurate credit file information on a consumer's credit report and
refusing to correct the information in a timely manner - resulting in
the consumer being denied financing. These are some of the most
obvious forms of violations.

Outside of the obvious violations that I have just noted, I would
say a strong consumer violation complaint would consist of a
'documented' proof of loss. This could be a loss of employment
due to inaccurate adverse information that includes 'Sealed' or
'Expunged' information especially if the information has appeared
in a CRA's system that you had previously notified (in writing)
that the information was sealed or expunged. The denial of
financing, residential rental or leasing due to inaccurate 'adverse

information' obtained in your background, and or inaccurate information appearing on a consumers credit report, are just a couple of examples of Fair Credit Reporting Act violations.

The (FTC) Fair Trade Commission imposes fines and penalties for violations against the (FCRA) Fair Credit Reporting Act on behalf of consumers. I personally feel that proven 'documented' loss would be your strongest case against a company. However, penalties can also be assessed when your credit file is 'fraudulently accessed' without your permission. Make sure that you retain any documentation supporting your violation complaint. Examples of supporting documentation would be a 'letter of denial' of employment due to adverse information obtained in your background or letters of denial for financing listing the Credit Reporting Agencies that provided the 'inaccurate' credit report. Documented proof of a violation is of great importance.

To file your claim of consumer privacy violations you can either access the (FTC) Fair Trade Commissions website and complete the consumer complaint form online or consult with an attorney. There may be some date limitations on filing violations so act fast when they occur, especially denials of employment or credit financing due to inaccurate information.

Your Credit Information - Some Do's and Don'ts When Seeking Financing

Do's

- *Know what is on your Credit Report;* are 'paid in full' accounts stated correctly, are account balances stated correctly, paid-on-time or delinquencies - make sure no account that is paid on time is shown as delinquent or late.

- *Pay off Accounts or Credit Card Balances.* Understand that making minimum payments on time, but never paying off accounts can be viewed negatively, by some creditors.

Try to pay off revolving accounts.

- *Reduce your number of 'Open Revolving Accounts'.*
  Understand that a high number of open accounts (revolving
  debt such as credit cards) even if the balances are zero can
  affects your ability to purchase or refinance a mortgage, or
  to obtain a lower interest rate - since those open accounts
  are considered as open lines of available credit (or in some
  creditors eyes, open lines of debt).

Don'ts

- *Don't negatively affect your Credit Score.* Do not allow
  any financing company to randomly submit your credit
  report information to a series of financing companies. Each
  of those companies may generate a new credit report on
  you. This can occur during auto financing and mortgage
  financing. When financing, have the financing company
  state in writing or give a verbal agreement that they <u>will</u>
  <u>only fax your credit report</u> to the respective companies for
  financing consideration, or present your own combined
  credit report for finance consideration. Generally, multiple
  'inquires' into your credit report, that occurs within a short
  period of time, will lower your credit score. I have
  witnessed the lowering of consumer scores in the past when
  a consumer sought auto financing during the financing of a
  mortgage and multiple credit inquiries appeared on their
  credit report.

- Don't apply for financing of 'any' other items during the
  financing of a mortgage or mortgage refinancing, this
  includes auto financing,

(HIPAA) Health Insurance Portability Accountability Act – What You Need To Know About Your Medical Records

Your health information is protected by Federal Law, however we do have companies and individuals violating this law. Within the past year, I have encountered a company that is currently supplying background information on consumers and is now supplying (selling) consumer's medical records. How are they able to get away with that I wonder? As a former Director of Operations for a Background Checking Company, and as a consumer, this is clearly a HIPAA violation but this company continues their brokering of consumer medical records today.

The (HIPAA) Health Insurance Portability Accountability Act provides protection of your medical information and defines the rules and regulation on who can *view* or *receive* your medical information. This Act or law also provides the provisions that allow consumers to take control of your medical information by defining who can have access to your medical information and for what purposes. The law also requires companies to disclose their privacy policies prior to engaging in data transactions with users or consumers. *Clearly, this law does not state that a company can buy or sell your private medical records information to any client of theirs who logs onto their website.*

One interesting comment, since a great percent of background information is riddled with inaccuracies how exactly in this 'background company' in a position to not only sell a consumers medical records to who ever requests them via their website, but how are these medical records being validated? *They are not. Period.* I personally cannot imagine that physicians are selling medical records since privacy statements are required upon medical service being rendered. Nevertheless, greed is greed. Could these medical records be purchased from Health Insurance Companies? If so, then I would state the same, these medical

'An Invasion of (corporate) Locust' by Darlene R. Miles

records are still not validated for 100% accuracy. After working as part of a project team for a Health Insurance Provider, I had an opportunity to view consumer-billing inaccuracies for medical services provided and billed. In addition, I have witnessed cross contamination of consumers names, addresses, and coded procedures billed. I have experienced the same types of documented systems errors from a medical provider following a consumer's 'simple' medical physical while the consumer was completely healthy. So what does this say about the accuracy of unauthorized 'sold' medical records?

Medical coding errors are created everyday. Everyday at the physician's office who is rendering the medical service, and when medical billing coding is performed at the health insurance billing companies. So what does this say? A company is currently selling medical records under what they state is a consumer 'Risk-Based Management Service', also known as 'Consumer Risk-Based Analysis' to their clients. Who exactly is creating the Risk? The company as a supplier, or the consumer who is potentially denied access to health insurance policies, life insurance policies, employment, or even financing, due to a comprehensive background check that includes unauthorized and potentially incorrect consumer information, or what ever these companies' clients are attempting to verify, or validate - with improper authorizations from the consumer. This is utterly ridiculous.

Where there may be companies that I feel are not complying with the HIPAA Act there are states that have taken the enactment of this law seriously and have worked diligently to comply with the Federal Government.

While working as a consultant on a state's project, I worked on the project that consisted of a medical systems revision and enhancements to the states medical providers system. The system revision included revisions the states Medicaid and Medicare Provider System in order to comply with the then newly created HIPAA Law, rules and regulations. I had the opportunity to gain a wealth of knowledge about the HIPAA law. When this law was enacted it was a challenge for all states to immediately comply, but they worked to comply with this privacy law. To assure compliance the government imposed deadlines that were weighted heavily with large fines for non-compliance.

This law gives the consumer rights over 'Your Health Information'. Rights such as:

- As a Consumer, you have the right to decide *if* you want to give your permission before your health information can be used or shared for any purpose, this includes marketing of your information.

- You have the right to receive a notice that clearly states *how* your health information may be used and shared.

- You have a right to receive a report on when and why; your health information was shared for certain purposes.

- You have a right to obtain a copy of your health records.

- You have a right to have your health records corrected (and errors do occur).

Providers that must comply with this law are; most doctors, nurses, pharmacies, clinics, nursing homes, hospitals and many other health care providers. The compliance also includes Health Insurance companies, HMO's, most employer group health plans, and certain government programs that pay for health care such as Medicare and Medicaid.

Your Information That Is Protected:

- Any information that your Doctor, Nurses and other health care providers put into your medical records.

- Any conversations with your doctor about your care, or with any other medical staff member.

- Your Medical Billing information.

- Most other health information that is held by those who are defined as providers under this law.

Nevertheless, we now have Background companies selling consumers medical records without signed authorizations. Consumer's medical records should not be brokered, as if it was a product, it is not. After all, if a company is authorized to obtain a consumers medical records, those records should be requested with proper consumer authorization, and directly from the consumer's medical provider. Not from a data broker who has obtained consumer medical records illegally. Most importantly, the potential of FCRA violations are so great for these violators when consumer medical information is obtained or accessed, and sold through scrupulous means. After reviewing the quality of consumer background information at all levels and for years, there is never a 100% guarantee of accuracy. Therefore, what does this say about unauthorized consumer medical records?

Reporting HIPAA Violations

If you feel that any person or persons, agency or organization covered under the HIPAA Privacy Rule has violated your health information privacy rights or committed any other violation of the Privacy Rule, you may file a complaint with the Office of Civil Rights (OCR). The OCR has authority to receive and investigate complaints against covered entities related to the Privacy Rule. Please go to the *Office of Civil Rights* website to file your complaint. Please note that there are timeline limitations on some claims, so if you feel your rights have been violated, please file quickly. Your claim must be filed on paper either electronically from the website or by mail; other options may be available so visit the website quickly.

(DPPA) Driver's Privacy Protection Act of 1994 – Protecting Your Drivers License Information - Understanding Your Rights

Congress passed the Driver's Privacy Protection Act as an amendment to the Omnibus Crime Act of 1994; it restricts the public disclosure of personal information contained in state department of motor vehicle ("DMV") records. While Driver's Privacy Protection Act generally prohibits DMV officials from knowingly disclosing personally identifiable information contained in department records, it delineates *several broad exceptions*. In January of 2000, the Supreme Court unanimously upheld the Act in the case of Reno v. Condon. The Court held that personal, identifying information from drivers' licenses and motor vehicle registrations is a "thing in interstate commerce" that can be regulated by Congress like any other commodity.

However, my experience has been that you can obtain any information that is available in a consumers driving record, transmit that information to the requester (purchaser) who may state that they have read the DPPA Law, and have a 'fiduciary' reason for the request. Here is what I found from the U.S. Code as defined for the term 'fiduciary'.

1104. Fiduciary duties
    (a) Prudent man standard of care
    (1) Subject to sections 1103 (c) and (d), 1342, and 1344 of this title, a fiduciary shall discharge his duties with respect to a plan solely in the interest of the participants and beneficiaries and—
    (A) For the exclusive purpose of:
    (i) Providing benefits to participants and their beneficiaries; and
    (ii) Defraying reasonable expenses of administering the plan;
    (B) With the care, skill, prudence, and diligence under the circumstances then prevailing that a prudent man acting in

a like capacity and familiar with such matters would use in the conduct of an enterprise of a like character and with like aims;

(C) By diversifying the investments of the plan so as to minimize the risk of large losses, unless under the circumstances it is clearly prudent not to do so; and

(D) In accordance with the documents and instruments governing the plan insofar as such documents and instruments are consistent with the provisions of this subchapter and subchapter III of this chapter.

Interesting?

People lie to obtain consumers information everyday without 'Permissible Use' or a valid Fiduciary reason, and without penalty when caught.

The (DPPA) Drivers Privacy Protection Act in summary states that,' In General' – Except as provided in subsection (b), a State department of motor vehicles, and any officer, employee, or contractor, thereof, shall not knowingly disclose or otherwise make available to any person or entity personal information about any individual obtained by the department in connection with a motor vehicle record.

Section (b), in summary, states 'Permissible Uses' Personal information referred to in subsection (a) shall be disclosed for use in connection with matters of motor vehicle or drivers safety and theft, motor vehicle emissions, motor vehicle product alterations, recalls, or advisories, performance monitoring of motor vehicles and dealers by other vehicle manufacturers, and removal of non-owner records for the original owner records of motor vehicle manufacturers to carry out the purposes of the Automobile Information Disclosure Act, the Motor Vehicle Information and Cost Saving Act, the National Traffic and Motor Vehicle Safety Act of 1966, the Anti-Car Theft Act of 1992 and the Clean Air Act. The Act provides in detail when consumers drivers license information can be accessed and for 'what use' the information can be used.

Where I see a challenge with this law that negatively affects consumers is the section of this Act that permits the Resale of a consumers driving records information. The act does still require that the 'Reseller' (generally a Background Checking company) discloses the 'Permissible Purpose' and must identify each person or entity that receives driving records information for a period of 5 years.

Even with this provision, driving records information is being accessed without Permissible Purposes.

The law goes further to state 'Additional unlawful acts', in summary, would be unlawful for any person knowingly to obtain or disclose personal information, from a motor vehicle record for any use not permitted under this Act. These 'unlawful acts' include 'False Representation' which would be any person that makes false representation to obtain any personal information from an individual's motor vehicle record. The Act also defines 'Penalties', Criminal Fine and Civil action for violators.

In my attempt to provide consumers with a summary of information regarding this Act I have provided a summarized version of this Act only. It is important to understand how your driving records information is and should be protected. I ask that you log onto the Drivers Privacy Protection Act website for complete details on this Act.

Reporting DPPA Violations

To report any Drivers Privacy Protection Act violations, I would start with your states Department of Motor Vehicles website. Please be prepared to provide documented proof of the violations. You may also be required to provide the named source, and or supplier of the report.

U.S. Patriot Act and How It Affects Consumers

The brief summary of this Act as stated is; 'To deter and punish terrorist acts in the United States and around the world, to enhance law enforcement investigatory tools, and for other purposes. *Be it enacted by the Senate and House of Representatives of the United States of America in Congress assembled...*'and so it goes.

You wonder how this Act affects you as a consumer. My greatest exposure to this Act was as a project team member on the enhancement of consumer Banking Systems. When this Act was enacted, it required certain validations of a consumer's information that currently existed on already established bank accounts. The additional requirement was to validate the consumer identification at the time a new bank account is opened. This Act goes further requiring that if a consumer's information could not be validated, the financial institution be required to act and report the incident to the appropriate authorities. The Act also required that additional banking system enhancements be created to monitor transactions and to identify those transaction as recorded against a consumer's bank account activity. The monitoring of a consumers banking activity would include wire transfers, large and cash deposits and more. I have summarized some of the Sections of this Act that I have found to be of most interest.

Banking Systems and the Invasions

My involvement with this Act was to implement the government imposed banking application systems enhancements to comply with the Act as stated by law. The Banking project was to incorporate banking application code changes where each existing consumer's personal information would be validated. The validation of an existing account required that certain consumers information exist on all bank accounts. Strangely, since some bank accounts may have been decades old some accounts were incomplete as it relates to consumers current personal information. The bank must validate each consumer's bank account information.

'An Invasion of (corporate) Locust' by Darlene R. Miles

The validation includes all consumers' information, information such as; name, address, social security number, and going forward, driver's license number amongst other identifying factors or the bank would be in violation of the imposed new regulation. This required that the banks generate a file of all accounts, duplicate accounts, and validate the status of each consumer. *Going forward the bank is to imbed the appropriate system coding that will permit the monitoring (in detail) of the transactions for any government entity, upon request...hummm, and we say there are privacy laws?* I clearly understand the need to prevent terrorism, but the average consumers should not have such requirements imposed, nor experience such an invasion of banking privacy.

What is now occurring within the banking industry is that some of the banks representatives are taking this Act and its powers beyond the stated privileges, or better yet, interpreting this Act and its powers to suit their ill behaviors. Some bank representatives are not only adhering to the government's requirements, but they are extending their powers by conducting 'Comprehensive Background' checks on consumers. Banks are now using one (CRA) Consumer Reporting Agency also know as a 'Background Checking' company, that I feel is invading the lives of consumers by providing consumer background information that is clearly outside of the scope of this Act. Information such as employment history, family and sibling information – up to six degrees of separation, your assets, your professional licensing information, drivers license, legal history (Traffic, Criminal and Civil), your neighbors information to include their addresses and phone number, cellular phone numbers (which should always be private) and last but not least, your medical records. Yes – your medical records as an option, if selected as part of the comprehensive consumer report. This is crazy but this Act has armed these crazies with powers that I hope someone will use in reverse on them.

Additional provisions of this Act are to follow in the next paragraphs.

Surveillance Provisions

This provision was not a direct requirement or part of my project as a Consultant, but I found this section of the Act to be quite interesting. The Act provides the provisions and authority to intercept wire, oral and electronic communications relating to computer fraud and abuse offenses. It also provides the authority to share criminal investigation information and of course the interception and disclosure of wire, oral and electronic communication.

Money Laundering and Related Measures

This Act provides the provision that permits 'Special due diligence' for correspondent accounts and private banking accounts' and Forfeiture of funds in United States interbank accounts. This provision continues with, 'Verification of identification', which was one of the provisions that directly affected consumers accounts, old and new accounts.

Bank Secrecy Act
(System Automation and Validation)

Now here we are. This Act directly affects the consumer, their information and how the banks or financial institutions are to report consumer's information back to the governing entity. Some of the Provisions within this section are outlined as follows:

- 'Penalties for violations of geographic targeting orders and certain recordkeeping requirements, and lengthening effective period of geographic targeting'. Part of this requirement and as addressed in the banking application and system application code changes - required that the bank provided a way to validate all customer information, have the ability to retain those validations and that the effective period of those validations had no end date.
- The Provision also includes a requirement to report

suspicious activity (*yes, your transactions*)

- Reporting of suspicious activity by underground banking systems
- Establishment of a high security Network *(I wish.)*
- Increase in civil and criminal penalties for money laundering
- Reports relating to coins and currency received in non-financial trade or business
- Efficient use of currency transaction report system

This Act goes on and on to cover, Borders, Currency Crimes and Protection, Enhanced Immigration Provisions, Removing Obstacles to Investigating Terrorism – Disclosure of Educational records, Amendments to the Victims of Crime Act of 1984, increased information sharing for Critical Infrastructure Protection, Strengthening the Criminal Laws against Terrorism, and Improved Intelligence.

The Act and provision summaries that I have provided here are summaries only; they are not the actual 'stated' legal provisions. I wanted to provide an overview of this act by making note of the provisions that affect a consumers banking privacy.

What the U.S. Patriot Act does is to provide the added security to monitor any potential 'funded' terrorism. What has happened, in addition is - we consumers have now had our banking privacy rights taken away. We have no remaining privacy rights when banking with a financial institution, after all – what other financial institutions are there? A shoe box? I tried the shoebox but decided to deposit the cash instead, no joke? *(As you can see, my use of a question mark in the place of a period is my only expression of some of these extremely invasive, ridiculous acts against consumers???)*

(SOX) Sarbanes Oxley Act and How This Act Affects Automated 'Consumer' Systems

As a consultant, I have had the pleasure to work with a client who has complied with the strictest of requirements and controls imposed by the Sarbanes Oxley Act (SOX). What is SOX? Sarbanes Oxley Act was put in place after the series of corporate failures such as Enron, WorldCom and others. What the SOX Act requires is that any publicly traded company complies with the appropriate rules and regulations when making changes to their automated software applications, that those software application changes be documented clearly, and that the company, if audited can produce the appropriate documentation of those changes along with the impact to consumers or investors. Who does this act affect and where are you the consumer immediately affected; Banking, Cable, Automated Medical Systems and more – any publicly traded company or corporation is affected by SOX.

Now for the official definition of Sarbanes Oxley Act:

■ The Sarbanes-Oxley Act was passed to provide greater oversight of financial management and included a whistleblower provision.

■ GLBA defines new security standards for the financial world to follow. Why?
- (A). to better protect customer information from a privacy standpoint and address the problem of identity theft.
- (B).Identity theft is now a major problem for financial institutions.

■ 1. Compliance provisions include:
- A. Financial institutions must institute verification procedures from individuals asking for information.
- B. Recommended procedures include calling the customer, customer letters, verify telephone etc.

'An Invasion of (corporate) Locust' by Darlene R. Miles

73

- C. Security safeguards must also include written policies/procedures to safeguard information.
- Reporting suspected identity theft to affected customers and law enforcement.

The Sarbanes Oxley Act was passed to require greater oversight of financial management. Scandals like Enron and WorldCom prompted the act. It included a "Whistle Blower" provision. Part of the act reads that publicly traded companies must establish a system for employees to report suspected or auditing misdeeds.

Section 301 of the Act, requires procedures for publicly held companies to report confidentially and/or anonymously problems regarding:

- (1) Questionable accounting
- (2) Internal controls
- (3) Auditing matters
- (4) Ethics violations
- (5) Internal theft

Even though there are regulations that govern how companies should enact controls around our personal information, it is still not occurring with all corporations. I will address some of those areas and bad practices throughout my book.

How to Protect Your Personal Information from Abuse of any Privacy Law or Acts

Review and challenge any 'unsolicited' Inquires that appear on your credit report yearly. Understand that employers along with credit companies will access your credit report information randomly and without your approval. These inquires sometimes appear with strange company names or the actual company name that sought to gain access to your information.

Report any abuse of theft of your personal information immediately. Document and report in writing to the credit reporting agencies that an abuse has occurred and that you did not authorize access to your credit information. You may also be required to file a police report.

Do not sign blanket or blank background check authorizations. Most companies do require background checks that do now include your credit information. I understand the need to have access to Criminal and Driving Records information for employment purposes, however – a consumer's credit file should not be randomly accessed after your hire date. Place a deadline on your signed authorization document. You do not want anyone randomly accessing your information without seeking a new authorization from you. Place termination dates on your consumer disclosures for background information.

Medical records, do not sign 'blanket' authorizations for your information to be sent anywhere without written notification to you by your physician. Make sure that there are specific details on the use of your medical information, and who is to have access to your records as a result of your signed authorization. On the Medical Authorization form, draw lines through statements that do not apply to you or to your office visit, also draw lines through statements that you do not authorize, initial your revisions on the document, and request an immediate copy.

Doctor's offices now request written authorizations, from consumers in order to forward medical information or medical history to insurance companies for medical claims payment. Generally, physicians have created extremely 'broad' authorization forms to save time and money. Because most authorizations are so broad, it is important that consumers read the authorization form and make any revisions to it in writing. Consumers should place authorization restrictions for medical information access to only the information association with the current office visit. Sadly, medical information is getting into the hand of data brokers and resellers. I do not feel that consumer data resellers should ever have access to consumers' medical records information for reselling purposes. Data brokers and resellers currently sell high levels of consumer personal and financial information to the highest bidder and the accuracy of any of this data, especially illegally obtained medical records - is never guaranteed.

Do not authorize insurance companies to use your medical information for any other purpose other than to pay your medical provider. Remember to 'edit' those medical authorizations by drawing lines through the information that does not apply to your doctor's office visits. Initial those changes and request a copy of that authorization in the event that your medical information is later released without your authorization.

Return those Privacy Notification 'Opt-Out' forms to block the sharing or reselling of your information. This includes Opt-Out statements from your health and dental insurance companies since they to will sell your personal information.

Chapter 5 - Background Checks – What You Need to Know About Your Personal Information

As a Manager and while working with consumer Background Information I had to clearly understand how our system developers would compile data, and develop and code the various web based application that were utilized by our clients. I also had to have a clear understanding of how information was obtained by our company that was to be resold to our clients. Consumers would be surprised at the level of personal information that is captured and retained by various resellers/brokers databases on a daily basis, and this is what was considered as consumer background information.

This gathering of consumer information goes much further each time a consumer performs a transaction (purchase from a store via check, credit/debit card or use those wonderful grocery points cards), or submit a response to a 'consumer' questionnaire, company rebate, purchase a home, rent an apartment, purchase an auto, update your drivers license, obtain a professional license, purchase utilities, become ill (yes sick with a serious illness), move, get a new job, get married, get divorced, have children, renews a license, apply for credit and of course commits any legal offense - your information is being retained and a historical path is being updated. *(Yes, a run-on sentence, but you get the picture.)* Interestingly all of the above information can be obtained from just one background source and in a compiled comprehensive report, within seconds – be it correct or incorrect information, it is all available and being viewed by most companies without authorizations from the consumer? Consumers obviously have had, until now, no idea of the levels of information (correct or incorrect) that corporations are needlessly requesting on consumers.

When I state correct or incorrect, this is the world of the data brokers and resellers – you don't really know what you are getting but yet, the compiled 'comprehensive' consumer information is bought and resold as though it is factual information. I will talk more about this process of consumer information validation later.

Additional types of background checks may also consist of what is called the employment screening process. Employers often use different companies that conduct employee-screening tests, these tests including drug tests, personality assessment tests, and background checks, all of which are legal as long as the employer does not base the tests on religious beliefs, sexual practices, or race.

Where Does Background Checking Generally Apply

In a technological world as we live, it applies to every business entity, and most consumers are now, also conducting background checks. Most Human Resources departments within most large corporation clearly follow the Privacy and Consumer Laws when conducting consumer background checks. What I have addressed throughout my book, are those companies, corporations and or company personnel who chose not to adhere to privacy laws, nor do they respect the privacy of consumers. The following are some of the areas where background checks are usually conducted.

- Education Verification
- Employment History Verification
- Criminal Records Search
- Civil Records Search
- Driving Records Search
- Nationwide Background Search
- Credit History Check
- Sex Offender Search
- Professional License Verification
- Drug and Health Screening

These are just some of the areas that background checks apply. As you can see a background, check can be conducted to validate several areas of a consumer's life. Generally for an employment verification a prospective employer may request an Education Verification, Employment History, Criminal, Civil, Driving Record and possible your Credit History Record. Generally, background-checking companies are combining the Criminal Background check with a Sex Offender Search. The Nationwide Background Search generally includes a nationwide criminal check and may include the Sex Offender Search. However, I do not feel *any* background company has automated access to all courts and counties in the United States so the accuracy of a Nationwide Background Check is generally questioned by me.

For those consumers with Professional Licenses, validation of those licenses are now included in background checks.

Nationwide Background Checks – What You Need To Know About the Accuracy of This Information

As a former Director of Operations, I would cringe when a client requested a so-called 'Nationwide Background Check'. This was a product that was sold to our clients as a fast and inexpensive way of obtaining consumers criminal history. Generally, this report would take 1 to 3 days to produce. What was most interesting was that we utilized several sources to compile this type or report and with no true guarantees that all of the information was accurate. To guarantee accuracy was humanly impossible, but this product was sold. This national check included all fifty states, Canada and Mexico. Can you imagine a true report from Mexico, but it was also included and sold.

One very important note here is that there are no 'consumer accessible' nationwide sources or repositories that house this type of consumer search information. The indication of no 'consumer accessible' nationwide source is noted because there is a national law enforcement database that is only accessible to the federal government.

What was even most challenging was that most of cities, counties, and even states do not have any form of criminal automated reporting systems. One Nationwide Search may consist of some automated information, some human intervention (which was quite costly) where our investigative source would engage a person to physically go to a court to check the record then return any information found. Now you might think this was a good step in the process – until we found that we were being billed for searches that were never performed.

What was even most challenging was that a complete Nationwide Criminal Background check could consist of not only a criminal search, but also any arrest records, and civil records that may be tied to the criminal case, any state cases, and it included any federal court cases – where applicable. In addition, most courts have began to restrict access to some consumer information, and in most cases the most important validation criteria such as a consumers date-of-birth or social security number. With consumer 'like-names' it was humanly impossible to validate the information but our office would still report the information that was found to the client. Can you image the lack of accuracy in compiling this type of information in a three-day period, in a 'so-called' automated process? Apathy….No!

Every court reports information differently and in some situations in quite strange data formats, let's not address the inaccuracies from court to court. Of course, there are no governmental laws that require that information be reported in any specific format. While working as a Court Systems Consultant I also experienced the level of inaccuracies from court to court in their timeliness in reporting case dispositions to their respective states. Some cases went unreported for months – so with that being said.

The Correct 'Background' Information Gathering Process

Now, I would say that there is a way of obtaining a more accurate Nationwide Background Check for consumer but it does require time and generally more money then the average company is willing to spend. A more accurate nationwide report also requires that the company obtain the correct authorizations from the consumer and not attempt to circumvent the process by utilizing fraudulent (non-authorized) sources to check consumer's background history. If a credit report is required, it should be stated on the consumer authorization. If a driving record is required it should also be stated on the authorization and of course if for any reason a consumers medical record is required, it should be stated on the authorization. A company should include in the requested authorization that a consumer provide all names used for the specified number of years and all address history.

I would personally begin by checking each city and county for all records (arrests, criminal, civil and traffic cases) with and without a date of birth, then with a date of birth and compare the results. I would also check for like-names and spellings. In addition, I would also check the respective states federal databases for any prison records. For consumers driving records, get the authorization from the consumer, go directly to the state, and request the consumers driving information. I saw too many 'brokered' 'resold' and 'sold-over' consumer driving records that came in with inaccurate or missing information. In addition, I must note here that even the states report inaccurate driving conviction information but if I were using a source, it would be the state direct for a driving record.

What I would not do, *unless you have an 'open mind'* and would not draw any quick conclusion; is not to utilize any 'so-called' sources of 'so-called' comprehensive background checks, since I would not rely on sources who sell or broker information without consumer authorization, *especially a consumers medical records information.*

Last. If 'Adverse Information' is obtained, follow the consumer laws that are set and allow the consumer to respond before any action is taken against them. The requester would still have a sense of validation of 'Adverse Information' with the consumer. For a driving record, it may require validation of conviction with the respective court.

What Information Can be Shared - Background Checks

Unfortunately, all consumer background information is now accessible. There are Background Checking Systems that can provide a consumers background information that can consist of your information from the time that you obtain a social security number, to your date of death and every detail between. The information includes detailed information on every state that a consumer has lived, every driver's license renewal, every auto titled in your name, to every parcel of property that you have owned and more, and companies are using this information every day. That is a little scary, but these systems exist and are being used by banks, financial companies and everyday consumers to access a consumer's private information – and consumers need to be aware of it.

Some 'standard' information sharing that currently exists from State to State is multi-state access to Driving Records and Criminal Records information. In addition, states do access multi-state criminal and warrant databases. I do feel these two areas of information sharing are necessary in an age of threats of terrorisms. What I feel should be protected in consumer information, is a consumer's medical records information and personal credit information. Since there are clear privacy laws to protect these types of consumer information, consumers must begin to monitor these areas more closely.

Consumers can monitor credit reports for any fraudulent inquires by companies who may access credit files without authorization. You can also refuse requests for access to your medical records information since there are companies who are currently selling consumer medical records information to background checking companies, and to other resellers.

Consumers can return those 'Opt-Out' statements that are receive annually from banks, insurance companies, health insurance billing companies and credit card companies. Consumers can turn off or 'block' Internet 'Cookies' on your computer to stop the capture of your personal and credit card (purchase) information, and to stop the sharing of your personal and purchasing history. The process procedure to turn off Cookies is available in chapter 4. *There are steps that we can all take to guard our privacy and stop this madness of so-call consumer information sharing.*

An additional step to protecting your information is to obtain a Post Office Box as an additional address. By obtaining a Post Office Box, you will protect your privacy and block the compiling of additional address history information. There is a (CRA) Consumer Reporting Agency currently reporting all address history on consumers. This includes anyone who receives mail at your specified address. Anyone can conduct an address history on your address and obtain the names of every individual who lives there. Invasion is clearly invasion and this is completely ridiculous. There is also a credit reporting company who records and reports your personal information from the time you were first reported to their credit bureau. Is it really important to list where a sixteen year old lived at the time they obtained their first credit card if that information is fifteen years old, not really? Strangely, this credit reporting agency will not remove old addresses information when consumers request the removal and is currently reselling that information (correct or incorrect) to background checking companies. This 'address history' product can be hazardous for any person who has been stalked, or prefers not to provide information that may be over ten years old. This is an invasion of privacy since some employers *do* go back further then the stated 10 year period on consumer's background checks, even though they may indicate that only 7 years will be accessed on the written request to the consumer.

A 'False' Background Check Can Happen To You – What To Do

As a former Director of Operations of a Background Checking company, I had the unfortunate opportunity of experiencing the results of many false, inaccurate, and incomplete consumer (information) background checks. What do I mean when I say false, inaccurate, and incomplete, background checks? Most consumer data, or information is entered into a system by humans, and humans make mistakes all the time. Mistakes at times occurring when a court representative is entering court case disposition information for traffic, criminal or civil case, or by a creditor entering incorrect consumer account information. Additional mistakes occur everyday with the inaccurate imputing of a consumer's social security number, the date of birth, the misspelling of a consumers name or an incorrect address, and these are some of the key factors in a background search.

A greater problem exists with consumer background information due to the levels of background information Resellers that exists in the United States. Everyone who wants to be a provider of consumer background information, now is? Consumer information is bought and sold by these resellers everyday. Consumer information is combined into various databases to create a 'so-called' super database of consumer information. Consumer data is scrubbed (*certain information removed*), replaced (*where a search result has incomplete data, companies will add 'what is assumed correct' data to complete a search result for a client*) and thus manipulating the produced background information. These background companies chose to do what ever they want to do with consumer data, and without the client or customers knowledge. Every supplier of background information wants to prove to their clients that they have the largest database of consumer information with the greater numbers of Local Municipality, County and State coverage's – but they don't. *It is impossible while using an automated system to produce accurate results.* Now you can better understand why consumers continue to have inaccurate background information appearing in their background checks, it has happened to me, and it can happen to you. *And yes, there are more accurate ways of producing a consumer's background check - but in order to produce accuracy, it takes time. Companies or CRA's are more interested in volume sales of consumer information rather then in increasing their rate of accuracy.*

Additional 'false and inaccurate' consumer information can also be obtained when other consumers are attempting to commit fraud by using another consumer's information (identity theft). Use of a consumers name, address, or even someone's social security number in the commission of a crime or driving violation, and these records remain as fact until they are invalidated.

What I considered as a 'false' background check was the return of negative background information attached to an individuals name as though the negative information was fact. This happens every day. What I consider as 'inaccurate' information, is information where there may have been some form of a conviction in a consumers background but the conviction information was entered incorrectly. And what would be considered as 'incomplete' would be no true cross-reference of information in order to validate a consumers information, missing information such as an incomplete social security number, missing letters in a name, no valid date of birth or address for the consumer.

Where I seemed to find most mistakes was in the court systems throughout the United States, yes – the Courts. Errors in data input occurs daily in the courts - be it when a Traffic offense is entered by a Police department representative or once the citation is forwarded to court personnel for further processing. Court systems are riddled with errors. Because of most court errors resulting from Traffic offenses, Driving records also have a high number of errors. These Driving record errors are created at the court or conviction level and are transferred to the various state Division of Motor Vehicles, and again – with errors.

No Guarantees of Accuracy

Most companies requesting background information on consumers do not understand that not all consumer background information is guaranteed 100% accurate, especially smaller companies. I seem to have had my greatest challenges with smaller companies when explaining the rights of the consumer or prospective employee when negative background information is received. I personally believe that it is humanely impossible to guarantee and produce 100% accuracy in consumer background information without some form of manual assessment or intervention, but companies continue to sell their background products as though there are guarantees. When consumer background checks were conducted in-house by my staff, I could randomly perform quality checks on data to validate accuracy. How many companies take that initiative, not many?

Each time a company or financial institution requests a background check on a consumer, written authorization should be obtained from that consumer, and sometimes the authorizations are not obtained by the company before making the request or logging on the our website to make the request. This is a consumer violation and against the Fair Credit Reporting Act. The random validation of the appropriate authorizations was a part of my auditing and validation process, but some violators did, and do get away with their violations in fraudulently accessing consumer information.

Our (CRA) Consumer Reporting Agency provided consumer background information via a web-based system. With some direct access to various entities, such as courts or state motor vehicle department, you cannot see how the background information is being processed, or the level of accuracy of that information. With clients who log on via the Internet to access and request, background information a company cannot validate all authorizations. In addition, a company may have direct access to the information source or reseller but may not be able to validate the accuracy of the consumer information. Nor can companies validate where the information was obtained, or if the information has been purchased from other resellers. I know this statement is somewhat confusing, but it is just as stated – resellers have no idea where consumer information truly originates.

This problem exists all over the United States for such providers and resellers of consumer information. There are no guarantees that the consumer information is correct, all the time.

What you need to do if a 'False Background Check' is returned on you:

- Immediately inform the company or individual that requested the background check that the report is inaccurate.
- Request a copy of the original background check. By law, it must be made available to you and without a fee.
- Request the name of the provider of the background check.
- Dispute the background information in writing with both your employer and the company that requested the background check, and with the provider of the information.
- Inform the provider of the background information (company) that you are aware of the Fair Credit Reporting Act and that they have to respond quickly with a correction to the false background information. Review the (FCRA) Fair Credit Reporting Act, consumer rights to become familiar with the Act. You may also review the FCRA section of this book for summary guidelines.
- Request that the employer or company not consider the negative information and to request another background check from another source, if possible.
- And last, if you have been a victim of identity fraud or have

been informed in the past that 'false' negative consumer information exists on you, or you have a 'like name', Smith, Jones, etc., that may produce an incorrect background check – inform the company who is requesting a background check on you before it is conducted. Since some (CRA) Consumer Reporting Agencies, employees do not understand how to read background information, or may come to an incorrect conclusion quickly - inform them at the beginning of the process.

When Violations Occur with a Consumer Reporting Agency - Where to Report the Violation

The (FCRA) Fair Credit Reporting Agency has drafted the rules and regulations regarding consumer information reporting. The (FTC) Fair Trade Commission imposes the penalties for violators.

A Consumer Reporting Agency or CRA is any company that has access to and supplies or resells a consumer's information. This could be a credit-reporting agency or a background checking company. What the FCRA states is the requesting agency must have an authorization to access a consumer's information and the responsibility to report that information accurately. If errors, incorrect or incomplete information is found, the consumer must receive an 'Adverse Action Notice' listing the consumers rights and in a timely manner from the date that the adverse information is reported (in summary).

What is most important is the Fair Credit Reporting Act also states that the consumer or employee must receive a 'Pre-Adverse Action' notification at the time the request for background information is made. Most employers or entities requesting background checks fail to present this piece of documentation to the consumer prior to requesting a background check. The 'Pre-

Adverse Action' notification, in summary, will document the rights of the consumer in the event negative or adverse information is found in a consumers background check. Since the Act clearly states that a 'Pre-Adverse Action' notification should always be presented, in my opinion, this would be an FCRA violation. If this situation applies to you, please contact the Fair Trade Commission. No consumer should be denied his or her rights.

To report a consumer violation, go to the (FTC) Fair Trade Commissions website to complete the complaint form. You may also want to consult with an attorney.

What Is Considered a Violation of Consumer Rights Based On FCRA and FTC

In my assessment, the most severe violation would be the accessing of consumers information (non-public information) without authorization for the consideration of employment, promotion, purchase, or investigative reasons. Interestingly this violation is committed regularly. I have seen violations committed by Background Checking companies who supply consumer's information to their customers without signed authorization or have the necessary precautions put in place to assure consumers privacy when accessed via web-based systems, especially with access to consumers credit information.

How Can Consumers Find Violations

The first location and most accurate location would be to start with your credit report and look for any credit inquires that you have not authorized. You will generally find two sections on your credit report regarding inquires. One inquiry section may list companies or agencies that have requested and obtained your full credit report. The other inquiry section will generally list those companies who have only requested your name and possible address. I feel, the name and address request should also be considered an invasion of privacy but credit reporting agencies (credit bureaus) sell consumers information daily. *Back to the Inquiries.* Look for any company name and phone number (since phone numbers now appear on the credit reports) that you did not apply for credit with and nor give authorization to access your credit file. In most cases, the company that fraudulently requested your personal credit information will not respond. Report the violation to the Credit Reporting Agency that submitted your authorized credit file to the fraudulent company, and also report the violation to the Fair Trade Commission, you may also consider reporting the violation to your States Attorney General, since this could also be identity theft. You should also request from the credit reporting agency (bureau) that the "Inquiry' be removed from your credit report since the request was not authorized and can affect your credit score. Make sure that you keep a hardcopy of the original credit report displaying the violation (inquiry) since this will be your evidence of the original violation.

When FCRA violations have occurred, companies have had to pay heavily in fines for those violations. One background checking company, Choice Point was fined heavily for violations along with several mortgage companies over recent years. Some mortgage companies are guilty of *fishing* for loans by accessing consumer's information without authorization; to me it is all identity theft. Protect your information and report violations when they occur.

Who Uses Consumer Background Information

In an age of systems automation and data sharing, nearly every business entity is now conducting background checks; Banks, employers, rental and leasing companies, investigators, insurance companies for auto –home and life policies, health insurance companies for medical records, auto financing companies, and of course the federal government.

While managing a background checking company our largest client base was employers and hiring recruiters. Which companies would I say utilized background check to re-certify consumers annually, would be employers. Our company created a background product that would automatically check the backgrounds of a company's employees yearly and flag any employee that had any Criminal conviction or high level driving offenses. Other types of industries that randomly generated background checks on consumers were banks, financing companies, and of course investigators. You may think that after being employed with a company and one initial background check was performed at your hire date, that there would be no other background checks performed? Be assured that several companies now perform several background checks on employees annually and that sometimes includes your driving records and your credit information. Companies will label these types of annual employee background checks as 'employee re-certifications'.

Background Check Authorizations – What You Need To Know

While working with consumer background information I found that several companies would randomly request repeat background checks on their existing employees. It became apparent to me that old authorizations were being used during random audits of our clients. Authorizations that were sometimes years old would be forwarded to our office as a tenant or employees signed release for background information. This background information would sometimes be used for multiple areas of a consumer's background. Background information requests were for such information as driving records, criminal, civil and or credit reports. The authorizations were valid but 'open-ended' authorizations and had to be accepted by our company and not questioned.

I found it somewhat appalling that an employer would not renew their request to conduct a background check and of course there are no known 'statute of limitations' on a signed release authorizations.

We consumers forget that an authorization was granted to a company or business entity to conduct a background check, for whatever the reason - be it employment, leasing or banking. Where we fail is at completion of the business transaction or employment verification process, the signed release or authorization remains open and available.

Remember to withdraw those authorizations after the transaction is completed or employment ceases. You may also cancel those authorizations after you are employed. These checks can sometimes include your credit and believe me I have seen where employers randomly request credit checks along with a consumer's criminal, civil and driving records background check. This information request continues even after employees are hired and sometimes after they are released. *Remember to cancel or withdraw authorizations after the initial information is obtained.*

Chapter 6 - Companies – How to Validate or Test the Quality of Background Information

This section is my attempt to assist companies in validating consumer background information. With so many incorrect, inaccurate and incomplete background checks being returned to companies that negatively affect consumers, I am making the following suggestions to validate consumer information.

What most companies do not understand is that background checking companies' broker information daily. Some background checking companies use old outdated information with no regular updates. Some background checking companies rely on 'checker', individuals that will go to a specified court to conduct a records check in person (or not), and some companies rely on poorly managed state repositories. However, the company's source of information, one easy step to test a background checking company is to generate the same background checks from your selected companies, using background checks that you know are filled with negative information that has been manually verified by you. The check should be against as many aspects of background information (validated) by you as possible, information such as education, credit, civil, traffic, and criminal information. I would begin by requesting validation of those checks directly from the state source such as directly for a department of motor vehicles, and a criminal or traffic records check directly from a courts database to validate your findings. You can perform the same step by contacting the consumers 'stated' college for education verification and so on. These validations will take a little more time but should produce information that is more accurate. Of course, these requests are made once you have obtained the proper authorizations from the employee or consumer.

The next step is to review the information received to see which background checks (companies) produced the correct information.

'An Invasion of (corporate) Locust' by Darlene R. Miles

An excellent test of a background or consumer-reporting agency or company is to conduct a Nationwide Background check on a consumer where you know a conviction occurred in a small court. Perform this type of validation of consumer information quarterly or at least twice a year to verify that the company's supplier of information is not being tainted. Keep an open mind, do not accuse an employee of having a negative background check without providing the consumer or employee with the opportunity (per FCRA rules and per the Adverse Action Notification) to prove that the information is incorrect. Generally if the information is correct the consumer or employee will accept your notification and not challenge the information, but if challenged – you most provide them the time to do so. In addition, each consumer or employee has a legal right to have a copy of the background information and the name or source of the provider, and at no cost to him or her. If the information is incorrect, the provider MUST correct the information, provide a correction notification to the supplier (broker), and resubmit a corrected background report to you (the employer) and to the consumer. Be aware, most background checking companies do not go this far... on the behalf of the consumer -but they must, by law. *They must also block or flag the incorrect information from future background checks, not allowing the incorrect information to pass through their system again or risk the possibility of legal action.*

Companies and 'Adverse Action' Consumer Notifications

Must companies are not aware of the appropriate 'Adverse Action' consumer notification procedure. Please consult with the (FTC) Fair Trade Commission for detail compliance. In the meantime, I have summarized the consumer 'Adverse Action' consumer right notification procedure, which appears in the 'Adverse Action and Consumer Rights' section of my book.

Sample 'Adverse Action' Consumer Notification

Sample 'Adverse Action Letter

Dear Sample Consumer, xxx-xx-1234

Thank you for your recent application to:

At this time, we are unable to approve your application.

This adverse action has been taken in accordance with the requirements of the federal Fair Credit Reporting Act, 15 U.S.C. 1681m(a).

This decision was based on:
[ ] Information contained in a consumer report(s) obtained from or through (The Named Source and Phone Number Here), which may include credit or consumer information from one or more credit reporting bureaus or consumer reporting agencies.

[ ] Information obtained from a source other then a consumer reporting agency. (You have the right to disclosure of the nature of this information, upon your furnishing proper identification, if you make a written request to us within 60 days of receiving this letter.)

[ ] Other:_____

In evaluating your application, information obtained from or through (Named Source Here), which may include credit information or consumer information from one or more of the credit bureaus or consumer reporting agencies, may have influenced our decision in whole or in part. These consumer-reporting agencies and /or credit bureaus did not make the decision to take adverse action and are unable to provide specific reasons why adverse action was taken.

YOU HAVE CERTAIN RIGHTS UNDER FEDERAL AND STATE LAW WITH RESPECT TO YOUR CONSUMER REPORT. IF ANY PERSON TAKES ADVERSE ACTION BASED IN WHOLE OR IN PART ON ANY INFORMATION CONTAINED IN A CONSUMER REPORT OR CREDIT REPORT, YOU HAVE THE RIGHT TO A DISCLOSURE OF THE INFORMATION IN YOUR CONSUMER FILE FROM THE AGENCY THAT PROVIDED SUCH INFORMATION, IF YOU MAKE A WRITTEN REQUEST TO THEM AND UPON YOUR PROPER IDENTIFICATION WITHIN 60 DAYS OF RECEIVING THIS DENIAL. THE FEDERAL FAIR CREDIT REPORTING ACT IS ALSO PROVIDES THAT YOU BE ENTITLED TO OBTAIN FORM ANY NATIONWIDE CREDIT REPORTING AGENCY OR CREDIT BUREAU A FREE COPY OF YOUR REPORT IN ANY TWELVE-MONTH PERIOD. YOU HAVE EAT RIGHT TO DIRECTLY DISPUTE WITH THE CONSUMER REPORTING AGENCY AND/OR CREDIT BUREAU TE ACCURACY AND COMPLETENESS OF ANY INFORMATION FURNISHED BY THAT AGENCY OR BUREAU AND TO PROVIDE A CONSUMER STATEMENT DESCRIBING YOUR POSITION IF YOU DISPUTE THE INFORMATION IN YOUR CONSUMER FILE. IF YOU BELIEVE THE INFORMATION IN YOUR CONSUMER FILE IS INACCURATE OR INCOMPLETE, YOU MAY CALL (Named Source Here and Phone#) WILL INITIATE THE REINVESTIGATION OR ANY DISPUTED INFORMATION OBTAINED THROUGH THEM AND WILL REINVESTIGATE ANY DISPUTED INFORMATION OBTAINED FORM THEIR DATABASE.

Authorized Signature: _____
Date: _____

'An Invasion of (corporate) Locust' by Darlene R. Miles

Chapter 7 - Consumer Information Sharing from State-to-State and Company to Company

The sharing of consumer information generally starts with the companies that we consumers conduct our day-to-day business with. Every time consumers make a purchase with something other than cash, consumers create an opportunity for a company to capture, share, and sell your personal information. Each time consumers use those bonus or advantage 'points' cards issued by retailers, banks and drugstores we put ourselves in a position to have information captured and shared regarding our purchasing habits. Each time we log onto a website our information is captured in the form of 'cookies' and stored. This stored information includes the products that we have viewed, request a price for and or purchased with our credit cards, your personal information, user ids, and passwords are recorded and stored in a database.

By not frequently deleting computer temporary files and stored 'Cookies' off our computers, and not completing and returning those so-called 'Opt-Out' documents sent to all consumers yearly, we position ourselves for additional information sharing of our personal and consumer purchase information.

What company's generally will state on most of their 'opt-out' annual documents is that they will only share consumer information with their corporate partners or something such as that? Well understand that after working with several companies automated systems, *everyone* is a corporate partner for the right price. This is why we consumers receive such high levels of junk mail, junk email from those 'so-called' another corporate partners....hummm.

Other more serious forms of information sharing are the use of nationwide database systems that are used by law enforcement agencies. I personally feel that their systems are most accurate and provide the necessary tool for law enforcement to perform nationwide criminal and driving records checks, and of course without any written authorization required from the consumer.

Consumer Credit Information Sharing (Reselling) and Opt-Out Information

All three of the credit reporting agencies, TransUnion, Equifax, and Experian currently sell consumer information. The selling of consumer information can be conducted at all levels to include the types of account content that currently resides on your credit report. These accounts can be defined as, mortgage loans, auto loans, credit cards, college loans. These credit-reporting agencies will group types of account and consumer information and resell consumer information for profit.

To OPT-OUT of the credit reporting agencies selling of your consumer credit information for what they define as 'firm offers', and for a period of 5 years - consumers must call the following number:

- 1-888-5-OPT-OUT or 1-888-567-8688

The Opt-Out number and service will then forward your request to all three credit-reporting agencies and by law, your request will stop the reselling of your information to companies of offers, for five years.

Your may also chose to place a Security Freeze on your credit file that will override the OPT-OUT process. When a Security Freeze is placed on your credit file, no one will be able to access or sell any of your credit file information at any level. You may place a Security Freeze on your credit file for one or seven years. Please refer to the chapter on 'Protecting Your Credit Information'.

Driving Records Information Sharing (History)

Most state agencies will retain up to 10 years of driving history, keep that in mind. In some cases, the number of years can be greater then 10 years for historical information. Several background companies gain access to consumers driving records information via specific agreements with a particular state and some companies broker (purchase) driving records from other companies (I do not agree with this process). Being a part of the building process of several state relationships, I had the opportunity to view the very strict contracts that most states provide to resellers of their driving records information. While some states do not permit the reselling of consumer driving records information there were always other sources ready to provide that same information to a client or reseller. This is an example of brokered 'resold' information that could have been tainted with errors, and believe me in most cases it was.

Criminal and Civil Records Information Sharing (History)

Criminal information sharing, at its best quality, is most accurately housed in government or federal databases that are not accessible to consumers. Criminal information that is made available to consumers or companies generally consists of a host of 'so-called' nationwide systems that I do not truly believe in. Any sharing of criminal or civil records is available via public records of the respective cities, county or states that house those records.

Even though most employers will request from a consumer the authorization to check only 7 years back on Criminal or Civil information, they generally obtain all that they can obtain. In most cases, the volume of information received is out of anyone's control. What I mean by out of anyone's control, is when a request for background information is made, it is generally made with the broadest request, or should be, then narrowed down.

What I mean by a broad request, a request that would by made initially by 'name only', then name and social security number, alias names and combined date-of-birth. Obviously a 'name only' request may result in a high volume of information returned but does at least provide the requester with as much information as possible that may exist. A first request as a 'broad name-only' request is always recommended since some courts, for privacy reasons, block the display of social security numbers and sometimes dates-of-birth.

A responsible person will analyze the information received very carefully and not make any immediate assumptions of guilt or innocence until the (volume) information can be further verified.

Chapter 8 - Background Information – How to Successfully Expunge and Seal Negative Background Information

From State to State, City to City, Court to Court, or Judge to Judge the handling of Court Case Expungements or Sealed cases was handled a little differently. The consistency that I found was that each court had an Expungement process that was offered to consumers.

As a then Court Systems Consultant, my job was to make sure that our Court System application was able to accommodate every courts Rules and Regulations along with the compliance of the State and Local Statues as law were enforced. I not only conducted the sales presentations of our firm's automated court system applications, I was also responsible for any additional court systems requirements, system modifications, system implementation and court personnel training that was required. I would draft the client's requirements and translate those requirements into developer's specification for our team of developers. The developers would then perform the necessary systems coding (*writing of new applications or enhancement of a current application*) to comply with the needs of the court. These enhancements could consist of a new court *legal form*, a new *State Statute,* or *Local Municipal Law change.* In addition, I also wrote the 'User Documentation', for the various court applications that were used by court staff, Clerk of Courts and Judges, and the procedure to implement or utilize new enhancements - and so on. It was interesting to see that each court processed their court cases, local statutes and charged fines/fees a little differently from city to city. The uniqueness between the various courts kept our consulting firm and me quite busy.

Over the years, I have had several people ask about the Sealing or Expunging of Court Case Information so I have added some information about that subject, and based *solely* on my experience working with the courts and <u>not</u> as a legal advisor.

The topic of Expungements and Sealing of court case information was also a hot topic with consumers while I was the Director of Operations for a consumer background information company. I found that this topic would reappear weekly when negative information (assumed expunged or not) appeared in the backgrounds of consumers applying for employment, opening a bank account (in some cases) and/or attempting to rent or lease an apartment. Generally, by the time a consumer would be speaking with me, my staff had already presented the background information to the requester. Obviously, the consumer felt hopeless and that it was too late to help them. At this point, their negative and assumed expunged information had been found and was in the hands of their employer, prospective employer, rental office, or bank.

I have added this Expungement section because I personally feel it is never too late. I want to arm consumers with information, who have had an occurrence in life where a criminal or civil offense has been hindering them from successfully moving forward. Mistakes do happen and I believe in second chances. I am not an attorney and do not proclaim to be one. The information that I am providing is based on public information and my experience working with the courts throughout the United States.

What does it mean to Expunge?

Expunged information is the removal or sealing of negative court case information. Criminal, civil or traffic case information that you may not want on your record for life. Some courts will Expunge a record if your case was Dismissed only and use the term 'Sealing of a Record' when you are found Guilty. Some courts will initially Seal a record and wait for several years before completely Expunging the record. This 'wait' period is sometimes imposed as a Probationary period to monitor a consumer's behavior and to assure that the consumer does not appear in their court for another offense or conviction for that specified period of time. While some courts will initially grant the 'Sealing' and 'Expungement', at the same time without stipulation – some courts do not. Please also understand that in nearly all cases a fee is charged by the court for the Expungement of a court case.

Most courts or local municipalities conduct their own hearings. This will include the case scheduling through case disposition of their own court cases within their own jurisdiction. However, there are situation when a case is forwarded to another jurisdiction or higher court. If this situation occurs, make sure that <u>all associated records</u> are expunged, *from every entity*; be it a *jail record*, an *arrest record,* or *lower court record*. If by chance any articles are written about your conviction, you will want to also have those items sealed if possible. However, articles are generally considered public information and may be a little difficult to Seal. Believe me they can also come back to haunt you in later years, but are not generally chosen as 'background checking' documentation.

When external artifacts (newspapers, journals, etc.) may have any information regarding your conviction, I would suggest that you engage an attorney if the judge is not willing to list those items in the Expungement order. *All records and sources of information, to be expunged are always listed on the Expungement order, especially an arrest that also has a jail record.*

While working as a Court Systems Consultant I did experience situations where consumers did have court cases in other jurisdictions while requesting an Expungement in another. If this situation applies to you, do not be hesitant to apply to a number of courts for Expungement. It is your right to do so. *Make sure that you understand the Expungement rules for your State, County or Local (City) Municipality. Detailed information can generally be found on your courts website or by contacting the court directly. Only rely on information that is in writing, not on a conversation*

with a Court Clerk since most courts will provide the
documentation on their Expungement procedure.

The Process of Notification – Your Protection

YOU MUST KEEP THE COURT ORDERED EXPUNGEMENT
documentation for life, in the event the record reappears again.
You must also contact all the local area and top national
background checking companies, and <u>forward a copy of the</u>
<u>Expungement</u> to those companies via certified mail. By mailing
certified, you will then have a returned receipt for your records if a
FCRA violation occurs later by their release of your background
information to anyone. <u>(Please see the FCRA Violation section of</u>
<u>my book for additional information.)</u> The proof of receipt of your
legal Expungement will become your added protection in the
future if the record resurfaces in that company's computer system.
Understand that, even though the court may issue an Expungement
order, they will not notify anyone on your behalf. All that you
have done by receiving the court order to Expunge or Seal your
information, is to receive the legal order of protection (my use of
words there).

Most consumers are not aware that public information is bought
and sold faster then running water, and that consumer information
remains out in the ozone for years. The only way to assure that
your expunged information is removed is to *be proactive and*
remove it yourself. An unfortunate situation for you would be if
the negative information re-appears when that big job is on the line.
Be proactive and make sure that background companies have your
court ordered document on file and your information blocked from
their system.

A final note on background information. Information is bought
and sold daily between courts, and consumer-reporting agencies
too include credit-reporting agencies. This also includes driving

records information. Most agencies sell their information, and in most cases to Resellers, who turn around and resell the information again, and again. With that being said, protect your information. *If a problem occurs, a Traffic citation, a bogus Arrest, get this taken care of immediately.* I have seen in the courts where certain Felony Convictions were expunged. So do not wait. The longer you wait the faster the information moves. A traffic citation, in most states converts to a warrant for your arrest when not paid. An arrest record can stop you from gaining employment or leasing an apartment. These issues are serious.

Verifying the Removal of Negative Background Information

Situations occur in life that can result in negative consumer background information, a DUI, an Arrest in college, a 'false arrest', or even a civil action that was never removed from your records. First of all you want to apply to the courts to have negative information removed; Expunged or Sealed then protect your rights and verify that no sources or suppliers of consumer background information continues to supply that negative information on you to anyone.

The verification of the removal of negative information can become a second job for you, for a period of time. The process can be lengthy, drawn out and time consuming. Nevertheless, you must protect your right to employment, residential and or commercial property leasing, and the ability to obtain financing. Based on my experience working with background information and privacy laws, I have some suggested steps to save you time.

The first step would be to submit your request for Expungement and/or Sealing of your record, and *all associated records*, to the court. After the court Expungement is completed, request via public records from the court, your own information to verify that all associated case information has been removed. The court may also have 'public access' terminals where you can walk in and search their database for your prior conviction information. In an age of Internet access, you may also be able to log into the courts database via the web. Make sure that you print a hardcopy of your inquiry into your 'name search', since there should be no records available from your prior conviction.

The second step would be to submit your court documentation to as many background checking companies in your area and nationally via certified mail for a return receipt. Once you have submitted your Expungement documentation, request a verification document from those companies, or perform your own background check on yourself from those companies to verify that the information has been removed from their systems. You want to perform some type of verification for a period of time by randomly accessing your background information, from those same companies.

The background report should not include your Expunged or Sealed information after you have submitted your Expungement documentation to these background-checking companies. If your information reappears these companies are in violation of the Fair Credit Reporting Act. You should make the verification requests from the same companies that you forwarded the court Expungement documentation to, to validate their systems accuracy of expunged records. Pay for the reports if necessary. This task will potentially save you thousands in finance interest (since banks use background checks) and future employment opportunities. I would suggest that you perform this task for two to three years or however long you chose. The records had better be blocked or removed from their system, or an FCRA violation has been committed and it would be time to file a complaint with the Fair Trade Commission.

The validation from each company that you receive also becomes the current state validation (documentation) of your information in their companies system. Also, recommend to the supplier of background information that they 'block' this negative information in their systems from future consumer searches. When Expungement documents are received at a background checking company the company should not only remove any reference to an expunged conviction, they should also place a 'block' on future receipts of that conviction information. Sadly, some companies fail to block the information from future receipts and the record reappears.

Why do I say that you should request validation that the information is removed for a period of time? All companies receive or purchase new records from various suppliers of consumer information; courts, state drivers license bureaus, and other brokers of consumer information. The negative (expunged) or incorrect information does not often get reported back to the supplier that the information they are supplying is no longer valid or is incorrect. Background companies do not often take the necessary steps to assure that corrections are sent back to the original suppliers, even to the courts.

You the consumer must take the initiative to correct your own information and document that you have supplied the (CRA) Consumer Reporting Agency, or background checking company with the corrected or expunged information.

The key to this process is to act quickly following any conviction or arrest. The longer you want to expunge a record the faster the information is moving through the hands of resellers.

Associated Records

When requesting an Expungement of any kind it is most important that the judge or court issuing the order to Expunge also include in the written order, the order to remove any associated records. Associated Records such as; arrest records, records retained in personnel files, and or jail records should be removed, expunged, and or sealed. The order should also include any civil records associated with the original charge or charges since restitution can sometimes be required and is a part of the original conviction or case. I have seen where associated records do appear later in other systems, be it a Jail system or in a Civil case resulting from the original charges.

To assure removal you must make the request of the court to remove all associated records. Also follow up with the agencies that are listed in the Expungement to validate the removal of the associated records, since mistakes can happen and records not be removed. Have the associated entities perform a search on your case number, your name, social security number, and address to assure that no records exist in their system. Request written validation, such as a system 'printout' that states 'no records were found' as of the date of your request.

Follow-up is also important with these entities. Wait 30 days then make the request again since systems are generally updated daily and monthly. Make the same request again in approximately six months, again to be assured that no data updates have occurred that may have contained your expunged or sealed information.

Expungement of Records (Who is Eligible?)

I could almost say that based on my experience as a Court Systems Consultant almost anyone is eligible to apply for an Expungement. Generally if you are a first-time offender who has only one conviction for either a felony or a misdemeanor and has no charge or charges pending with that court, you are were eligible. Each judge and court sets his or her own guidelines. You may not be eligible if you were convicted of certain crimes, including murder, rape, vehicular homicide, and crimes committed while you were armed. However, I have seen where a murder conviction was expunged but later re-appeared in a background check.

The laws regarding Expungement vary from Judge to Judge, city to city, county to county and State to State. What is important to know is that everyone has a legal right to apply to a court to have a conviction expunged. Expungement guidelines are generally available by contacting the court of conviction or an attorney. I would personally contact the court first to gain an understanding of the process. I would say, if you fall outside of those court 'standard' guidelines, submit your request anyway, in this case, I would probably utilize the assistance of an attorney, – and it does not hurt to submit your request.

Expungement of Records (When Can You File?)

I have seen where consumers have filed their Expungements immediately following the conviction, if no probation was required. If probation was required, following a conviction, some courts were a little more restrictive. I have seen in the courts, as our firm developed the various court systems, Expungements were generally granted two to three years from the time a consumer completed probation, parole or straight release from prison for a felony.

As part of the Expungement process, some courts would require that the defendant would have completed the payment of all court costs, fines, restitution, and or any community service that was imposed. In some cases, a court may only grant the Expungement after one year from the time you were convicted of a misdemeanor. At least two years from the time that a grand jury failed to indict you and the jury's report of "no bill" was returned. Any time after you were found not guilty, or your case was dismissed, and that information has been recorded in the court's journal, it can become eligible for Expungement.

Expunging Juvenile Records

Juvenile records are not available as public record after you reach the age of 18; however, records are viewed by the public all the time. If you committed an offense as a Juvenile, you can have those records Expunged or Sealed. It is not always an uphill battle for you.

In most cases with little assistance, you can process the paperwork for the Juvenile records Expungement on your own or with a little assistance from an adult. If you are doubtful, please always consult an attorney. The attorney should be able to provide you with some assurance that they *will* be able to produce the required outcome for you, which is your successful Expungement. If they cannot guarantee that outcome, then search for someone else, this is not rocket science. The process requires that you or your attorney comply with and understand the court rules and procedures for requesting Expungement and Sealing of Juvenile records.

If the court has a *'two part' process;* part one is the Expungement of the record and part two is the Sealing of the record, have the entire process included in the attorneys quote and fee. Do not just expunge a record if the court also has a Sealing process. Generally the record can be expunged which means it will no longer be made available to the public but can only be completely removed after a probationary period which is the final 'Sealing' of the record.

Understand that most courts do not utilize both methods. Most courts will expunge the record, which indicates complete removal.

The final outcome of the ultimate removal 'sealing' of the record may depend upon you. Since the court will monitor your behavior, in some form, you do not want to get into any additional trouble with the courts. At least not in trouble within the same municipality, city, and county or state (which ever applied to the record removal) that you are requesting.

Expunging Criminal Records

What is most tragic is that there are millions of consumers with criminal records of some kind. From what I have observed, while working with the courts and as a Director of Operations was that most of the criminal cases were non-violent criminal cases. A criminal record does not have to be limited to high-level crimes. A criminal case can also occur while driving. When these types of records occur, it can be very crippling to the consumer, loss of the right to secure employment, denial of certain types of financing, denial of access to lease an apartment, or even your right to vote.

This process does not have to be an uphill battle. What is even most unfortunate is that most criminal cases result from the consumer's inability to secure the appropriate legal representation at the time that they are charged with the offense. In my opinion, the ability to secure legal representation can in most cases result in a lesser charge and or possible dismissal prior to a trial, and obviously dependent upon the type of offense. Of course, the securing of an attorney will cost the consumer but I tell you, it is better to have the appropriate legal representative to fight than to be at the mercy of the court without it. Please also understand that even if a case is dismissed a court record is created so these records should also be considered for Expungement, they do appear in background checks.

In prior sections of my book, I have talked about types of convictions that I have seen expunged, with that being said – start your process of removing these types of records from your past. What I have seen in the past, while working as a Court Systems Consultant, were a great amount of arrest for the silliest of situations. Some Arrests occurring on college campuses for drunkenness, or even for college Protesting. Protesting, hummmm - sounds a little nonviolent to me, but still damaging to a consumers background. Other convictions, especially on college campuses were convictions for marijuana or bar fighting, get them all expunged before some potential employer uses those convictions against you, and they will. Start the 'clean-up' process quickly.

Remember that the first step in the Expungement process is to contact the court for their details of their Expungement process. Again, each court is different. What may work in one court may not work or apply in another court.

Expunging Civil Records

Civil records can be as disabling as any other court record. Most consumers are not aware that certain civil records can also affect the ability to secure employment since these records are also included in background checks. A Civil case does not involve a 'charge' as in a Criminal offense; however, a civil case can be tied to a Criminal case for money damages. Civil cases will generally involve cases where individuals sue each other over money issues. If by chance a consumer has been named in a Civil, case resulting from a guilty plea on a Criminal case then that guilty disposition (generally) becomes part of the Civil Case information of record. In addition, a plea of 'no contest' to a misdemeanor charge can also result in a civil case if money damages for restitution are filed in civil court. In this case, the court records will generally reflect the plea on the misdemeanor case and is now directly tied to the civil action. So, with that being said – you want to apply to the court to have a Civil case Expunged if the court of jurisdiction has applicable Expungement provisions.

A Civil record can be recorded at the federal, state, and local municipality courts level, or even by the military so when considering the Expungement process, remember that you will have to address the appropriate court or engage an attorney who specializes in this area. In addressing civil records, you may also want to address any civil records that may contain incomplete or inaccurate information.

Sample Expungement Form

The sample Expungement that follows is one of the most complex Expungements orders that I have seen while working with courts and consumer information. This is one of the types of court-automated forms that my former Consulting firm would create for our court clients. This form is a sample form and has been modified to reflect inaccurate statutes, and inaccurate ordinances. Do not be alarmed by the volume of content on this form; just be armed, with information.

As I previously stated, each court conducts their own Expungements so make sure that you review the Expungement order in detail. Do not be quick to sign a document that you do not understand. Consult an attorney if necessary.

IN THE SAMPLE COURT OF NAMED COUNTY,

IN THE SAMPLE STATE NAMED:

: CRIMINAL
DIVISION

v. :

: Docket Number:

MOTION FOR EXPUNGEMENT OF RECORD

AND NOW, comes the Defendant, and files this Motion to Expunge Record, averring in support thereof as follows:

1. On _____, Defendant was arrested for_____

_____ by the _____ Police Department and taken before Justice _____.

2. On _____, Defendant was accepted into the Sample Court Program

by Judge _____ and was given _____ Months of Probation; _____ license suspension and costs and fines.

3. Defendant successfully completed the Sample Program and paid all costs and fines in full.

4. Pursuant to Rule XXX of the Rules of Criminal Procedure, Defendant now wishes to have his/her record expunged in accordance with the provisions of the Criminal History Information Act, 01 STATE HERE. C.S.A. et. seq.

WHEREFORE, Defendant respectfully requests this Honorable Court to enter upon the record herein the Expungement Order attached hereto.

Respectfully

submitted,

_____

_____

Consent:

_____

District Attorney of Named County

IN THE SAMPLE COURT OF COMMON PLEAS

: OF NAMED
COUNTY,

v.:

: Docket Number:
: OTN:
:

ORDER OF COURT

AND NOW, to-wit, this _____ day of _____, 2007, upon consideration of the within Petition and on Motion of Expungement, it is ORDERED and DECREED, that the above-named defendant, whose date of birth is _____ and whose Social Security number is _____, for the charge(s) _____ Criminal History Record Information Act, 01 State C.S.A. § 9XXX3 as et. seq.,

'An Invasion of (corporate) Locust' by Darlene R. Miles

AND TO ACCOMPLISH THAT PURPOSE, IT IS SPECIFICALLY ORDERED THAT:
1. Counsel for the Defendant shall:
1. Serve two certified copies of said Petition and Order upon the arresting agency.
2. Serve one copy of the said Petition and Order on the District Attorney of Your County, and, if this Order involves Expungement of a case or cases finalized in the District Courts (where there was a dismissal, discharge or other final disposition at the District level, and no bind-over appeal to, or other disposition in a court of record), serve one copy of the Petition and Order upon the proper issuing authority or authorities.
2. The Clerk of Courts of Your County shall note the Expungement on the records of the within case(s), if the case(s) were finally disposed of in the Sample Court of Common Pleas.
3. The arresting police agency, upon receipt of two certified copies of the within Petition and Order from the Clerk of Courts, shall:
1. Forthwith forward one copy of the within Petition and Order to the , State Police Central Repository; and,
2. Note the Expungement on the records of the within case(s) maintained by their department, and expunge from any local RAP sheets or their equivalent maintained by said police agency any reference to the within case(s); and,
3. Within thirty (30) days of the receipt of this Petition and Order, file with the Clerk of Courts of Your County, an affidavit stating that paragraph 2 of this Order has been complied with.

4. The said State Name Here State Police Central Repository shall:
1. Expunge their records in accordance with this Order; and,

2. As required by the Criminal History Record Information Act, 01 State C.S.A. § XXX0 (d), "notify all criminal justice agencies which have received the criminal history record information to be expunged" of this Expungement order; and,
3. Within thirty (30) days of receipt of this Petition and Order, file with the Clerk of Courts of Your County, an affidavit stating that paragraph 3 of this Order has been complied.

5. The District Attorney and any issuing authority, upon receipt of; this Petition and Order shall note the Expungement on the records of their offices, if any, relating to the case(s).
IT BEING FURTHER ORDERED, HOWEVER, THAT NOTWITHSTANDING THE ABOVE AND IN ACCORDANCE WITH THE CRIMINAL HISTORY RECORD INFORMATION ACT, NOTHING IN THIS ORDER SHALL BE CONSTRUED TO REQUIRE:

A. The Expungement of public records which are exempt from Expungement by 01 State C.S.A. § 9X000 (e), namely, "(o)original records of entry complied chronologically, including but not limited to police blotters and press releases that contain criminal history record information and are disseminated contemporaneous with the incident", "(a) any documents, records or indices prepared or maintained by or filed in any court in the Commonwealth, including but not limited to the minor judiciary", "(p)posters, announcements, or lists for identifying or apprehending fugitives or wanted persons", or (a)announcements of executive clemency." 01 State C.S.A. § 9XX14 (a).

'An Invasion of (corporate) Locust' by Darlene R. Miles

B. The Expungement of non-criminal history record information which is exempt from Expungement by 01 State C.S.A. § 9XX91, namely intelligence information (defined in 01 State C.S.A. 9XX02 as "information concerning the habits, practices characteristics, possessions, associations or financial status of any individual", investigative information (defined in 01 State C.S.A. § 9XXX3 as "information assembled as a result of the performance o any inquiry, formal or informal, into a criminal incident or an allegation of criminal wrongdoing and may include modus operandi information), including medical and psychological information or information specified in 01 State C.S.A. § 9XXX3 as (Other than as specified in 1 above, this includes: "(c)court dockets, police blotters (including any reasonable substitute therefore) and information contained therein").

C. The Expungement of information required or authorized to be kept by the prosecuting attorney, the central repository and the court by 01 State C.S.A. § 9XXX3 as (c), relating to diversion or pre-conviction probation programs such as Accelerated Rehabilitative Disposition.

BY THE COURT:

_____

Consumers Attempting to Hide Negative Background Information

The attempt to 'hide' negative background information does not work permanently. However, I have seen some good attempts. I have seen situations where a consumer would provide an incorrect social security number to attempt to hide negative information. This may initially work until the correct consumers name appears in the social security validation database, yes, there is a database that validates social security numbers. I have also seen where consumers may move from state to state to avoid address verification history in a background check. Now this may work for local offenses since most companies will only request a background check based on the cities or states that the consumer provides as current and prior residences. It is important to know that the negative information may appear in a nationwide background check, note the word *may*.

I did however encounter one quite interesting attempt at hiding negative background information. This attempt occurred with a consumer from the state of Florida. The conviction was for Manslaughter. Yes, I said Manslaughter (someone's death). This was one of the most serious convictions that I had seen as a Director of Operations of the consumer-reporting agency. How did I see the 'so-called' hidden information, you ask? The record was not 'successfully' hidden nor was it (as stated to me) expunged from the court systems. The consumer was already employed in a high-level position and was due to be promoted to an even higher position when the information reappeared on a new background check.

With a possible promotion pending, the consumers company requested a new background check from the local recruiters. This recruiting company utilized our company's website and database for their background checks. This was also the company who originally processed the first background check for this consumer.

At this point, the second request for a background check was being conducted by a different representative in that same agency. This second representative then obtained the correct conviction information. Not only was there a criminal record for Manslaughter but also prison time served for that conviction. My, was this interesting. Under FCRA (Fair Credit Reporting Act) rules, this consumer had a legal right to contact the supplier of the information, which was our company, and the consumer did. This consumer contacted me several times originally stating that the information was expunged by the courts. I contacted the State of Florida regarding the 'time served' occurrence and the courts to verify the status of the conviction. All information reported on this consumer was correct. The records were not expunged. I also found that this individual had a series of other convictions in their background information that were not initially supplied in the information source.

What had occurred was the consumer contacted a representative of the recruiting firm that was engaged by the consumer's employer to conduct the employment background recertification. This office representative 'blocked' and deleted negative information from the content of the background check, and forwarded a clean report to the employer. This investigation went on for several weeks involving the employer, recruiting company and our office. This individual was dismissed from their position.

What this consumer and office representative clearly did not understand was that the agency directly logged into our database of information when conducting background checks, and that the information would eventually reappear again. What had occurred with the representative was the 'saving' or storing of the original altered background check on the area office computer. The 'old' background information was not used when the new office representative requested a recertification background check.

With daily and weekly updates of new information being received, with some direct connections to court databases and with the storing of existing information, this consumer's conviction would remain available for future reference. Thus, there was no legal Expungement of any records, only an attempt to hide the negative information. *A background recertification is generally conducted at employee promotion or by some employer yearly.* What employers are looking for when they recertify their employees are for any new criminal convictions, DUI's and or civil actions occurring since your hire date. Some employers will engage background-checking companies who may have an automated process to 'flag' employees that have negative information appearing in their backgrounds. Be aware of this employment background activity – it does exist.

As stated previously a background check is only as good as the sources of supplied information, some good, some bad, some accurate and some inaccurate. I would say that if you have negative information in your background clean it up. Have the record or records legally sealed and or expunged this is the best approach. Attempting to hide a conviction will only come back to haunt you at the most inopportune times. (Please refer to the section on Expungements for more information.)

Disputing Negative Background Information

The FCRA (Fair Credit Reporting Act) requires that information be reported accurately and that the consumer be able to obtain a copy of any negative information from the employer or the source that supplied the information. If the information is incorrect, you must be given the opportunity to prove the inaccuracy and obtain a corrected file free. When a company does not comply with the FCRA rule, the complaint is filed with the FTC (Fair Trade Commission).

Legislation enacted does place time limits on the amount of time that the source, supplier, or consumer reporting agency has to respond to a consumer inquiry on inaccurate or incomplete background information. These time limits are imposed as guidelines before a violation can be imposed. Understand that I have seen where incorrect information was reported on consumers, multiple times because the information remains out there until it is removed. These background checks are generally based on public information and generally entered by people. People are not error proof. Your social security number can be entered incorrectly by one digit resulting in inaccurate or negative information being reported on you. Your name can be miss-spelled and again resulting in negative information being reported, especially on your credit file. You can have (Jr.) junior as part of your name and the negative information from a (Sr.) senior is reported against you. Make sure your employer understands the law.

Generally, employers rely on incompetent background checking companies for their background checks. These companies, especially resellers, are not always accurate. While some employers do conduct, their own background checks they may not understand how to read the information. It is important to know that with so many privacy concerns some courts are not reporting case information with social security numbers or even with a consumers address. Without a consumer social security number or the ability to validate an address, it is a challenge when validating a background check. Companies or employers who conduct their own background checks must understand how to utilize other resources to cross-reference check the information. Most recruiting companies and employers do not understand the validation process for incomplete information but will report the incomplete information obtained as fact to the consumer and potentially deny employment. In some situations, employers will not grant the consumer the courtesy or right to know that negative information was gained in a background check. To save the employer time in processing paperwork the employer will just deny employment. I would suggest that if a background check is requested as part of an employment process, that the consumer request a copy of that background check - if you are not hired. Generally if a consumer passes the employment application process and reference check, the last step is to perform a background check. If you are denied employment at that point, you may never know that negative information exist in your background. I would not make a request until after the denial of employment. In addition, of course the denial of employment does not always result from a negative background check, so keep that in mind.

It is important to note that consumer information is bought and sold daily, generally from unknown sources (don't that sound interesting), sometimes hacked information from several other companies systems (isn't that a black hole), and so on. You have the legal right to have a copy of any background information obtained on you by anyone.

Adverse Action Letter Received Resulting From Background Checks

While working with consumer background information, I found that very few employers understood consumer rights. Most employers, residential leasing agencies, or background checking companies (resellers) who utilized our systems did not understand consumer rights and would immediately terminate or deny employment without explaining the rights to the consumer both verbally and in writing. The following is a summary of the consumer rights per the (FTC) Federal Trade Commission.

An 'Adverse Action' letter is generally issued because of negative background information received in a consumer's background check, which may also include a consumer credit reports. Generally, an Adverse Action letter will document the denial of a job application, denial of a rental lease agreement or application, or the termination of an existing job at time of promotion.

Since 'Adverse Information' can appear in a consumer's background information accurately or inaccurately, before a consumer can be denied, that consumer must be given a 'Pre-Adverse Action Disclosure'. The consumer disclosure should include a copy of the background report, or what the (FTC) Federal Trade Commission entitles a 'consumer report'. You must also receive 'A Summary of Your Rights Under the Fair Credit Reporting Act'. The 'Summary of Your Rights Under the Fair Credit Reporting Act' is a document prescribed by the FTC. Since most companies or employers utilize a service, background checking company or credit reporting agency – whichever agency providing the adverse information should provide you, the consumer with the summary of rights.

In addition and based on the Fair Trade Commission, the employer must provide the consumer with a notice in writing, electronically or orally that an action has been taken in an Adverse Action Notice. The notice must state the name, address, and phone number of the company that provided the background information. The consumer must be notified that the agency providing the report did not make the decision to take or to issue the Adverse Action Notice and cannot specify the reason for the Adverse Action Notice. The consumer MUST also be informed of their individual right to dispute the accuracy or completeness of the background or consumer report. You must also be informed of your right to obtain a copy at no expense - of the background or consumer report within 60 days from the date of request. *Please review the detail of this information on the Federal Trade Commission website.*

'Blocking' Negative Credit Information from Your Background Check

There are times when employers require consumer credit information as part of a background check. As a former Director of Operations and manager of a background checking company, I do not agree – however, this is at times a requirement for employment. What is most strange about this 'sometimes;' requirement is that the potential employee may not know that credit is a part of the background check until it is too late. At time, employers may perform background checks that require credit checks on their employees that are already engaged in employment with that employer. So with that being said, and with a belief that every consumer should be clearly informed and aware of any requirements for employment, promotion or other - I make the following recommendation that any concerned consumer place a 'Credit Security Freeze' on your credit file, with all three credit reporting agencies.

With a Credit Security Freeze, no one, and I mean no one will have access to your credit file without your authorization. Once a Credit Security Freeze is placed on your credit file, it will require a written authorization from you to lift the freeze. A Credit Security Freeze can be placed on your credit file for either one (1) or seven (7) years. I documented how to place a Security Freeze on your credit file in Chapter 4.

Chapter 9 - Court Automated Systems (Traffic and Criminal) – What You Should Know

In this chapter, I will discuss court systems automation, and provide 'consumer' court self-help information that is not known to consumers. I will also provide you with key systematic information on the process of 'consumer court information transfer' *to* 'consumer background information', and how corporations are now utilizing this consumer information.

I must first start by stating that there may still be smaller courts processing their court case information manually, but for the greater percent of the United States, city, municipal, county and definitely federal courts – they are utilizing some form of court-automated case processing systems.

Court systems automation generally includes the definition of court state statues, local ordinances, fines, court cost, case disposition codes, court forms, agency distributions, and any other court parameters required. The automation process, in summary, also includes the automation of court docket controls and court financial reporting. The automation process, for our clients also included providing the ability for the courts to report court information electronically to higher courts and to the states Department of Motor Vehicle, for traffic violations. Our firm provided court automation for multiple cities within, of course, multiple states.

For nearly ten years, one of my responsibilities was as a Court Systems Consultant for my consulting firm. This role involved the sales, court systems requirements definitions, court systems implementation and court employee training. Obviously, you can draw the conclusion that our firm was quite small, at least for most of the years, and senior consultant performed many roles.

My key responsibility in the role of court systems consultant was to evaluate the courts requirements during the sales process and translate those requirements into an automated system that would meet the needs of the court. This task was sometimes challenging since most courts, even within a designated state, processed their court cases differently. In addition, each local court maintained their own local ordinances - in addition to the use of state statutes.

The discussion begins here. If you are issued a Traffic, Criminal, or Parking citation (ticket), *please* appear in court, on the court date specified on your citation. If you chose to pay the citation rather than appear in court, then pay the court imposed fine on time utilizing the court pay options, and by the court specified due date. Within the State of Ohio, and in most states, if you fail to appear or pay a simple citation (ticket) on the stated-due-date, a warrant will automatically be issued for your arrest and your fines or cost increased. In some cases, a Warrant may also be issued for a simple Parking citation (ticket), or for a high number of unpaid parking tickets. For unpaid parking tickets, this may also include the suspension of your vehicle registration or renewal. Do not choose not to appear in court, not pay the fine, or not contact the court because you do not have the money to pay the fine. Generally, and in most courts if you are issued a citation, the court will allow you to pay on a *payment plan*. However, it is important that you understand that the same situation applies, you must pay the payment-plan payments on time or additional court penalties will apply – the issuance of a Warrant for your Arrest. Ultimately, if a Warrant is issued, your fines and cost will most likely triple. If you are arrested, you will need to have that Arrest record (for a stupid Traffic ticket) Expunged and your additional court costs and fines have now skyrocketed to the Moon, due to the arrest and 'simple' citation that could have been paid on time and for less money. Get the point? The Expungement process was covered in depth in Chapter 8. I will discuss the issuance of Driving Privileges, and provide a sample Driving Privilege document in the next section of this chapter.

Citations – Traffic Offenses (Request for Driving Privileges and License Reinstatement)

It is important to first note that in some states, driving with a suspended or revoked driver's license can carry a fine of up to $5000 and or a year in jail. I will also start by saying that you should consult with an attorney if convicted of a DUI or any other serious conviction since Appeal periods may apply following your violation or conviction.

A driving license suspension can be imposed for a number of reasons. Reasons such as being suspected of driving under the influence of Drugs or Alcohol; an accumulation of traffic convictions that 'total' a minimum of 10, 11, 12, and up to 18 points against your drivers license; unsatisfied civil judgment resulting from use, care, or maintenance of a motor vehicle; failure to pay a fine or appear in court in connection to a traffic offense; under 18 years of age as a juvenile suspensions where a juvenile has been adjudicated unruly, delinquent, or juvenile traffic offender; for mental or physical impairment where you are deemed to be suffering from a physical or mental disability or disease that prevents you from exercising reasonable and ordinary control of a motor vehicle; upon a check with other states, an individual is found to be under suspension in the NDR (National Driver Registry); non-compliance of financial responsibility law - any driver and or owner who fails to show 'Proof of Financial Responsibility' and that it was in effect at the time of an accident or offense will lose their driving and registration privileges for a minimum period of time; and in some states for non-payment of Child Support, as some of the reasons across the United States that driving privileges can be suspended.

What is important to note regarding drivers license suspensions is that a court or state can impose a license suspension and you fail to receive the notification because of an incorrect address on record. Since the issuance of driving privileges is a state privilege, it is important that you understand your state driving laws when violations occur. These laws are available on your states department of motor vehicles websites.

While working as a Court Systems Consultant I found that most courts would grant *special driving privileges* when Drivers License Suspensions are imposed on a driver. The issuance of driving privileges does depend upon the type of violation that resulted in the imposing of the license suspension. The process to request driving privileges varies from court to court and is based on the types of suspensions. Generally, driving privileges are granted for first time offenders, and sometimes multiple offenders for 'court-imposed license suspensions'. The driving privilege, when granted can permit you to drive to-and-from work, to school, to church, and to scheduled doctor's visits' if specified on your driving privilege form. Most courts will charge a fee for this privilege. The courts will also limit the time that you can be behind the wheel of a motor vehicle, to the court specified, and approved times shown on your driving privilege document.

When granted Driving Privileges, following a Drivers License Suspension, you are generally given a written document that clearly specifies the 'time of day' and 'day of week' that you are permitted to drive. Generally, the permit will also include the descriptions of your driving privilege, such as 'to work', 'to the doctor' or 'to school'. If you are caught driving outside of those specified, and approved times, your privilege is generally revoked, and in most cases, an additional suspension period is added to your existing suspension. In some cases, an additional fine is also imposed.

In addition to your License Suspension, the court may have other requirements prior to the issuance of a Driving Privilege. For some driving suspensions, there may be a minimum period of time that the suspension has to be applied before driving privileges can be granted. A period of time such as 15 or 30 days after your violation occurrence date, even though I have seen courts override these specified dates, please check with your courts. The court may require that you also obtain proof of insurance, or an insurance bond. Courts may also require that all fines, court cost and any restitution for damages caused by you (if applicable) be paid in full, or that you provide proof that a payment plan is established. For all of these requirements, please contact your court of record where the license suspension has been imposed.

If you currently have a drivers license suspension imposed, contact the court or log on to the courts website, via the internet, to view the courts procedures for granting driving privileges. Do not wait. Do not allow yourself to be caught driving without either a drivers license or written driving privileges. Added penalties or additional (possible) suspensions are not necessary when *help* is available to you! Just check with your court.

Drivers License Reinstatement

The Drivers License Reinstatement process is generally a relatively simple process that you can handle on your own. In some cases, it may require the assistance of an attorney.
Drivers License Reinstatement would occur after you have satisfied the courts in reference to your original violation or conviction. Reinstatement can also occur prior to the reinstatement date resulting from a court Appeal of the suspension.

Unfortunately the reinstatement of your drivers license is not (in most states) in automatic process. You must contact your local state department of motor vehicles to verify the reinstatement requirements. Requirements such as proof-of-identity 'documents', and reinstatement fee amounts, or any proof of satisfaction of a civil judgments granted against you may be required at the time of reinstatement. On the next page, I have put together a 'Sample Driving Privileges Form'. This is a sample and a somewhat simple form that our firm would have put together for one of our court clients. This is a sample *only* since each court's form does vary. If your court grants driving privileges, they may also make their form available to consumers, for downloading from their website.

Driving Privileges Sample Form

Driving Privileges (Sample Form)
(Must accompany any Department of Motor Vehicles Forms)

Name: _____   Case#:_____

Employer: _____   Phone: _____

Employer Address: _____   City: _____

DOB: _____   License #:_____

DMV Case#:_____

<u>I work the following schedule:</u>

Days of Week	Start Time	Quitting Time
Monday	_____	_____
Tuesday	_____	_____
Wednesday	_____	_____
Thursday	_____	_____
Friday	_____	_____
Saturday	_____	_____
Sunday	_____	_____

I drive in the course of my employment_____Yes   _____No

I need other driving privileges for the following necessities:

Purpose Location   Date   Time
_____
_____
_____
_____
_____

CHECK OFF AND ATTACH THE FOLLOWING DOCUMENTS:
□ DMV Notice of Suspension   □ Receipt of DMV Payment
□ Letter from Employer   □ Copy of Insurance Card or
                                                    Insurance Declaration

'An Invasion of (corporate) Locust' by Darlene R. Miles

Citations – Traffic or Criminal Case (Payment Plans)

Did you know that all courts generally allow *payment plans* for Traffic and Criminal citations? If you are convicted or plead no contest to a citation or ticket the court will generally allow you a period-of-time to pay your fines and costs. Generally, this arrangement is given to you in writing or verbally by the court representative and in some cases without any added fee for the arrangement. If you ask for payment arrangements, I would advise that you obtain written arrangements from the court, or at least the first due date of your payment in writing. I would be a little leery of a 'verbal' arrangement but some courts will give you the arrangement 'due dates' verbally. I would at least wait a couple of days to access your case information online (if the court has a website) and print out your payment due dates from your case docket entry for your own protection. You do not want the court clerk to error and a warrant issued for non-payment, and you not have any form of documentation to support your arrangement with the court. If a 'Payment Plan' is granted you will be told, what dates your payments are due or at least when the first payment is due and when the balance must be paid in full. When the court grants this privilege, adhere to it, pay the amount due by the specified period of time or due date.

Please understand that the court is not in the collection business so if you think by not paying the fine and not receiving a collection call from a court representative that you have gotten away with not paying…you are wrong. In most cases, the court will automatically issue a Warrant for your arrest the day after your payment was due and without a courtesy call. If you can't make the payment due dates, go to the court in person to discuss your options, I would not trust any arrangements made over the phone with court personnel unless someone can fax to you the new arrangements, or the new arrangements are viewable via the court website. Of course, the best approach is to pay the court when the payments are due.

Citations – What Does the Fines and Cost Generally Consist Of?

As part of the court automation process, my former firm's responsibilities to our court clients was to create a court automated system that would allow the courts to define what the fines and court costs would consist of. In most cases a citation would consist of the court imposed Fines for the offense, Court costs, State Fees, Local Municipal fees, and generally a court Computer fund. Yes, the computer fund. This fund was to offset the cost of computer enhancements as additional software enhancements or computer equipment was required.

The court has the option to impose any fee and define any fund that a court, city, or county deems necessary. These fees and or funds are then embedded within the cost structure of a consumers citation costs. There were no rules and these amounts varied from court to court, and state to state.

Citations – Criminal and Driving Records Information - Where Is Your Information Reported After Recording?

The first action of consumer court information reporting occurs via public access and by background companies. In some cases, background companies will send representatives to the court to manually extract the information or they will purchase court consumer information on media and directly from the court. Where this action sometimes negatively affects the consumer is when these companies report court case information without convictions while cases are still pending and you have not been found guilty. The negative affect on a consumer's personal life is that this information becomes a part of your background report and can be viewed by employers, prospective employers, creditors, and potential leasing agents.

Citation information, following disposition, in most cases is reported to the highest court within your state after disposition. In most cases, courts will report their monthly court case counts and case dispositions to the State Supreme or Superior Court for funding and auditing of dispositions. Traffic case information is reported to the states Bureau of Motor Vehicles or Department of Motor Vehicles, generally weekly and sometimes monthly. This is the reporting of a consumers driving records information which consist of any Traffic and or Traffic/Criminal convictions information and any 'Points' assessed.

The Driving history information is stated to be visible to the public and for insurance company consideration, for 3 years only in most states, and 10 years for police access. However, as a former Insurance Agent I had access to consumers driving records information for up to ten years, and in some cases even longer. This was not by my specified request to have such access. The volume of historical years was returned to the agents via the 'principal' companies system that all agents utilized for the writing of consumer insurance policies.

The volume of reported driving history was the standard system format used by the insurance company that I wrote insurance business for. So keep in mind that several years of driving records history information may be viewed by an insurance agent or insurance company underwriter when quoting your insurance policy.

The police departments various systems can also view your driving information for an indefinite number of years so do not believe the hype... The so-called review of only the last 3 years of your driving records information for insurance consideration is not always true. Driver's records history is generally reported for a longer period of time then you think for insurance companies and for the police to view. Believe me some police officers will consider those prior violations when considering whether to issue you a ticket for a new violation.

'An Invasion of (corporate) Locust' by Darlene R. Miles

131

In reference to a consumers Criminal records, all that I can say here is that information never goes away until it is Sealed or Expunged. Even though companies will request background checks for a specified number of years, some systems will return all historical records that appear since some background searches are conducted by a consumer's social security number and or name only. I have discussed the Sealing and Expungement of records in length in my book, so refer to that section for additional information.

Chapter 10 - Banking Systems Automation – The Affects on the Lives of Consumers

As a consultant I worked on various automated banking applications, which included software specifications, design, software quality assurance, and the ongoing system enhancements to comply with government banking regulations. An important piece of information to share with consumers is regarding the level of information that is gathered on a consumer when simple banking transactions are performed. Banking transactions such as making deposits, withdraws, using the ATM, performing online transactions, phoning customer service and even when making transactions at a teller window, there are a series of automated systems that performs 'checks and balances' of various banking applications.

Banking systems are now designed to check a series of informational databases. These system validations occur very quickly and provide the financial organization with a host of consumer information. Some of the systems validations consist of such processes as, to check your credit worthiness right on the spot – 'Can I offer a credit card or mortgage loan to this person?', or does the systems display 'not eligible' for new credit. Interesting isn't it? Other systems will indicate if a consumer has been 'flagged' with a fraudulent bank history. Validations can range from the validation and use of the 'ChexSystems', systems which will validate your eligibility to open a bank account, or indicate if you have been reported to ChexSystems for any other reason. In addition, banks will also perform a criminal check to validate a consumers background as per the U.S. Patriot Act *(please refer to the chapter on Consumer Privacy for more information on the U.S. Patriot Act)*. The criminal check is not a consistent check but complies with the U.S. Patriot Act and based on certain types of consumer transactions. There can be a series of 5 to 10 different systems accessed when you make a bank transaction at or with a bank, so be aware of this activity.

Another important area to address is the consumer bank statements. Most large financial institutions staff an IT Department for the 'constant' banking systems modifications that are performed quite frequently. With so many systems modifications being conducted (nearly daily), to protect your information and privacy – I recommend that all consumers have their 'checks-and-balances' (literally speaking), performed quite often.

As in any other computer systems modifications – these systems are all developed by humans so I recommend that, you verify 'in detail' all bank account statement information. Bank Account information such as, accurate bank balance reconciliation, and check amount coding - which is the verification of the amount of the check, which is always coded, in the lower right-hand corner of a check after it has been sent to the bank for payment. Errors occur quite often in coding the actual check amount paid verses what was deducted from a consumers account. An example of an error would be a check written for $25.00 but the check was coded as $250.00, with $250.00 deducted from your bank account. The amount of the coded error would appear in the lower right corner of your check as 25000 when it should appear as 2500. Most consumers don't request to receive their physical (hard copy) paid checks, but opt to view their checks online from their respective financial institutions so these errors can go undetected unless you reconcile your accounts monthly.

In addition, I recommend that consumers validate all (ACH) Automatic Clearing House transactions that have been posted to your accounts. Most vendors are using ACH to automatically debit (withdraw) your online and telephone payments from your bank accounts and errors do occur. These errors can be costly so watch these transactions closely, this included the possibility of duplicate withdraws in error.

ACH withdrawals are also now being used by financial institutions when consumers mail payments by paper check. In this case, the financial institution scans your check that is mailed to them and electronically withdraws the funds from your bank account – generally on the date that the check is received. What is most interesting about the ACH process is that most department store are now utilizing various companies to provide their check validation and these companies are gaining access to consumers bank account and personal information. Be very careful when writing checks where you are required to sign away your rights in order to write a check for your purchase. When you are required to sign the credit card scan device, you are granting authorization to the 'processing company' to capture your personal information, bank account, driver's license and to access your bank account in the event any problems occur with your transaction. For more detail on the ACH process, please refer to that section of my book.

It is also important for consumers to be aware that even though there is a high volume of systems automation that occurs with banking systems, there is still a high level of 'human' bank account review and intervention. There are account reviewers assigned to view account activity and make a host of decisions based on a consumer bank account behavior; behavior such as the review of the number of transactions, review of the types of bank account transactions, review of the volume of cash deposits and NSF checks as a few examples. One very important note about the human intervention – this intervention includes the reporting of consumers to ChexSystems without any documented warning for NSF checks, this includes 'paid' NSF checks. Yes – Paid. There are banking representatives that will report consumers to ChexSystems and never inform you that you have been reported, so be aware of that information.

Where my banking client systems may have functioned soundly, and with an efficient IT department, I cannot say the same about several other banks whose banking systems have been hacked in the past and consumer information stolen. It is important that all consumers verify your bank account statements, transactions and balances, and be aware of the laws that now surrounds your banking activities.

Last, protect your personal information when choosing to write personal checks anywhere. Be aware of what information is being captured and stored, and by whom?

Privacy Policies and Online Banking – Protect Your Privacy

Nearly all financial institutions capture and share personal information about consumers. As a consumer, you should be able to obtain information directly from your financial institution on their practice of sharing consumer information. The financial institution should have a document that outlines the level of sharing of your personal information.

In July 2001, banks were required to provide a clear method for all consumers to 'Opt-Out' of their consumer information sharing. Opt-Out statements are mailed annually to consumers and must be completed and mailed back to the financial institutions. Some financial institutions will allow the consumer to log on to their website to complete the Opt-Out request in addition to mailing the information back to the financial institution. However, you chose to respond, just respond to the document in order to maintain your personal information privacy.

Banks do make millions on the banking activities of consumers, and are always looking for ways to make more money; after all banking is a business for profit. There are various groups within the banking industry that are sometimes called 'Lines of Business', headed by senior management with a goal to either 'enhance your banking experience' or to look for the next 'profit product to market', or to comply with new government banking regulations, however banking experiences and systems are changing daily. What I have come to appreciate is how these various banking system continue to work in sync and without losing all of our money. Just a little joke here. With so many banking systems, modifications begin developed and implemented, system automation and change is always in motion.

The capturing of consumer information occurs in several methods. One method of capturing consumer personal information is when a consumer visits the website of your financial institution. Most if not all financial institutions have an automated process in place to track web browser habits while you are visiting their website. You might wonder why a bank would want to track what you are viewing on their website or record any web links that you click on from their web site? It is marketing at its best. Some financial institutions want to know what the consumer is interested in for future Marketing. There are also situations where your personal information is captured and sold to 'Third-Parties' for a profit. However, the reason – just protect your information.

An additional step in securing your personal information is to only enter personal information on secured websites. A secured website is always indicated in the web browser address as *https:*, the *'s'* indicates 'secured'. In addition, you may want to turn off 'Cookies' or at least turn off your 'Third-party' cookies. Another choice is to set your web browser to 'prompt' for 'Cookie' access to your computer. You may ask why you would perform this task. Cookies are designed to either capture your information (at all levels) or to be implanted and reside on your computer. Cookies store personal information that can be transmitted back to a website automatically and upon accessing the Internet, or when visiting a repeated web page or web site. However, there is enough information bouncing around the world that we cannot control, so when we can – just stop some of the scrupulous web behaviors, by setting your browser controls to 'Prompt' you for access to your computer. As I do, just so <u>no</u> to strange 'Cookie' request. After all, would you allow strangers to reside in your home? I would say the same should apply to your personal information stored on your computer, protect it by denying access.

US Patriot Act H.R. 3162 and Banking – How It Affects Consumers

The U.S. Patriot Act *'in plain English'* is the authorization granted by the Government to allow various business entities to monitor consumer information. The portion of the Act that I am addressing here is the impact to consumer banking. The Act includes a multitude of provisions designed around protecting the United States from terrorist acts while capturing and monitoring consumer's activity and or banking transactions... hummm.

When this Act was enacted, it required certain validations of a consumer's bank account information that currently existed on already established bank accounts. The additional requirement was to validate the consumer identification at the time a new bank account is opened. This Act goes further requiring that if a consumer's information cannot be validated, the financial institution be required to act and report the (lack or validation) incident to the appropriate authorities. The Act also required that additional banking computer system enhancements be created to monitor transactions and to identify those transaction as recorded against a consumer's bank account activity. The monitoring of a consumers banking activity would include wire transfers, large and cash deposits and more. I have summarized some of the Sections of this Act that I have found to be of most interest.

The first paragraph of the Act reads as follows:

> *To deter and punish terrorist acts in the United States and around the world, to enhance law enforcement investigatory tools, and for other purposes.* Be it enacted by the Senate and House of Representatives of the United States of America in Congress assembled,

While working on the Functional Requirements for a banking application; *(Functional Requirements: How, will the system change or enhancement be designed? What, will be the impact to*

'An Invasion of (corporate) Locust' by Darlene R. Miles

other infrastructures?; When, does the Government require that these changes be implemented?; and Where, will the system changes/enhancements fit in the current environment?), for a former Banking client for which the United States Patriot Act requires that banks request, record and maintain specific information on a consumer when opening a bank account. A portion of this Act also includes the provisions that permit the monitoring or bank activity, deposits, dates, deposit descriptions, transaction history, reporting of suspicious banking activity and much more. Financial Institutions, by law had to modify their banking systems to allow the capturing of our banking information. The US Patriot Act also includes the provision to request this information without a subpoena or notification to the consumer. Please refer to the government website for the U. S. Patriot Act, for complete details of this Act.

Banks and Financial Institutions Use of Comprehensive Consumer Background Checks

What is a 'Comprehensive Background Check', you would be surprised at the level of information that financial institutions currently obtain on consumers and in most cases, without cause. Regrettably, certain government laws and acts have given financial institutions 'snooping' privileges. However, some financial institutions have taken these law changes a little too far.

Banks and other financial institutions are now using a 'reverse lookups' process to gain comprehensive background information on consumers. I have seen where these financial institutions are using this information without any 'necessary' cause other then that they can - and they do now have detailed access to consumer information which is completely outside of the scope of needed financial information. Several financial institutions are utilizing services that provide such information as, your address history, credit information, employment information, names of individuals living at your residence, the names of your associates, siblings, adult children, extended relatives, their addresses, the spouses, your in-laws and their addresses. In addition the information includes your assets, your driving license, traffic-criminal and civil records history, your professional licenses and registered affiliations – and yes, this volume of information a true invasion.

To explain what a 'comprehensive background check' consist of - here you are. It begins with, 'up to six degrees of separation of your relatives' your siblings, their names and dates of birth, their spouses names/DOB's, their addresses/phone numbers, their children names/DOB's and addresses, everyone's social security numbers, your neighbors on the left and right, their names, your assets, auto, licenses, professional licenses, address history from age 16 (approximately), drivers licenses, autos titled in your name, employment history, and any legal records…and more.

As a Director of Operations for a background checking company we utilized the same 'consumer invasion' source. Yes – invasive (invasion) source and sometimes 'inaccurate' source. I don't understand the need to conduct such comprehensive background checks on consumers but unfortunately some banking officials have come to the conclusion that these reports are needed. This is clearly an invasion in the lives of consumers and without a clear need. Most financial instructions have or have had access to a consumer's complete financial information and in most cases for years so why perform such an invasion? Why - Because they can.

Reverse 'Lookups' Performed by Banks and Financial Institutions – What Does This Mean To You?

A system automation process is currently being utilized by most financial institutions and it is entitled 'Reverse Lookups'. Banks are using an automated telephony (telephone) process to capture consumer phone numbers. These phone numbers consists of your work phone numbers, home phone number, or any other phone number that you utilize to place a call to a financial institution. These phone numbers are being utilized to capture personal information about consumers, your associates and more.

So you ask, 'What's in a phone number'? You would be quite surprised. Phone numbers are being stored and used to gain your personal information. Most financial institutions Telephony Systems (office automated call distribution systems) are now designed to capture and retain all phone numbers. These are the phone calls made by consumers when connecting to a call-center or customer service representative. Nearly all phone numbers are being captured, stored and used later (if necessary) to track a consumers employer information, residence, and or associates information. Residence information, be it your home or where you are living, or with whom? Additional uses for a consumers phone number history is for skip tracing of delinquent accounts or in some cases just being utilized by 'rogue' customer service representatives who think they have superior powers while diving into a consumers personal and background information. Financial institutions have the ability, while utilizing various systems to check the name listings that are registered against a phone number or company name then to dive into the listed individual's information, address, family information and more.

Now keep in mind that most work numbers also utilizes 'caller-id', even for private numbers so every number that is generally called to any employee's extension or placed from an employee's extension is saved to a company database. The employee extensions and phone usage is then available for any company administrator to view. In addition, how would I know this piece of information you ask? As a former Director of Operations, I was responsible for the installation and implementation of the new Telephony (phone) system, which included these abilities. This is a standard practice now amongst companies and if for no other reason, to monitor employee's behaviors. My method of madness was to have the ability to manage the call levels for my Client

Services Representatives so that no one representative would be overloaded with a high number of client calls. In addition, it did also serve as a tool to monitor those abusers of the company phone system, yes – that long distance 45 minute calls to relatives and parents that would tie up the phone queue process and force clients into voice mail? These standard phone systems will not only monitor call timing, but will also record all phone numbers and much more.

So with that being said, be careful when phoning any financial institutions 800 or, (or other) numbers to discuss your accounts unless you want the phone number that you are calling from to be stored as a contact number in the future. There are no longer, what we consumers called 'blocked-unpublished phone numbers', this includes your 'private' cellular number. There are new systems that unblock private or 'anonymous' and cellular phone numbers. There are companies who market and sell these numbers everyday to their clients and customers so be aware of that. No phone numbers are considered private anymore and that includes your cellular phone number.

Be aware that financial organizations are taking several necessary and unnecessary liberties with consumer's information. As I have stated in previous chapters, these behaviors are a complete invasions of consumer's privacy. Who exactly are these representatives that are accessing consumer information? Why are they maneuvering so deeply into a consumer's life? Most consumers with any type of historical relationship or historical payment information with a financial institution generally will not be a terrorist, at least I hope not. We work, we deposit our payroll, we pay our household expenses using our bank accounts, – and they have everything they need, why go any deeper without cause. I understand the need to combat terrorism but I would call this an 'unnecessary' invasive behavior, by financial institutions - a form of financial consumer terrorism.

What I suggest to consumers is that you yell as loudly as you can if this happens to you, and report this behavior to a superior or manager of the financial institution. This behavior has to stop. In addition, as I have stated throughout my book where are these companies storing this consumer 'personal' information that they are so boldly compiling. What controls have been but in place to dispose of consumer, personal information when it is no longer needed? Do they sell this comprehensive information, which can be quite extensively compiled on a consumer...most likely yes?

Consumers can put a halt to some of the 'Reverse Lookup' process by limiting the 'extra information that a company can obtain from you. Limit your contact to mail or email when you can. If you have to call them, call from home. After all, you do not want your cell phone, family's phone, boyfriend or girlfriends number to be placed on a callback list.

Now as I have stated before, I am not trying to provide ways to avoid paying financial obligations, obviously not. The compiling of consumer information is not limited to a consumer's delinquent account – its simple contact with financial institutions. What I am doing is providing the necessary information to limit this world of 'rogue' financial company's unnecessary capture of consumer information. So much for the 'Information Age'?

Personal Check Usage and Approvals – What You Need To Know

Most service providers, retailers, and grocers are now utilizing Check Approval Merchant Services to provide their check approvals. What consumers must be aware of is that several of these Check Approval Merchants for several larger retailers have had consumer personal and banking information stolen from their databases. These thefts are not just limited to system hackers breaking into their corporate systems but include the theft of consumer personal information by their own employees.

What is most dangerous about this check approval process is that the approvals granted to these merchant services is not limited to just validating a consumers check writing privileges, it includes access to the consumers drivers license information and direct access to the consumer bank account. In most cases, these services grant the check approvals and take ownership of the check amount of the purchase and process the payment. The 'taking or ownership' of the check amount may sometimes result in a direct debit of the consumers account. A direct debit involving some forms of ACH (Automatic Clearinghouse) transactions where the funds are drawn automatically from the consumer's bank account, while consumers are not aware of this invasive business practice.

If the check payment is not processed successfully, (funds not available or able to be drawn against the consumers bank account), these merchants will debit the consumers bank account until the check or transaction is 'made good' and this includes the merchants drawing of their fees to process these transactions – what ever the amount. These transactions can occur over and over again and sometimes resulting in multiple banking fees to the consumer.

What is quite unfortunate for consumers is that the retailers are not informing consumers of these business practices nor are they informing consumers of their Check Approval Merchant relationships that are now allowing these entities to capturing (steal) and store   consumer information without authorization.

Be aware of the check writing approval process when writing personal checks. It is not just a matter of writing a personal check anymore – it is now an issue of, *'how much personal information about your life and direct access to your bank account do you want to provide to strangers who may not protect your personal and bank account information'? And yes, that was a run-on sentence, but the impact was established.*

Debit Card Usage

It is my personal recommendation that you not use your Debit card randomly for purchases. Retail agencies are now retaining your banking information forever in their systems. Just kidding about the forever, but close to forever. They are retaining Debit and Credit Card information with no end date – that sounds better. As a consultant, this was one of the projects that I worked on as a project manager. The system project was to design the capture and validation of Debit and Credit Card usage for banking and retail customers. From a banking standpoint, it is necessary to validate and place the necessary security controls for the consumer. However, as a retail company I feel they are going too far in the level of information they continue to retain on a consumers Debit and Credit card information.

Use a Credit card rather then your Debit card. Your Debit card provides access to your bank account and bank account balance. When these retail stores system or online purchase agents systems are hacked, your bank account information is then stolen. When systems are hacked, the hackers then have access to your bank accounts, full access. It is bad enough to be notified that your information has been stolen, driver's license number, credit card, checking account information, etc and a consumer then has to replace all of that stolen information. It is a headache let me tell you because I have had all of those items stolen in the past including the Debit card.

Be careful with your debit card. If this information is stolen or compromised have, it replaced immediately. This includes your driver's license number. You may have to get a police report before requesting a new driver's license number, but it is definitely worth it not to have all or your information out in the *ozone* somewhere.

Credit Card Usage and Your Security Codes

Some companies are recording and storing (stealing) consumer's security codes off the backs of your credit cards when you make a face-to-face purchase. I somewhat understand the need to validate the credit card security code for over the phone purchases, but in person purchases – that is a little crazy. There is currently an office supply company instructing their employees to key in a consumers three digit security code, off the backs of the credit card when making purchases at their store? This is utterly ridiculous, and an automated process at their cash registers.

Lately, most companies seem to (unfortunately) have their systems hacked at one point or another. If their systems are not hacked, they all seem to retain and sell consumer information to the highest bidder, or share internally with their so-called subsidiaries. Why record the security code off the back of consumer's credit cards? Just another loss of privacy and added potential identity theft.

Therefore, what this means is consumers have to periodically request to replace your credit cards, especially when you feel your credit card information has been compromised. Protect your credit information and protect your privacy.

ATM Usage

Banks have been trying to put certain controls in place to protect consumers from ATM Usage fraud. What has been occurring at some ATM facilities is the fraudulent attachment of foreign devices to some ATM's that can be used to capture and copy your Debit/ATM card information. I would recommend that you are very careful when using your ATM card at even your own financial institution. It has been reported where scam artist will attach foreign ATM Scan devises to an ATM machine, once your Debit or Credit card is swiped they have all your information that will allow them to create a duplicate card with your swiped information.

A clear sign to consumers, of a tampered ATM machine, is when any externally attached device has been attached to your ATM machine. Generally, these devices stick out or protrude from the swipe area of your ATM machine and are quite obvious to you if you have used this particular ATM machine before. Again, generally the device is protruding or external to the machine but can appear as a valid credit card swipe devise.

Generally, most financial institutions force you to insert your card directly into the bank ATM machine. The attached items that I am referring to are the sandwich type devices that stick out from the ATM machine. In addition, I would also not use ATM machines in strange places, such as a bar, restaurants, or a corner store where the ATM machine are not directly connected to a bank facility, this is my personal opinion. There are several vendors that place ATM machines in corner stores or other locations as 'stand alones'. Try to stick with your financial institutions ATM's, they are much safer. Also, beware of machines at grocery stores since some grocery stores have also been scammed and had some of their swipe machines replaced without their knowledge...yes, in a grocery store.

Last, for those of you who say, I will not worry since my bank will reimburse me for what ever I loose. Well, yes they generally will...nut...I mean, but - they sometimes will take up to two months to reimburse you and what if all of your funds have been stolen...hummmm? Just protect your funds. After all, they are your funds, not the criminals who are trying to find ways to get them.

ACH Transactions and Their Affects on Consumer Purchases – What You Need To Know

'ACH' Automatic Check Handling or Automatic Clearinghouse transactions. The use of ACH has for some time been a process used by companies and in banking systems. What is most surprising is the level of ACH transactions that are now being used by Retailers and Grocers. These companies are now using an ACH debiting system to obtain their funds from consumer's personal check purchases and payment transactions more quickly. These ACH transactions are sometimes being debited (subtracted) from a consumers bank account funds the very same day that a consumers pay for goods or services with a bankcard or personal check.

What an ACH means is the service provider; retailer or grocer automatically subtracts the funds from your bank account and in some cases the same day, when the transaction is made. ACH is a form of epayment or electronic payment. There are generally two ways payments can be transferred; (1) by wire transfer or (2) through an automated clearing house.

Have you ever made a purchase and the store scanned your check then handed your check back to you? Well that was a form of ACH epayment. Some retailers or grocers don't hand the check back but instead they will 'quietly' use a service to guarantee your check and that service will, (at the time of purchase) check your bank account to verify that the funds are available and sometimes immediately debit (remove the funds from your account) within 24 hours.

Be careful when using a check to purchase, do not always assume that you have a couple of days to make that deposit to cover that check that you just wrote. Also, be aware that some lenders are also processing checks when bills are paid in the same form. Keep in mind that check payments are being processed much faster then the old 7 to 10 business days of the past.

For those consumer payment 'Clearing Houses' (companies paid to process consumer payments for companies) that may take longer to process your payments - these are not considered what I call ACH payment methods. Do not begin mailing your payments later then you currently do if these 'mail in' payments types currently take 7 to 10 days to post. Continue to mail those types of payments and allow the appropriate mail and posting times as stated by your financial institution.

ACH Consumer Information Theft – Beware

Recently one of the largest consumer check verification and processing companies had consumer information stolen from their systems by an employee. The consumer financial information was then sold to data brokers. That company was Certegy Check Services, Inc., per their letter; 'a provider to U.S. retail merchants'. I happened to be one of their victims. The letter from Certegy Check Services stated the following: '*a service provider to U.S. retail merchants, was recently victimized by an employee who wrongfully removed and sold consumer information to a data broker who in turn sold a subset of that data to a limited number of direct marketing organizations. For your background, Certegy provides check authorization services to U.S. retail merchants and provides certain credit card-related services to the gaming industry. As a result of our investigation, Certegy believes that information regarding the above-indicated account was included in the misappropriated information*'. The letter goes on to state that the employee was fired? That's all, fired? This sounds criminal. Are we kidding here or what?

The account that Certegy Check Services was referencing in their letter to me, was my personal bank account? Yes, my bank account and personal information was now stolen again. Unbelievable? This ridiculous theft of consumer information was right in line with what I have previously stated as a companies 'lack of consumer information' protection. And here I go again. This was my trusting of retail, stores check approval process and what did I get in return? Interestingly, this company processes checks for nearly all high-end retail stores that are located in nearly every state throughout the United States so there is no reason to list them all. Consumers, please be careful where you right personal checks for purchases. You never know until it is to late where your personal and financial information was sent to or provided to when your check is scanned during your purchase process. In addition, you do not know how long that 'so-called' check approval company will store your financial information in their database. What is an even worse thought, is - whom will they now resell or lose your information too? Re-loadable Credit cards look better and better to me everyday.

As consumers the loss is much greater then just your bank account when information is stolen and sold to data thieves, a small percent of your personal life is also stolen. These check merchant approvers capture much more then just a consumer bank account information, they capture your drivers license information, name, date of birth, and address and now has a direct access to your bank account – and so does everyone else that your information is sold to.

ChexSystems - How Banks, Creditors, Retailers and Background Checking Companies Use This Service - What All Consumers Need to Know

There are various automated processes that financial institutions utilize to validate a consumers banking activity, check writing history and consumer personal information. One of those system automation processes is the use of ChexSystems to monitor, track, and validate a consumer banking activity.

In addition to financial institutions (banks, etc.) utilization of ChexSystems, ChexSystems also provides Risk-Assessment information as a 'reseller' and provider of consumer background information to their investors or clients who purchase this service from them.

Per the ChexSystems Consumer Report section entitled, 'Inquiries Not Initiated By Consumer Action', this *'extremely'* interesting statement reads as follows; *'Inquires Not Initiated By Consumer Action refers to inquiries resulting from transactions you may not have initiated, so you may not recognize the source. Members of our service with a permissible purpose include current creditors, pre-approved creditors, potential employers, and potential investors trying to assess risks. We report these requests only to you as a record of activities, and we do not include any of these requests on credit reports to others.'* Consumers, be aware of this consumer information usage and invasion of privacy.

Well…my comments are as follows regarding the usage of consumer information at the levels that ChexSystems provides, and to the multitude of companies and individuals that they chose to allow 'permissible-purpose'. First with my experience working with consumer background information, this 'so-called' array of entities who can have access to a consumers banking information adds more risk to a consumers financial and personal life. We consumers rely, or depend on, a somewhat private financial relationship with our financial institutions. Could you believe that just by opening a bank account and purchasing your personal and business bank account checks from the Deluxe Corporation that your personal information is being sold to everyone and anyone who wants it? I guess I should state it as ChexSystems states it; *'Members of our service with a permissible purpose include current creditors, pre-approved creditors, potential employers, and potential investors trying to assess risk's.* What is not clearly stated is the reseller's agreement?

The information that ChexSystems is providing, includes a consumer social security number, and it's date of issuance, along with the state who issued the social security number. This information also includes your drivers license number and state of issuance, your bank account, and bank routing numbers (supplied by Deluxe) along with your bank locations, check numbers and quantities along with the dates that those checks were purchased. This level of 'brokered' banking information is extremely unnerving.

I know and understand how these automated systems are developed. I also understand the various levels of information that is provided to a consumer and what is provided to your client. I have viewed the information that is returned to a bank from a ChexSystems inquiry, and received a 'hard copy' of their report. The relationships that ChexSystems provides to their clients is based on the product line of information purchased…it always is. This is the sales process.

This process of brokering consumer information to the sources that are listing on their consumer report is absurd, Investors – this means nothing to me as a consumer. What this statement appears to imply is if you become a 'member of their service' you can, as our clients did, *click* to access a consumer's information by stating whatever 'permissible purpose' that you chose. This is your information and my information and it is not protected – clearly not.

The term 'Risk Assessment' has a scope that reaches into infinity so let us now connect this word usage to the word 'Investor'. I would wonder how many of their clients identify themselves as 'investors' while assessing risk, by viewing and or reselling consumer information. Interestingly, there is one of the largest supplies of consumer Background Information and that so-called 'Risk Assessment' information in the U.S., and their information is not always accurate. I experienced the levels of their inaccurate information as a Director of Operations, and I will not provide this companies name in my book. I feel consumers have enough to contend with, with the various financial institutions, corporations, investors (?) and potential employers who are already utilizing the ridiculous source for consumer background information, as though their information is 100% factual, and it is not.

The only way consumers can stop these types of behaviors are to place a complete security freeze on your consumer file with ChexSystems. I provided the information to freeze your file for the maximum 'five-year' period allowed by ChexSystems.

The monitoring that is currently being conducted by ChexSystems is not limited to just your banking information, but includes all 'History of Checks Ordered'. This would be the ordering or your personal and business checks ordered from the Deluxe Corporation. The consumer report includes the quantity of checks order, the starting check numbers, the check order dates, and the bank name. The ChexSystems Consumer report also includes the validation of your driver's license number and the state of issuance. The report also includes your date of birth, social security number and the date your social security number was issued, along with the state of issuance. The report also includes 'Retail (Check) Information' history for five years. The 'Retail Information' section of the consumer report includes any 'Check Approval Merchants' who process check approvals transactions including ACH (Automatic Clearinghouse) check debits and personal checks that were returned as non-sufficient funds. The check approval merchants report to 'Shared Check Authorization Network' (SCAN) and SCAN reports the information to ChexSystems.

Neither ChexSystems nor SCAN validates any of the reported merchant 'non-sufficient funds' information for its accuracy so consumers may never know what the contents of their 'ChexSystems' consumer file consists of until you attempt to open a new bank account.

The reporting by check approval merchants is not limited to the reporting of *unpaid* (NSF) non-sufficient funds checks – unpaid checks issued to merchants. The merchant reporting to SCAN, then SCAN's reporting to ChexSystems also includes the consumers *'Paid'* ACH (check) transactions and personal checks that were originally returned as non-sufficient funds? What is most discerning about how either of these entities report consumer information is that any check-processing merchant can place negative check information on a consumers report and that information is not validated by either SCAN or ChexSystems? With no consumer negative check validation process in place, these two companies specify on their disclosures that 'the consumer has a right to request a reinvestigation of their information', now this statement is really a joke to me. If any consumer encounters a negative consumer report, that consumer is most likely performing some type of banking transaction. As most banking systems are designed, once a consumer is flagged negatively by ChexSystems – you remain flagged negatively by ChexSystems in the banks system for which you are attempting to do business.

The reporting to ChexSystems directly will also consist of a consumer's negative banking activity. Negative banking activity such as consumer closed bank accounts by financial facilities due to a consumers poor banking practices and the reporting of consumer check fraud.

For any consumer not to pay a check that was returned as non-sufficient funds obviously is not a good business practice. However there are situations that occur where checks are returned for non-payment or in other words, (no funds are available) and is sometimes out of the control of the consumer. What most consumers do not understand is the number of ways that a personal check can now be processed, and very quickly by merchants. In addition, most consumers are not aware that you can be reported to ChexSystems and not know that your name has been reported. A consumer can have a negative consumer report in the ChexSystems database for years and not be aware of that information until you attempt to open a new bank account.

Why I have chosen to write a chapter on this subject you may wonder? It is due to the fact that financial institutions, that make the decisions to return consumers checks, and sometimes for just a couple of cents off from the consumers checking account balance, and then report those consumers to ChexSystems is really strange behavior and sometimes systematic. The financial institutions sometimes go even further by reporting consumers to those 'no-named' Merchant Check processing agents who have representatives that report negative check information on consumers also, and will report this information long after they have successfully received payment from the consumer for the check transactions. This does not make since. Especially since not all Merchant Check Processing, companies report consumer non-sufficient funds information to ChexSystems, especially 'paid' information.

For financial institutions, there are representatives that monitor deposits and transactions. There are sometimes deposits held for no other reason then negligence on behalf of the bank representative. There is selective handling of which checks are to be paid and which checks to return, and when to post deposits - and most times, it can appear as malice on the part of that bank representative. *Sadly these horrible bank practices affect consumers with the least amount of funds on deposit, the average consumer.* How many consumers pay fees for returned items where the consumer is charged a fee, the deposit is delayed posting to your account and the item (check) is 'Paid as NSF', meaning the check was not returned but the bank charged a fee anyway? Then the consumer spends days trying to get the fee reversed and not be successful in doing so, this is a bad practice of most financial instructions but the behavior continues without challenge.

The use of ChexSystems is another harsh practice of financial institutions. Once a check is considered (NSF), non-sufficient funds on deposit to cover the check, fees begin to tabulate. Most consumers are placed into ChexSystems for the fees and the cost of the check, sometimes the fees can reach hundreds of dollars before the financial institution closes the consumers account and transfers that consumer's information into ChexSystems.

An example of a situation is the payment of a check for $250.00;

what ever amount available in the consumers account (and it could be $240.00) is deducted from the consumers account along with a fee of $30 to 40 dollars or more. Then the financial institution immediately begins charging a daily fee which can be as little ad $5.00 or as high as $10.00. Now if another check is presented against the consumers account then that check is returned and another fee added to the amount and so on. If the consumer, who may already be in financial trouble has to wait fifteen days or two weeks for a next paycheck by then the fees can be in the hundreds of dollars, and so it goes.

 What is sad is there are fraudulent consumers in the ChexSystems database and they should be there but for the average consumers who have been taken advantage of by a financial institution, this is what I find to be most sad.

What I want consumers to know is that this madness can be drawn to a closure. Do not give up!

If you are in trouble with your bank account, a suggestion; First make a payment arrangement with the bank to repay the money owed and hopefully before you are placed into the ChexSystems database for negative checking account balance. Yes, some banks will allow you to make payment arrangements. Stop any direct deposits that you have setup with that financial institution and immediately open another checking account, somewhere else, and as soon as possible with a cash deposit. Do not use a check from the financial institution that you now have troubles (did I really need to say that?). Understand that the bank where you have a negative balance will eventually close your account, try to avoid that situation but quickly establish a new bank account and repay what you owe. Keep records of the payments and try to get the bank to stop the daily charges for the negative balance or you may have a more difficult time repaying this negative balance. Do you see how quickly a consumer can be caught in this terrible mess of 'bad checks'? Be aware that some 'not so nice' bank representative will try to give you a hard time, approach them with kindness and patience even if you do not receive it back. There is nothing wrong with making a request to receive your agreed payment plan in writing from the bank representative. The documented payment plan may be your only proof of the arrangement with the bank. And don't feel bad, just hang in there. After all this is your attempt to salvage, your personal financial business and future check writing privileges.

Who Is ChexSystems

ChexSystems is a subsidiary of the Deluxe Corporation. Yes, Deluxe Corporation. The Deluxe Corporation is also one of the largest supplies of consumer's bank account checks. This would obviously and clearly explain the process of 'cross pollination' of consumer's bank account information and bank account check order detail which includes your historical bank account numbers, check numbers ordered and bank account names.

ChexSystems also reports consumer check processing historical information that is reported to SCAN. This information is reported by SCAN and ChexSystems without any form of validation of its accuracy and will appear on a consumers banking financial history until challenged by the consumer. This one connection, ChexSystems and Scan is an interesting form of cross-pollination. Where ChexSystems may state on their consumer report that 'They do not determine a consumer's check writing eligibility', they do however allow financial institutions to have direct access to ALL of a consumers ChexSystems detail – and again, be it accurate or inaccurate.

ChexSystems is utilized by most financial institutions to validate a consumers personal information at the time a bank account is opened. ChexSystems is one of the many systems that a bank would utilize to also check for consumer fraud; fraud such as the validation of a consumer name, drivers license and social security number match. In addition, banks check to see if consumers are reported by other financial institutions and for what reason.

The Process of Being Reported to ChexSystems - How Does This Happen?

The 'bad checks' process begins in most cases when checks are process quicker then a consumer funds are deposited. In some cases, consumers may think that they have deposited the funds but some banks 'batch' process deposits where the posting may take 1 to 3 days to post to a consumers account. I find this 'batch' process to be the most ridiculous I have seen for the average consumer to contend with and some consumers do not clearly understand why this happens. Sometimes funds post sooner and sometimes they post later. Consumers must understand how your funds and direct deposits are posted to your accounts before writing checks anywhere.

Understand that most retail department stores, grocery stores and others now immediately debit (withdraw) from consumers accounts when checks are written and right on the spot. These companies use an 'automated cash clearinghouse', or ACH withdraw service to guarantee the check. Have you ever seen were a retail company or grocer hands you back your check after that check is ran through an automated system? Those are the instances were your funds have already been drawn from your account on the spot and at least guaranteed and debited within 24 hours. Be aware of this process since fees can sometimes result from these types of transaction when deposits are made on a Friday and fund not "officially" post to your account until midnight on the next business day. Can you envision what this can do to your bank account in fees if you are shopping at several types of companies that debit on the spot, sometimes it only takes one situation especially if you pay bills on line and drive your account balance to almost nothing by the next business day?

Other situations that can cause a bank to report a consumer to ChexSystems is when you close an account and forget to allow all checks to clear your account, or even your   automatically scheduled withdraws such as monthly auto loans, utilities or monthly life insurance payments. Most of these types of automatic withdraws are not easy to stop but easy to start. So be aware that these types of transactions continuing after your account closes and can cause you to be placed into ChexSystems. It is not fair but some bank representatives who report consumers to the 'system of hell' just are not concern with the impact to a consumer's life. .

Banks Don't Always Notify Consumers When You Are Reported To ChexSystems

Some scrupulous bank representatives and check approval merchants will report consumers to ChexSystems without any warning and while you are an 'active' banking customer. You wonder how this can occur. Any banking representative can report a consumer to ChexSystems if you have NSF (non-sufficient checks) processed in your bank account. And yes, this includes 'paid' non-sufficient checks you can be reported to ChexSystems. Sadly, it may be years before you are even aware that the report occurred, so be aware that this ill practice exists.

I recommend that all consumers obtain your free consumer report from ChexSystems to be aware of your consumer check writing and banking privilege status. You can log on to www.consumerdebit.com to obtain your free consumer report. Keep in mind that you can be reported to ChexSystems by any merchant entity, valid or invalid and not be aware that negative information exists in your consumer file. If your report contains negative 'paid' information, you should contact ChexSystems Consumer Affairs to have the information removed. I have assisted consumers in the past to have 'negative paid' NSF check information removed from their ChexSystems report. This was of course for a bank account that was still open and being used by the consumer. If you have disputed negative information, you should dispute the information in writing. The ChexSystems website does not provide any phone numbers that lead to a 'live' support representative so here you are, the consumer affairs toll free number that is currently functional, and is 1-800-513-7125. For SCAN, their phone number is 1-800-513-7125.

If your request to remove negative information does not occur quickly, I would advise you to contact the (FTC) Fair Trade Commission and report the incident.

It's Never to Late to Re-establish a Bank Account

It is important to know that *not* all financial institutions, banks, or credit unions report to ChexSystems and there are some financial institutions that will give consumers a second chance to re-establish a bank account. Sometimes that second chance is called 'Second Chance' as a program for consumers with some banks. Call around to speak with various bank managers, you would be surprised who would be willing to listen and help you reestablish your financial privileges of having a checking or savings account. If calling does not get you the information you need, check online for banks that do not report to ChexSystems or for 'second chance' financial institutions in your area.

How Long Does ChexSystems Keep You in Their System

Currently ChexSystems will retain a consumer's negative checking information in their system for five years. Yes, five years so you do not want this to happen to you. If it does happen to you, I have armed you with the information to re-establish your financial privileges.

How to Seal or Freeze Your ChexSystems Consumer File (Access)

A 'Security Freeze' of ChexSystems information placed on your file will stop your information from being provided to background checking companies as a result of employer backgrounds checks and any other background checks. The freeze would have to be temporarily lifted by you if you decide to apply for a new bank account.

What is most interesting is that ChexSystems states on their consumer statement that they will still continue to sell consumer information even after the freeze. This statement troubles me, why not at least stop some form of information sharing.

Each consumer-reporting agency has different requirements for supporting information to issue a Security Freeze. An example of the supporting information is as follows.

1. Name
2. Address
3. Date of Birth
4. Social Security Number
5. Proof of current address such as a current utility bill
6. Payment of applicable fees to request a security freeze of your credit
7. If you are an identity theft victim and are requesting a security freeze, you must also include a copy of a police report, Identity Theft report, or other government law enforcement agency report, such as a DMV report.

ChexSystems requires that the consumer submit their request to Freeze your Consumer File on a Notarized document. The request should be mailed to their Consumer Relations department. The current consumer relations address is shown below, however, I do ask that you contact ChexSystems to verify the instructions and mailing address for a consumer information 'freeze' of your information.

ChexSystems
Consumer Relations
7805 Hudson Road Suite 100
Woodbury, Minnesota 55125

'An Invasion of (corporate) Locust' by Darlene R. Miles

1.800.513.7125

Also, be aware that the information and instructions on placing a Security Freeze is not readily available on any of their web sites. You will have to hunt for the information.

Chapter 11 - What Tools Creditor's Now Use To Compile Consumer Information (Secretly)

Service Providers - What They Can Find Out About You!

Not only are financial institutions utilizing 'Reverse Lookups' to obtain information on consumers but Creditors are also using the same tools. Did you know that a 'Reverse Lookup' could also occur with the use of your name? A consumers name can be entered into a database, and the 'name only' can produce a host of detail including your social security number, date of birth, address history and much, much more.

Did you know that every phone number that you use to call your creditor and service provider such as your bank or auto lender captures the phone number that you phone from... hummmm? Be aware that nearly all service providers and financial institutions now capture phone numbers and store those numbers in your contact file and later perform 'Reverse Lookups' by using those numbers to contact your or use those numbers to perform comprehensive background checks on you, your family and or your associates, and most cases without warrant (justification or need).

The creditors check generally begins with the names attached to you or the phone numbers that you might phone from or provide to the creditor. There are no longer 'blocked' or 'unlisted' private phone numbers. Creditors can obtain any information they want and it is as simple at using your name to gain access to your assets, your addresses, your neighbors, your auto and professional licenses, your relatives, your relatives their addresses and phone numbers and much more.

Some of the creditors, banks, and auto financing customer service representatives are taking to many liberties with consumer's personal information. Sadly, they are all (generally) using one service to perform most of these comprehensive background checks and something needs to be done about it. My question is where are they storing all of this personal information? What about those Privacy laws? How are they protecting consumers since most of these financial institutions have had their systems hacked at one time or another.

What controls do they have in place to protect consumers when they generate these types of comprehensive background checks? It only takes one hacker to gain access to a bank and auto finance companies servers to have access to thousands of consumers information at the level that we can be destroyed for years to come.

I feel these customer service representatives do not have the level of understanding of the damage they can potentially cause a consumer when they unnecessarily perform comprehensive background checks and expose a consumer life to a computer database. Why?

I also feel the companies that provide consumer background information and access to these reckless companies should be penalized along with the abusers of these 'so-called compilers of 'public information', while they make millions on exposing consumers lives and needlessly.

Use of Your Company Phone – What You Should Know

Are you attempting to hide from creditors by not calling them from your home number - so you call them from work or someone's home instead? Do you call from work to make arrangements to pay a creditor but did not stick to those arrangements, only to attempt to stop the calls for a period of time. Did you know that generally all phone numbers private and otherwise are being captured by creditors and provide the creditor with the ability to perform a 'reverse lookup' of your information included employer, or new employer. Do you want to get creditors calls backs to the phone number that you are contacting the financial institution from? No, you do not.

First, we consumers should try to take care of our obligation but when those situations occur and you are dealing with aggressive financial institutions or collections agencies then use my information to keep your privacy. Please understand the financial institutions already have quite a lot of information on all consumers already – why give them more? Don't call creditors from phone numbers that you do not want them to have access to because they all capture every phone number that comes in to their phone systems.

Now aren't you amazed at what a simple phone call can produce???

Creditors Reselling of Bad-Debt

Did you know that creditors sell their 'bad debt' accounts to the highest bidder when they are unable to collect from the consumer? This means that your unpaid bill can appear and re-appear sometimes years down the line. If you have had a situation, maybe after leaving college or suffering some financial difficulties where you had accounts that were placed into collections? I advise you to retain your proof of payment receipts, especially if your account was sent to an outside collection company.

While working with consumer background information nearly a third of our client base was collection companies. They do have the ability to locate you. And of course, you do not want to be relocated for a debt that has already been paid. Keep all records of payment on any account that goes to collections for several years. This would also include closed bank accounts for negative balances, since those accounts are also sometimes sent to outside collection companies along with the reporting to ChexSystems.

Chapter 12 – Insurance and What You Need To Know

Now this is an interesting subject. I obtained my insurance license in Property and Casualty and Life and Health in 2000. What drove me to obtain an insurance license, which was an extremely rigorous process, was that my insurance agent had under-insured my new home. My home was not even insured for the amount it took to build it, and that included what it would take to replace my home. Is that crazy or what? Since the consulting firm that I had worked for, for several years closed, and during the building of my home - I decided to take six months off from consulting to obtain my state insurance license.

You learn a lot in those insurance certification classes and even more when you open an insurance office and attempt to write policies. I have always felt that we consumers pay too much for insurance, and we do. Insurance is not designed to be used (repeatedly) on small claims and most consumers are not aware of that bit of information until it is too late, and they policies are cancelled due the volume of claims submitted over a short period of time. Too many insurance claims will get your policy cancelled, and sometimes very quickly after your third insurance claim. In my opinion, insurance is designed for catastrophic events. Events such as a 'complete or major-partial' loss of property (fires, tornados, etc.), damage caused by 'Mother Earth', a tree falling on top of your home (partial loss), flooding (if flooding is added to your policy), not the broken window and the use of homeowners insurance due to items being stolen off or from your auto. Comprehensive insurance claims are sometimes submitted to cover these types of damages. Be aware that this claims history is stored for years and can negatively affect you later when a more serious claim is submitted.

Comprehensive Insurance is defined as, coverage that repairs or replaces the policy owner's vehicle and personal property that was damaged or lost due to other situations such as fire, theft, flood or vandalism.

Minimum Coverage Insurance – What it truly means to you

Most states require that a licensed driver and vehicle owner obtain a minimum amount of bodily injury and property damage liability insurance before they can legally drive their vehicles. All states have financial responsibility laws for license drivers. This means that consumers involved in an automobile accident will be required to furnish proof of financial responsibility up to certain 'minimum' dollar limits. To comply with financial responsibility laws, most drivers purchase automobile liability insurance. The insurance industry and consumer groups generally recommend a minimum amount of $100,000 of bodily injury protection per person and $300,000 per accident since accidents may cost far more than the minimum limits mandated by most states.

What Insurance Companies Know About Your Household

All insurance information is historically retained from ALL insurance companies into a series of databases. These databases are made available to insurance companies and now to almost anyone who wants to pay for the information. Yes, as I stated – most anyone who wants to pay for the information.

Most people are not aware that your insurance claims and driving history information is so readily available when consumers attempt to move from one insurance company to another with negative information for claims and poor driving record history. Please understand that your insurance and driving history moves right with you. Another important piece of information to be aware of is - when you apply for an insurance policy, and do not list all drivers in your household, while attempting to save money by not listing that your teenage son or daughter will be driving your autos. Be aware that, their driving records information, and all other licensed drivers in your household (good record or bad record) appears when your driving record is generated. Systems that are used by insurance companies will not only produce in one consolidated report, everyone currently residing in your home, the system will also produce their driving records, and claims history. This is how attempted consumer fraud is found (in most cases) prior to a policy being written.

Insurance Rates Based on Where You Live 'Red-Lining'

Red-lining *(paying more for your insurance based on address and zip code)* does exist and it is not fair. In addition to red-lining, you have to fight those really smart 'pocket-protector' wearing actuaries (underwriters) who sometimes will override the insurance agent and quoted system premiums. When this practice occurred, I found it utterly ridiculous. Generally, the insurance premium quote is increased by hundreds of dollars, by the underwriting department and based on their individual assumptions of risk. I found myself fighting the insurance companies underwriting practices repeatedly for fair premiums for consumers, and sometimes winning to get original system-quoted insurance rates. In addition, I gave every discount that I could, and you know what that meant, I made little money *but* made 'Agent of the Month' my first month as an agent (hummmm), and was one of the top writers for most of the months as an agent. Obviously, my goal was to be successful as an insurance agent but it was not possible. I found it quite difficult to make money as a new, note the word 'new' insurance agent while trying to help consumers obtain lower rates for insurance.

Sadly, insurance companies are only interested in profit. That's where those pocket protector wearing actuaries come into play, they protect the interests of the insurance companies by trying to determine when you will drive, when you will have an accident, what your credit says about the person that you are (hummmm) and how expense your insurance rates should be with those factors into consideration, amongst many other considerations. Unfortunately, a new agency just does not initially make money on policy renewals as a new agent, only on new policies written which forced new agents to hold back on consumer multi-policy discounts. I decided a 'fair rated', low premium - consumer policy was more important, so I gave every discount that I could to consumers.

Don't Cancel an Existing Policy While Insurance Shopping

My advice is, if you are insurance shopping do not cancel an existing policy until the new policy is officially received from your new insurance agency. An agent can give you a quote and that insurance quote be returned (mailed) to you at a much higher premium then originally quoted by the agent but now from the underwriting department. What I consider an even worse action by the insurance company is that underwriting can deny your insurance after the agent has issued you a temporary insurance card and taken your premium. All that you will get is a 'Letter of Cancellation' from the insurance company that now places you at risk with no coverage and now searching as an uninsured consumer, this happens frequently.

Insurance and Your Credit History

Did you know that your credit history and credit score affects your insurance rates? As a former Insurance Agent, I feel this practice with insurance companies was, and is unfair. I do believe that a consumer's insurance claims history should be used to determine rates; I guess I should say a consumer's abuse of insurance claims and any fraudulent claims information should be considered. No one wants to pay for the abuse of insurance, but I don't think using credit is a good factor for every consumer to consider what premium rates should charged, but it is used as a factor and make a lot of revenue for the insurance companies.

In addition, another factor being utilized is the conviction for being caught driving without insurance. The penalty for that action is now and within most states the consumer being assigned to maintain a Bond or assigned a SR-22 requiring that you maintain insurance minimums for a court specified period of time, this penalty will also severely affect your insurance rates greatly – and even more then poor credit.

Insurance Deductibles

In my opinion, it is generally best to have a higher insurance deductible. Higher insurance deductibles will save you money on your insurance premiums. Of course, you need to have access to funds equal to your insurance deductibles in the event of a loss. Having the funds available or saved that are equal to your largest deductible is recommended.

Higher deductible, in most cases, can save you hundreds of dollars each year on your premium and should project a good consumer image with your insurance company. That image projected, with a higher deductible such as $1000, or $2000 on your homeowner insurance shows that you, as a consumer are not interested in submitting small frivolous claims. Believe me you will not be quick to submit small claims when the initial claim amount is out of your pocket, or deductible amount. Your insurance premiums will also then be a little more manageable (smaller).

In reference to auto deductibles, $500.00 is a good deductible amount. I have difficulty understanding consumers who have no deductibles. Why give more money to the insurance company when paying a higher, no-deductible insurance premium. Try saving the deductible amount or at least making sure you have that amount on a credit card somewhere, but just do not give it to the insurance company as a 'no-deductible insurance policy'.

Insurance – Discounts

Insurance discounts do exist so make sure that your agent gives you discounts for multiple autos insured, auto and home insured and security systems in your home - these are some of the standard consumer insurance discounts. In addition, a discount may generally apply when insuring your 'student' child who maintains a certain grade point average. The student discount will save you hundreds since coverage for teen drivers is so costly. After all, the parent can impose the 'good GPA' continued discount to the student's right to drive the household vehicle. If the GPA slips then so does the right to drive. Nevertheless, remember, by law all licensed drivers must have some form of insurance coverage. So dropping insurance coverage for a teen driver is not an option However, allowing that teen driver to obtain a drivers license is. Be aware of the financial obligations as a parent when your teen becomes licensed to drive.

There are hosts of other insurance discounts so check with your agent or check the insurance provisions for discounts at their website. Sadly, some insurance agents do not grant applicable insurance discounts since they reduce their own revenue when doing so.

Insurance – Auto Insurance

Don't drive without Auto Insurance - You know the law

Do not allow yourself to be placed in the position to have to maintain a SR-22 or insurance Bond, which is basically permission for the insurance company to place you in a high-risk insurance category and charge you the maximum for your insurance premium. Please understand also that if you have been told by the courts to maintain insurance for a specified number of years for driving without insurance, and now have an Insurance Bond or SR-22 appearing on your driving record, you are required to maintain insurance for those specified years. Please understand that information appears on your driving record. If you drop your insurance coverage your agent will gladly report that drop to the (BMV) Bureau of Motor Vehicles or (DMV) Department or Motor Vehicles, and the state will gladly, and automatically, extend your penalty years required to maintain the SR-22 thus requiring that you pay much more for insurance for several more years. In most cases, the cost of insurance doubles your monthly premium. *Tough it out and pay as required*. If you are not a homeowner request at least the state minimum coverage, this will reduce the premium cost but also limit your insurance coverage limits. Which I do not recommend (state minimums of insurance), but at least it is affordable. If you are a homeowner, do not settle for state minimum coverage in auto insurance, this is not enough coverage if you are ever in a multiple car accident. Minimum coverage is generally only 12.5/25.7.5 in Ohio and 25/50/10 in New York. These amounts represent bodily injury and property damage maximums for each occurrence (each accident). I will talk more about state minimums in a later chapter.

SR-22 is a form of Financial Responsibility Insurance that is issued on a Certificate and is filed by an insurance company with the state, stating that auto liability insurance is in effect for a particular individual. Required when insurance is provided to and individual who was in an accident or was convicted of a traffic offense and was unable to show financial responsibility for a state required approved about of time (specified years). The SR-22 requirements vary from state to state and if the insurance is cancelled before the stated required about of time, generally additional years of required coverage is added to the original requirement.

Insurance Quoting Factors

These were some of the quoting factors that were used by the company that I wrote policies for. I did not agree with these factors but they were used by underwriting to quote consumer insurance rates. Regrettably, there are several factors that are used when insurance quotes are generated. One factor is your zip code; additional factors would be your address and city, and then your age, marital status, the state that you live, and any prior or current insurance coverage. 'No prior insurance' is not good since this would clearly indicate that you do not have insurance at the time that you are acquiring new insurance. No prior insurance will negatively affect your new policy rates. Applying for insurance with no current insurance policy in place will place you in a higher rated policy verses a lower rated premium. You are considered 'high risk' to an insurance company when you are a licensed driver and do not have any form of auto insurance, obviously. Additional factors are your number of accidents and understand that some insurance quoting systems will display driving records history and accident claims history back further then the stated three years, sometime up to 10 years. Other factors would be your gender, any other licenses driver in the household, etc.

One important factor here is to understand that the insurance company has access to information on every licensed driver in your household so not listing a license driver or children that have obtained their license will not reduce your premium. The key is any licenses driver who reports your address as their address will appear on your report for the insurance company. If you have a 16-year-old licensed driver or a child of teenage years with a driving permit, their information will appear on your insurance driving records inquiry.

Other quoting factors that are considered by insurance companies are:

- Your driving record is paramount
- Recent accidents even if they were out of your control are looked at
- The residential area that your policy will be held
- The make and model of your vehicle
- Numbers of prior claims, comprehensive and otherwise

Insurance companies create profiles based on their past experiences, so any correlation, no matter how accurate or inaccurate become cause for concern to an insurance company.

Insurance – Other Drivers of Your Vehicle

Make sure you review your policy for the coverage of 'other drivers'. Every auto policy indicates who is covered when driving your vehicle. You policy may state that only drivers over the age of 25 are covered (only), take this statement seriously. In addition, we all know that you should never allow an unlicensed driver to drive your vehicle, if you do, be prepared to pay legally if any accident occurs while this individual is in possession of your vehicle. You are liable along with the unlicensed individual. Please review the details of this provision on your policy section.

Insurance – Homeowners

Now this is an interesting subject. For consumers looking to purchase a home, condo or looking to rent an apartment I recommend that you obtain a quote for insurance for the areas that you are considering from your insurance agent prior to moving into the area, house, condo or apartment. You will be surprised what rates you will get from area to area and state to state. This is an import factor since insurance can cost hundreds or thousands based on your dwelling (home) zip code. In addition, don't think over insuring is of benefit, I personally only want protection from catastrophic events not to submit small claims for little incidents such as broken windows, falling gutters or someone driving on your lawn (of course by accident). Try to only use your insurance for big events, 'Acts of God' (storm damage), fire damage, etc. Please also note that I am not trying to discourage any consumer from submitting claims for insurance damage. I am only trying to explain what affects our insurance rates and too many claims within a three (3) or five (5) year period of time will get your policy cancelled. Even though I do not agree with the insurance companies on this practice of canceling consumers based on the submission of claims, they do. So submit claims when you can afford to fix or repair the damage. We all know what we can afford or not afford. Just be aware of what the insurance companies and I mean companies (all) are looking at when pricing our premiums. That's all☺

Another very important factor to consider when insuring your home especially if this is a new home, condominium, or apartment that you are purchasing. Some properties can have a high claim history prior to you taking position of that property. Understand that the history of that property is also retained in insurance databases even if the property was not insured by the company that you are contacting for a quote – yes, those 'shared' claims databases. This of course can be of benefit to consumers in some situations, especially if the property has had 'black mold' or fire damage in the past that has resulted in a high number of claims to repair. It does not hurt to request an official quote or claims history or a property before taking position of it.

Verify Claims History on the Property You Want To Purchase or Insure

Most consumers are not aware that the claims history of the property you want to purchase can affect your ability to insure the property after your purchase. Insurance companies retain claims history for all claims and will shun away from properties with a history of at least one claim of water or mold damage and or a high volume of property claims. Obtain an estimate from your insurance company and allow them to run a claims history report on the property, be assured they will, and this will be to your benefit.

Most companies that collects and stores this information, collect both claims, and damage reports history. Now if you are the seller of damaged property all that I can say is …hummmm.

Insurance Claims Information is Shared – Auto, Home, Health

While I was an insurance agent, I experienced an interesting consumer attempting to apply for new insurance with claims history for the same household damage, which appeared to have occurred yearly for the prior three years? As a new agent, this appeared as insurance fraud. Why would the same claim be submitted for the same damages year after year? In addition, since the claims history was being entered into the 'shared' claims system all insurance companies could view this information. There is no way the system would allow the writing of this policy.

What most consumers do not understand is that insurance companies do not want to have to pay insurance claims. In addition, nearly all policies are reviewed by insurance underwriting prior to issuing. In my personal opinion, insurance really should be used for serious catastrophic claims such as

'An Invasion of (corporate) Locust' by Darlene R. Miles

complete and partial loss of property and of course those 'Acts of God'; storms, tornados, etc. Consumer must understand that when you contact an agent for the first time to request a quote for homeowners insurance, the agent has a responsibility to the insurance company that they write policies for, to obtain a claims history on you and the property. Every insurance claim that you file, be it homeowners, auto and health is stored to a national database and is accessible to the agent. This claims history is also reviewed by Underwriting after your policy is written by the agent. The process of additional review of claims history also occurs at the 'Renewal' of your policy. With high claim history, you may be denied new policy coverage, or rated extremely high on your premium. Do not think by moving from insurance company to insurance company your claims history does not follow you. It does.

Insurance companies maintain claims history on you as an individual and on your property. The information maintained on your home or property can cause you to become uninsurable, and without your clear knowledge of the past history of your property.

Consumers are not aware that the property you may be about to purchase may have had a serious water or mold damage claim and that claim history was recorded. It only takes one serious claim for water or mold damage for an insurance company to deny your property and you insurance coverage for your property.

Insurance – Renters Insurance

You may not own the place where you live, but you still will need insurance protection for your belongings.

Renters Insurance is for anyone who rents a home, or apartment. Renters insurance will protect your personal property against fire, theft, and vandalism. Renters insurance will also protect you against liability lawsuit filed against you when anyone claims to be hurt on or at your apartment. One important piece of information to know is, Liability insurance will generally protect you if someone is injured on your property or damage occurring to another person's property. Liability protection will generally cover incidents that may occur at your residence or by you when you are away from your residence.

Generally, an insurance company will grant discounts on both a renters' policy and combined auto insurance coverage as a multiple discount when you purchase those policies with one insurance company. This may not apply to all states so check with your agent for insurance company discounts.

What Affects Renters Insurance Rates

The price of renters insurance varies by company and by. Some of the quoting factors are:

- The number of coverage's that you purchase
  - o Loss of use
  - o Total or value of your property, jewelry, furs, etc.
  - o Medical payments
- Your deductibles
- Your property location
- Prior claims history

What Affects Homeowners Insurance Rates

Sadly, my first comment would be that your rates are affected and determined by where you write the initial insurance policy. You are probably, wonder what I am stating here. I have seen where a consumer requested a quote from a newly licensed agent and received an extremely high quote. Why you ask, this agent is only receiving commissions on new policies, and is not willing to discount the consumer's policy because it cuts into the agents profits. In most cases, a new agent may not receive commission on renewals until after two years. Not receiving commissions on renewals for two years would mean that the new agent has to work very hard to build a strong renewal base of policyholders so that when the two-year renewals kick in they will receive consistent revenue moving forward.

Now this was not my case. Even though I did not receive renewal renewals, as an agent I discounted everyone that I could and still made Agent of the Month as a new agent. However, I did not make any money. I was determined to discount everyone that I could since I feel we all pay too much for insurance.

Now back to what affects your insurance rates. Some of those items are your past claims history within a five year period (some insurance companies look at as many years of history that are available before approving the new policy). Credit history, to determine how likely are you to commit fraud, or if you have many liabilities, or do not pay your bills on time along with the number delinquencies reported on your credit report. In addition, your current state of insurance, or existing insurance (are you insured at the time that you are requesting a new quote or have you not had insurance in place). Your coverage limits, value of your home, the condition of your home (are any visible repairs needed), the condition of the exterior stairs and railings to assist visitors and decrease accidents. Is there any broken concrete on sidewalks and of course, the condition of the inside of the home – all of these factors are considered and evaluated when obtaining a new home policy or used by the insurance company when determining if the insurance company will write your policy. If attempting to obtain a new insurance policy, have your property up to par – all repairs completed. If there are over three exterior stairs outside that leads up to your property, make sure that you have a hand railing (which applies in most states). Exterior railings, when there are over three stairs leading up to a consumers property is a requirement with most insurance companies. This requirement will also help to protect you from lawsuits and prevent accidents resulting from falls due to no exterior handrails.

Homeowners Insurance and Certain Types of Pets

Some insurance companies will not insure your home if you have a dangerous pet. Some dogs that are considered dangerous are; Pit Bull, Rottweiler, and Doberman. Additional dogs can be labeled dangerous if they have bitten humans in the past.

Keep in mind, to add coverage for your pets you will still have to go through the same screening process, with the same qualifying questions regarding your demographics (male or female), your date of birth, your credit rating (yes, credit rating), information about your property (own, rent, new purchase), value of your home, claims history and more.

Get your insurance quote before purchasing what is considered a dangerous pet.

Insurance is designed to help protect you from losses – So hold the Insurance Company to it!

I wanted to provide more information on what is considered as 'Losses' and the various 'Coverage's' that appear on a consumers insurance policy. It is important to understand these coverage's. The worse situation would be to need the insurance coverage and not understand them or have them in your policies.

Here you are:

Losses are occurrences that caused direct physical damage to property or injury to persons, whether covered by insurance or not.

Property Coverage Information

Coverage's are generally one of the most complicated areas for consumers to understand and are generally not reviewed carefully; even I am guilty of that. What I put together are some simple examples of 'coverage's' that can appear on your property 'dwelling' coverage section of your policy. I do advise that all consumers' review their coverage's carefully since this is what the insurance company is stating that they will pay for your loss if that occurs. I also advise that consumers review their coverage's periodically, especially after home improvements or large purchases (over a period of time) to assure that you have adequate insurance coverage.

Another review of coverage's may be when your college student goes away to college and takes a portion of the house with them☺ Will their (your) property be covered away from home? Make sure you know your coverage limits.

Personal Property – Coverage B

- The personal property you have in your home such as your clothes and furniture.
- The personal property you have with you when you are away from home in many places throughout the world, while traveling for work or on vacation.

Coverage for your personal property may include losses caused by:

- Fire or lightning
- Weight of ice, snow or sleet
- Explosion
- Aircraft and vehicles
- Smoke

'An Invasion of (corporate) Locust' by Darlene R. Miles

- Sudden and accidental tearing or bulging of heating or cooling systems
- Windstorm or hail
- Theft
- Riot or civil commotion
- Falling objects
- Vandalism or malicious mischief
- Sudden and accidental water discharge from plumbing or appliances
- Freezing of plumbing systems

Loss of Use – Coverage C

This coverage provides payment for certain losses when your home is damaged and rendered uninhabitable because of an insured loss.

Additional Living Expense

This covers the actual loss incurred for increased expenses over and above what you normally spend for food, shelter, and related items for the shortest time required to repair or replace the premises, or for your household to settle elsewhere up to 24 months.

Inflation Coverage's (Watch this one!)

This coverage automatically increases the amount of your insurance coverage's on your personal property as inflation changes the cost of living. The changes are based on the movement of an inflation index and are reflected in the premium at each annual policy renewal.

What I've seem with this 'Inflation Coverage' is that it is

sometimes used to calculate your 'Replacement' Cost at very high amounts that increase your premium each year or sometime every six (yes, six) months, if the insurance company has your policy on a six month renewal period. Watch Replacement cost closely. Do not let the insurance company over quote at a ridiculous amount just to charge you a higher premium. You can request from your insurance agent that your Replacement and Inflation Coverage amounts be reduced to reasonable amounts. Your Replacement cost provides payments based on the cost to repair or replace the damaged property at the time of loss, if actually replaced. Look at your policy and premiums over a period of a couple of years to see how the amounts have changed. If you have thrown old declaration pages away, look through your old check registers or even ask your agent for your premium history. Just do not over pay, keep your money in your pocket.

Personal Liability – Coverage L

This coverage provides payment for your legal liability up to the limits in the policy for damages because of bodily injury or property damage caused by an occurrence to which your insurance applies. In addition, it may provide for the payment of your defense against these claims or suits.

Medical Payments to Others – Coverage M

This coverage pays medical expenses up to the limits in the policy for people who are on your premises with your permission and are accidentally injured. The coverage also extends to people accidentally injured by your activities. However, the coverage does not pay for medical expenses for you or members of your family who live with you.

Losses Sometimes Not Insured Unless Specified

While most homeowners and renter's policy provides comprehensive coverage, they sometimes do not provide coverage for *every* loss. All property coverage's are subject to the **Losses Not Insured Provisions of your policy**. It is important that you understand this section. You do not want to need coverage and find that you do not have it.

Some examples of losses that can sometimes not be included but are not limited to:
- Water damage caused by flood or underground water.
- Earth movement including earthquake or landslide.
- Damage caused by nuclear hazard.

Review your policy for your complete list of losses not insured.

Some Optional Coverage Information

Coverage's available for an additional premium include but are not limited to:

Personal Articles Policy

This is special worldwide coverage in the amount needed for your valuable possessions such as furs, diamond rings, art, etc.

Personal Liability Umbrella Policy

This is for a million dollars or more of personal liability protection for many situations, which may not be covered by your basic insurance. Generally, an insurance company will only offer this type of policy if your home and auto is also covered with the insurance company and if you maintain a certain dollar limit amounts on your existing homeowner and auto insurance. You generally cannot write an 'Umbrella' policy if you only maintain state minimums on your auto insurance policy.

I highly recommend this coverage. It is generally a yearly inexpensive premium. The cost is generally around one hundred dollars per million dollars, for personal liability protection.

- Earthquake damage.
- Waterbed liability.
- Increased business property.
- Incidental business liability.
- Increased liability limits from lawsuits.

Please check with your insurance agent for additional information.

Other Terms You Should Know About Insurance Policies

Loss Settlement Provisions--Personal Property

Limited Replacement Cost Loss Settlement

Provides payment based on the cost to repair or replace the damaged property at the time of loss, if actually replaced.

Depreciated Loss Settlement

Provides payment based on the cost to repair or replace damaged property less depreciation at the time of loss.

Personal Property Special Limits

While the Personal Property Loss Settlement provisions determine the loss payment on your personal property, it is important that you know that special limits apply to certain types of property.

For example:

- Money, bank notes, coins (including collections) – specified on your policy
- Property used or intended to be used in business - specified on your policy
- Cash On premises (certain dollar amount specified on your policy)
- Cash Off premises (certain dollar amount specified on your policy)
- Watercraft and equipment (specified on your policy)
- Securities, checks, traveler's checks (certain dollar amount specified on your policy)
- Trailers (certain dollar amount specified on your policy)
- Stamps, trading cards, comic books (including collections) – (certain dollar amount specified on your policy)

Theft loss of:

- Jewelry and Furs (certain dollar amount specified on your policy)
- Firearms (certain dollar amount specified on your policy)
- Silverware and Gold ware (certain dollar amount specified on your policy)
- Rugs, tapestry, wall hangings
- Aggregate (cumulative)- (total dollar amount specified on your policy)
- Home Computers (certain dollar amount specified on your policy)

Antiques, fine arts, painting, statuary, and similar articles that cannot be replaced by new articles, and property not useful for its intended purpose, is limited in coverage to its market value.

'An Invasion of (corporate) Locust' by Darlene R. Miles

187

Higher limits on some of these items are available through optional coverage's.

Deductibles

The deductible is the portion of a covered loss that is your responsibility. Although deductibles vary by state, they are typically available in amounts such as $250, $500, or $1000.

For example, if you had a $500 deductible, you would need to pay $500 of the covered loss or the amount of the deductible will be subtracted for your loss total. For auto deductibles, those are generally required to be paid before your vehicle is released to you after a covered repair. In other words, you have to pay the deductible before you get your vehicle.

Generally speaking, higher deductibles lower your premium, but increase the amount you must pay out of your own pocket if a covered loss occurs. Ask yourself how much you are willing to pay in order to save on premium?

Insurance Property (Homeowners) Replacement Cost – Watch This One!

Watch the stated Insurance Property Replacement calculation that appears on your insurance policy. What is 'Replacement Costs", you ask? Replacement cost is the insurance company's assessments, of how much money it will cost to replace your dwelling and if stated in your policy, replace your personal belongings.

The insurance companies will increase the Replacement Cost yearly. The increase is not always to your benefit. Just imagine building a home for $160,000 in the year of 2000 then by the year of 2006, the insurance company has increased your property replacement cost to $429,000, while the appraised value is less then $300,000. First of all the insurance company increased your insurance premium payment with each of these increases in replacement cost. Do not be impressed with a high replacement estimate from the insurance company.

Here are two items to think about. Number one – what is the balance of my mortgage or mortgages? You would want to make sure that your insurance replacement cost would cover those mortgage(s) balances. Second, approximately what will it take to rebuild my home if you had a complete loss? And last, can I afford the taxes on a $429,000 dollar home in the neighborhood that I live if I had a complete loss of my property due to a fire, tornado, etc.?. Would you actually build a $429,000 home if you had the chance? Can you afford the mortgage payment on $429,000? I personally feel the high replacement costs that are calculated by the insurance companies are revenue-generating tools.

A final comment on this issue, look what happened to the homeowners in the states of Louisiana, Mississippi, and other Gulf states after a complete loss of their properties. Most top rated insurance companies denied consumers claims for complete loss. Watch your pocket. Do not over insure your property; it serves no benefit to your pocket. When you reduce your Homeowners Replacement cost to be in line with actual replacement cost, you will save money monthly on your ever-increasing monthly or quarterly premiums.

For those of you who escrow your insurance premium, the same situation applies. Check to see what your property replacement is being calculated at and how much it is costing you monthly since you may not pay close attention to your policy when escrowing. Understand this note, when your insurance premium increases it does affect your escrowed insurance payments.

'An Invasion of (corporate) Locust' by Darlene R. Miles

Insurance Rates Based on Types of Vehicle Purchased or Owned

Insurance coverage for new verses pre-owned autos will vary but keep in mind that coverage for sports cars are generally quoted at higher rates. Additional factors that may be considered are; the value of the sports vehicle, your demographics (male or female), your age, your address, your zip code, and of course your claim history – amongst some of the factors.

Motorcycles or 'Bullet Bikes' – High Premiums Generally Apply

Most insurance companies do not care to insure what is considered as a 'Bullet-Bike'. These motorcycles are considered as extremely fast racing motorcycles. There are more accidents that occur on these types of bikes and consumers do seem to ride much faster, which is clearly what these bikes are designed for …speed.

Be aware that your premiums may be quite high for insurance coverage for these types of adult toys…hummmm.

Insurance for New or Teenage Drivers

The law states that when you become a license driver, you are required to have insurance coverage; this includes our teenage and new drivers. Please be aware that the insurance companies are aware of all license drivers in your household. Please do not think that by not listing a teen driver that teen will automatically be covered by your auto insurance policy, they won't – and as a matter of fact you may even have a provision that no driver's under the age of 25 can drive your vehicle. Please review your policy carefully. If your auto policy provision excludes drivers under 25 years of age, and that individual causes an accident in your auto, they will not be covered. In addition, you may be sued for damages that were caused, and so on. Please insure all teenage drivers and make sure that anyone driving your vehicle has insurance and is a licensed driver.

Insurance and Other License Drivers in Your Household

Did you know that Insurance Company is aware of all License drivers in your household?

Do not think that you can get away with not reporting all possible licensed drivers living in your house. If the driver is reporting your address as their address of residence, their driving record is automatically available when your driving record is generated by the insurance company, so be aware of this. Some consumers try to 'hold out' on adding their teen drivers to their policy due to the high cost of insuring teen drivers. Be aware that all licensed drivers living in your home will appear on a consumer report. Save yourself the trouble and insure everyone as driver's license is issued. As for others living in your residence, if they have bad driving records, do not allow them to drive your auto.

What Is High Risk Insurance and What You Should Do About It

Several top insurance companies offer high-risk insurance coverage for consumers, then there are those high-risk insurance companies that only offer consumers high-risk insurance.

What is the difference? Not much, except as a former agent the consumer stands a better chance of having lower rates through a 'standard policy', and of being insured at a later date. With a clean driving record and no lapse in insurance coverage most consumers can move successfully into a standard rated policy with one of the top insurance companies or even leave a high-risk insurance company after a period of time, thus lowering your insurance premiums.

What can place you into a High-Risk Insurance Situation?

Some of the following situations can place you into a high-risk insurance situation as a consumer:

- Multiple auto accidents
- Multiple tickets or citations, this includes traffic and parking tickets
- Multiple tickets or citations that went unpaid
- Lapse in your insurance coverage (driving uninsured)
- A teenage driver and not being added to an adult policy
- Bad Credit (yes, bad credit)
- DUI or multiple DUI

I would try, if possible, to stay away from the high-risk insurance companies. Obtain the quotes from the higher-risk insurance companies but also obtain quotes from the top rated insurance companies. I personally feel that you will be better off over a longer period of time. You will also increase your chances of creating good insurance claims and payment history with a top rated company that can later offer you lower standard not 'sub-standard' high-risk insurance rates.

Car Insurance Limits – What You Need To Understand

Automobile Financial Responsibility and Compulsory Limits by State (As of October 2006)

The limits that I display on the worksheet are what you would hear stated as 'State Minimums'. Just referencing one of the lowest limits stated below for the state of California - the state limits for California are listed as 15/30/5; fifteen thousand maximum bodily injury per person, thirty thousand maximum per incident for bodily injury (doesn't matter how many injured or the total cost of those injuries) and a MAXIMUM, yes maximum of ($5,000). Five thousand for Property Damage for each accident. Please tell me what will happen if you hit a Mercedes, BMV, or a high priced SUV, where rear-end damage cost is nearly $5000.00 or more to repair? I will tell you what may happen without sufficient cover limits, you can be sued in court for damages, and your wages possibly garnished via a civil action if you do not have the money to pay damages. Part of this civil action may also be a conviction in traffic court of a license suspension if you cannot pay the damages, and that is just the result of the Property damage. What if there are personal injuries resulting from the multiple car accident where _everyone_ gets out of the vehicle holding their head or neck…hummmm???

I caution you when considering purchasing state minimum insurance as auto insurance coverage, especially if you have assets that can be taken by the court - such as your home. Strangely and in most cases, State Minimums will cost nearly as much as your higher limited insurance. I advise that you at least stay somewhere in the middle on higher limits of insurance such as 50/100/50.

State 2007	Bodily Injury - Per Person	Bodily Injury - Per Incident	Property Damage - Per Incident
AK	50,000	100,000	25,000
AL	20,000	40,000	10,000
AR	25,000	50,000	25,000
AZ	15,000	30,000	10,000
CA	15,000	30,000	5,000
CO	25,000	50,000	15,000
CT	20,000	40,000	10,000
DC	25,000	50,000	10,000
DE	15,000	30,000	5,000
FL	10,000	20,000	10,000
GA	25,000	50,000	25,000
HI	20,000	40,000	10,000
IA	20,000	40,000	15,000
ID	25,000	50,000	15,000
IL	20,000	40,000	15,000
IN	25,000	50,000	10,000
KS	25,000	50,000	10,000
KY	25,000	50,000	10,000
LA	10,000	20,000	10,000
MA	20,000	40,000	5,000
MD	20,000	40,000	15,000
ME	50,000	100,000	25,000
MI	20,000	40,000	10,000
MN	30,000	60,000	10,000
MO	25,000	50,000	10,000
MS	10,000	20,000	5,000
MT	25,000	50,000	10,000
NC	30,000	60,000	25,000
ND	25,000	50,000	25,000
NE	25,000	50,000	25,000
NH	25,000	50,000	25,000
NJ	15,000	30,000	5,000
NM	25,000	50,000	10,000
NV	15,000	30,000	10,000
NY	25,000	50,000	10,000

'An Invasion of (corporate) Locust' by Darlene R. Miles

194

State 2007	Bodily Injury - Per Person	Bodily Injury - Per Incident	Property Damage - Per Incident
OH	12,500	25,000	7,500
OK	10,000	20,000	10,000
OR	25,000	50,000	10,000
PA	15,000	30,000	5,000
RI	25,000	50,000	25,000
SC	15,000	30,000	10,000
SD	25,000	50,000	25,000
TN	25,000	50,000	10,000
TX	20,000	40,000	15,000
UT	25,000	50,000	15,000
VA	25,000	50,000	20,000
VT	25,000	50,000	10,000
WA	25,000	50,000	10,000
WI	25,000	50,000	10,000
WV	20,000	40,000	10,000
WY	25,000	50,000	20,000

'An Invasion of (corporate) Locust' by Darlene R. Miles

Automobile Coverage Information

As is with Property coverage's, the complication does not get any easier with *Automobile Insurance coverage's*. I put together a simple explanation of automobile coverage's that should appear on your insurance policy. I do advise that all consumers' review their coverage's carefully since this is what the insurance company is stating are your limits in coverage's and the amounts that will be paid if a loss occurs. I also advise that consumers review their coverage's periodically to monitor any insurance company modifications, or reduction in limits on your policies.

Coverage Descriptions

Bodily Injury and Property Damage Liability

The 'Bodily Injury' coverage defines the maximums paid to Each Person, with a maximum paid for Each Accident. Generally, the higher limits are $100,000 Each Person, $300,000 Each Accident.

The Limits of Liability Coverage for 'Property Damage' generally appears for Each Accident and for the higher limits, appears as Each Accident $100,000.

Appear as 100/300/100

The above are examples of higher limits. Where consumers seem to struggle is with the understanding of what limits to add to their automobile policies. Here is an example of a states minimum requirement for auto insurance:

- Your auto insurance limits are: $12,500, $25,000 and $7,500 – This example equates to, $12,500 For any Bodily Injury for each person hurt in an accident per occurrence

- $25,000 Total paid for all injured parties (combined) for that one accident occurrence
- With a maximum Property Damage paid to all parties, per occurrence of $7,500

Appears as: 12,5/25/7500

With the example above, if a multiple car accident occurs by an insured consumer with such minimum coverage, both the individual and individuals left with damages, and the insured may be in financial trouble without enough insurance coverage.

In today's society, most new vehicles cost an average of $15,000 to $30,000 dollars new. If you cause a multiple car accident with damages that exceed the $7,500, you can be sued for the remainder of the damages, and lets not speak of any medical or bodily injuries. Why drive with only the minimum coverage when most higher limit policy may only cost $50 to $100 dollars more per month.

Medical Payments

This section of your policy will list the 'Limits of Liability' coverage for 'Each Person', for Medical Payments. These medical payments can be quite useful following an auto accident and are in most cases paid directly to the insured for medical expenses.

Deductible Comprehensive

This section of your policy will list the Deductibles for your Comprehensive portion of your policy and for your Collision portion of your policy.

- Comprehensive insurance is generally used when items are stolen from or off your auto.

- Collision insurance is for property damages to a vehicle.

Uninsured Motor Vehicles

This section of your policy displays your limits for any Uninsured or Underinsured Motor Vehicle Accidents.

Again, limits apply to this section, and are generally matched to the limits that you carry for your Bodily Injury/Property Damage Liability coverage's.

Additional Auto Coverage's

Additional coverage's may be added to your policy such as:

- Emergency Road Service
- Car Rental/Travel Expenses

These additional coverage's also are displayed with 'Each Day – Limits' and 'Each Occurrence – Limits', so view you policies closely.

Selecting an Insurance Agent

This may be as important as the policy that you write with an agency. You should build a good relationship with your insurance agent and part of that building process should be your gained knowledge of insurance as a whole. Learn as much as you can about insurance so that you will not pay for insurance that you do not need. Understand that most insurance agents are in the 'selling' business. They only make money on renewals of your policies or new policies written. Some agents are more concern with retaining your business, especially if you are a 'good insured' policyholder (not submitting frivolous claims all the time). While other are mostly concern with the number of policies written each day. I personally would be concern with both areas of business - writing 'good consumer business' (policy term here), and taking good care of existing policyholders.

If you have not already begun to build a relationship with your agent, here are some key important factors to consider; does your insurance agent work 9am to 5pm or is your agent generally not available in the office? Does your agent have an office assistant who is knowledgeable or just a seat warmer? Okay, a receptionist and not licensed to add a policy when you need one added, how's that☺ Does your insurance agent respond quickly to your needs and request, or do you wait several days for a reply?

Your insurance agent is an important person in your life and you need to be able to trust that you will be sold only what you need in insurance, not what everyone else's needs are.

Your insurance agent needs to save you money on discounts for multiple policies and address growth when it occurs in your life, business, and family.

Your insurance agent should have such a relationship with you that when a new vehicle is purchased, they will cover your existing vehicle for the maximum period of time while adding your new vehicle without charging you for both vehicles…this should be a standard behavior, but it is not with all insurance agents. It is with mine☺

Look for an agent with history and not with consumer (negative) claims such as listed negatively with the Better Business Bureau in your area. Look for me....just kidding. I wanted to serve the people and give insurance away - *free*, if only I could have.

Shopping For Insurance

Most consumers prefer not to have to shop around for insurance but I truly recommend it. When I initially began, the process of shopping for insurance my heart raced as though I was going to purchase a new car and was concern with the negotiation phase. Approach shopping for insurance with the same enthusiasm and intensity as you would anything else that affects your life. Understand that what you save up front in premiums will save you dollars in your pocket, into the future.

When speaking of shopping for insurance, I do not mean just calling around from the phone book; it sometimes includes a face-to-face meeting with an agent. If by chance the face-to-face intimidates you, then use the phone and call several companies to compare exact coverage's. Write the information down or have it emailed to you unless you have photographic memory…hummmm, photographic of what - the conversation? Write the information down.

You want to be adequately covered if you get in an accident or have a dwelling claim. In addition, you certainly do not want to pay more for insurance than you should. Maybe waiting for an agent or insurance quote to be beamed into your living room is not the best approach, be proactive.

Researching Insurance Companies via the Internet

For those of you who are somewhat savvy with the Internet you may want to use a comparative insurance service that will perform a lot of the work for you and produce the insurance comparisons. I still feel there is nothing like individual contact with various insurance companies to get a feel of the agent and office support, which are all very important when you have a claim. I can (almost) guarantee that you will receive several different quotes when you call an insurance company, which is why it is important to do so.

'An Invasion of (corporate) Locust' by Darlene R. Miles

Sometimes you will find that you will save hundreds per year. One important note here is; I *would not cancel my existing policy* until you receive the physical policy in the mail from the company. This does not mean the paper quote form the agent, I mean the actual policy from the insurance company. Why you ask? Sometimes Underwriting will increase the rates (without cause and with cause) after an agent has given you a written quote. This is one action I constantly fought for my insured and one of the reasons; I felt I could not be an agent. We all pay too much for insurance and if an automated system produces a quote and that quote is presented to your customer, then the quote should stand, sometimes it did not. And believe me I fought with Underwriting when the consumer's rates were sometimes changed during the underwriting process to get the customer the original quoted lower rate. In some cases it was what I call 'Red-Lining' a consumer because of their zip code or unfair pricing because due to the age of the consumer. Whatever underwriting issue - I would fight for what I felt was right for the consumer, and some agents will not do this. If it was not a requirement in the automated quoting system, then it should not have applied in underwriting or increased the consumer's insurance rates.

Here are a couple pointers to consider when shopping for insurance:

- How much insurance do I need to cover my vehicle? Minimum requirements vary from state to state, so what are your state minimums, you must have at least the state minimums. (*Read further first before making a decision here.*)

- Do you have assets to protect? If you have assets to protect — and that is all that the insurance is doing — protecting your assets then purchase enough liability coverage. For instance, if you purchase $50,000 of bodily injury liability coverage but have $100,000 in assets, attorneys could go through your assets (treasures) in the event of an accident in which you are at-fault and the other party's medical bills exceed $50,000.

- How much insurance should you buy beyond your state's minimums after considering your assets (and obviously, those assets are not in your car☺)?

- What is you personal financial situation? If you are in an accident, will you have medical coverage? This option is available with your policy as Medical Coverage in addition to Bodily Injury.

- Another issue is that the limits of any uninsured and/or underinsured motorist coverage that you purchase cannot exceed the limits of your liability coverage. *This coverage can be quite valuable, as it will cover lost income if you are out of work for several months after being injured in a major accident.*

- Your driving habits may also be a consideration. If your past driving records history is filled with fenders benders (accidents), if you have a lead foot (speeding tickets) or a long commutes in bad traffic, then you should get more comprehensive coverage.

Insuring Older Vehicles

Be aware that you may not have to purchase the same amount of insurance for an older vehicle. Normally your 'full coverage' insurance includes Collision (auto repair or replacement) and Comprehensive Insurance (covers any other vehicles you may hit) coverage, if your auto is an older model you can chose to only carry Comprehensive coverage and not the Collision. Why not carry both you ask? If you have an older model year vehicle what can be valued at a couple thousand dollars, chances are you will not get replacement value for your vehicle. Check with your agent for documented details on the replacement cost of your older vehicle. I have seen where an individual purchased a 1992 vehicle from an auction for less then $500 and insured the vehicle for full coverage, comprehensive and collision but the insurance company only paid the book value, which was around 1000 dollars. The individual had repainted and upgraded the vehicle. The consumer had also added several accessories to the vehicle, new wheels, etc.; this consumer paid the insurance premium for this vehicle for two years at the rate of $150.00 per month. The consumer was in an accident where the vehicle was totaled and the insurance company would only pay the book value for the auto. The book value was less then 1000 dollars even though the consumer's investment was much greater then 1000. Check with your insurance agent before adding both Collision and Comprehensive coverage on an older model or high mileage vehicle. Since some agents may not be completely honest, read your policy closely.

What I would recommend is that you place the Collision portion in the bank and gain interest on the money, if you can afford to. If you have a good driving record and you drive fewer miles then the average person then why pay for both Collision and Comprehensive? Of course there are those individuals who pay the maximum premium with small deductibles and submit every little claim possible, while watching their monthly premiums go up and up like a helium balloon...hummmm???

Now, if there is a sense of security in paying monthly premiums for both Comprehensive and Collision for your older vehicle, then please do so. This is only my option and information.

Fight for as much replacement value as possible, keep an updated photo of your vehicle (at least yearly), and at least try to fight for a replacement of the *actual* (total loss) vehicle then to take the cash payout.

Consumers please understand that you may not always get the amount you expect from the insurance company when a claim for a total loss is submitted. Read and understand your policy

'An Invasion of (corporate) Locust' by Darlene R. Miles

'coverage's', and hold the insurance company to them.

Now that you have made several practical and philosophical (thoughtful) decisions, it is time to start shopping. Begin by setting aside about an hour for this task. Bring all your records together - your current insurance policy, your driver license number, and your vehicle registration. Drink plenty of coffee, coffee only – you definitely need to have all your faculties at hand – no alcohol during this process☺. Have a comfortable speakerphone and your computer ready for the job. Also, have lots of paper in the printer. It will help to print out your quotes when you can.

If you chose to begin your insurance shopping via the web, be careful since there are several insurance companies out there. You can, in most cases enter only your name and address without entering your drivers license and social security number when requesting a quote. I advise that you do not enter any personal information that can be 'hacked' or stolen during this 'shopping' experience.

Generally, all that is needed for a quote is your zip code, age, driving history (number of ticket over a period of time), etc. Stick to that type of information. Be as vague as possible but not to vague that you will not get the actual quote that, you need. Keep good notes or save the quotes on your computer hard drive. Use the same parameters (information and guidelines) for each site, if you vary, the results may also vary. Be prepared to spend enough time to gain good comparisons of companies and remember this process will save you money. When you complete the process list the quoted amounts from each policy and see what amounts you just saved yourself…that savings should make you quite happy. Again, set the time aside and work the process until you are done (period).

Two web sites that you can visit while insurance shopping is Insweb.com or Edmonds.com. These are pretty decent sites. You should also use the top named insurance sites for which I will not list their names here but I did work for one of them and was not happy with their consumer business practices. Stay away for no-named quoting sites that request personal information such as your driver's license number, date of birth or social security number. Do provide that kind of information; it should not be needed on an Internet site. Now if you are speaking directly with an insurance agent then that type of information is required in order to provide the quote. Please also keep in mind that some sites will request general information and return the quote to you at a later time. This was the type of site I utilized for my agency. On the other hand, your quote can be emailed at a later time, generally within twenty-four or forty-eight hours from your request.

Another note regarding website quotes. Some sites will wheel you in with general information but continue page after page after page. Be sure you want the quote and maybe only provide an email address rather then your actual phone number, name and address, otherwise – when submitting your home phone you have just given access to a comprehensive background of information – sorry! Just be careful. I talk about the use of phone numbers in later chapters regarding a company's use of 'Reverse Lookups'.

Here are some 'parameters' to use when insurance shopping:

- How is the insurance company rated by A.M. Best or Standard & Poor's?
- Is there a local office/agent to support or process any claims?
- What discounts do they offer; multiple cars or multiple policy discounts?
- Does the company have 24 hours support for claims?
- What payment options are available to pay your premium; monthly, quarterly, online, etc.?

Add to the list based on what is important to you and keep good comparison notes.

The last evaluation would be after receiving the quote, contact the actual agency to speak with the agent. Listen intently to that agent or their office representative to determine (at best) what type of service you could expect from that agent and their staff. Last, do not be too quick to take the cheapest quote for insurance. Make sure that you have rated that agency and clearly understand what their claims process is. Don't' be quick to write a policy with a company that may not fix your auto accurately or in a timely manner. Review the agencies repair or restoration policies. Check for any policies restrictive. Do their repair policies require that you use their specified repair services?

Make sure that the company is reliable and available to you. You can always find the lowest premium, but it may not be immediately obvious how to determine whether an insurance company is reliable.

One way to check for reliability is to check with your local Better Business Bureau or your State Department of Insurance website. Generally, the State Department of Insurance for each state will list any consumer complaints. Do not think that a big named insurance company is always a good choice. It will be the agent that you will have to work with, not the company directly. It will be this person, the agent, who may screw up your policies or rates. I have experienced big named companies including my current company where a former agent, writing for the same insurance company did not insure my home correctly. I now have another agent with the same company who is an excellent agent. See the difference.

Find out if the insurance company has any requirements on where you can have your vehicle repaired, or if damages occur with your dwelling that you are limited to their repair companies. You may not want this as an option. Some companies may only allow 'aftermarket' parts, not new auto parts to repair your vehicles.

If you have a claim, be careful not to sign your rights away. You may want to contact an attorney for guidance before signing any

Arbitration Agreements. Do not give up your right to go to court.

Life Insurance - What We All Should Know

A bad visual, but visualize if you were to die and leave your family with nothing, what would happen to them? How could they survive financially?

Life insurance is designed to leave your loved ones in a state of survival after your departure (death). It does not matter if you purchase a Term Policy (Life Insurance Only) or a Whole Life policy (Life insurance policy with cash value). Please at least leave your family with enough money to bury you. The ideal policy should be equal to several years of your income. Questions to ask yourself, 'how old are my children and how long would I want to support them after my death?', 'how long will it take my spouse or significant other to get on his or her feet after my death, and what expenses will they incur after my death that they can not afford?' 'How many years are remaining before my children will reach college age?' You may not be in the position to 'financially afford' exactly what you need to purchase based on these calculations. You can however purchase an amount of life insurance coverage close to what you need. A Term policy is always the cheapest option for maximum benefits.

Health Insurance and Shared Information (Employment Checks)

Did you know that Health Insurance information is now available in background checks? Yes, it is. I feel this is a complete invasion of privacy. When you sign to allow a company to perform a background check, look for the inclusions. What does this background check include? Is it Criminal, Civil, Traffic and Credit or does it include something else such as your medical records? An 'open' signed release is an 'open' signed release. Be very careful. If an employer has a need for medical records, I probably would not work for them. Not for any other reason then that, your medical information is private information. If there is a need to have access to you medical information for insurance, purposed then those records should come directly from your doctors not a broker of background information.

Also, remember to cancel those signed releases after information is obtained otherwise, the employer or whomever requesting your information can continually generate background information on you at will.

Health Insurance and Shared Claims Information (Employers)

Employer's insurance premiums are generally calculated based on the number of employees, age range of employees and prior claims history. Some employers use Private Insurance or 'Private Insured'. What this means is the employer has access to your claims history. Be aware of this. Even in large corporations, claims history is reviewed annually for increase in premiums. Nothing is private. If you want to keep health information private, pay the complete cost out of your pocket and do not use your regular physician.

Health Information and Shared Information about Consumers Serious Illnesses

Insurance companies will not tell you this but all insurance companies share a database of information on consumer's health. Recently one of the sources of background checks started providing consumers Medical records as part of the information they now sale to Insurance companies. In my opinion, this is a clear invasion of privacy, and they are (for now) getting away with it. What is even most ridiculous is - these are brokers of consumer information, and the accuracy is not guaranteed. One way of keeping your information private, at least for a while, is to not use your health insurance for your office visits.

Physicians 'Medical Authorization' Form – What you need to know

All information recorded with your health insurance provider, outside of the physician providing the medical care is stored to a database. If you will recall, when you visit a physician you are asked to sign a 'medical authorization' to allow the physician to submit any of your medical information to the insurance company for payment authorization. When those medical records are submitted the information is retained and eventually sold. Clearly sold, since medical records information is somehow getting into a non-medical provider's system (data broker) to be resold to anyone who clicks the 'checkbox' to the question of 'please indicate your reason for obtaining this information', that's all it takes, and physicians have all consumers sign a HIPAA Privacy statement, what a joke. After seeing what I've seen in the past - if you think you are sick with anything you do not want public, first pay for the visit (is my recommendation), don't submit the claim to your insurance company and don't use the insurance to fill any follow-up prescriptions, those are recorded by insurance claims companies also. Consumers are entitled to privacy so until the law catches up with the invaders, these are steps you can take to protect your privacy.

Health Insurance and Claims Information (Your Policy and Benefits)

After being involved in the development of Health Insurance Claims (Billing) Systems I realized the number of errors that occur. Always check your payable health insurance benefits. As most automated systems that exist from one insurance company to another, are riddled with software defects and human coding errors. Check your insurance company's payable benefits (payments) often against your policy payment booklets (insurance coverage details). Since I have seen in insurance claims systems, a high percentage of claims errors when insurance claims are paid. I recommend that every consumer verify every insurance claims invoice received from your Health Insurance Billing Company.

Health Insurance and Claims Information (Hospital Billing)

I have seen situations where surgery was performed on an individual where certain repairs (surgeries) were performed to an individual's arm, which included the repair of multiple tendons. Each of those tendons can be billed at several thousand dollars each. The hospital over billed and stated that there were a higher number of tendons repaired, by an additional number of four. This error increased the hospital bill by $11,000.00, and this individual did not have insurance coverage. It is extremely important that you check with your doctor to receive (in writing) what surgery was actually performed. You should then verify all charges from the hospital and other medical providers, for that date of service. Sadly, there are a great percent of errors in most automated billing system. Medical billing system errors occur everyday.

Health Insurance – Group Health Insurance Rates and How Your Job May Affect Your Rate

Did you know that Health Insurance companies quote a companies group rates for insurance based on the health of all employees in the group. This is the 'Sales and Marketing' part of the health insurance business.

If someone (a co-worker) is seriously ill, it can affect the rates that you pay for your group rate of insurance. There are generally other factors, but this is (generally) one of those strong factors. In most states, which include the state of Ohio but exclude the state of California, insurers can raise group rates up to 40% per year. In the state of Pennsylvania there is currently no cap on the annual increase, insurers can increase rates up to 100% if they desire. Keep these factors in mind.

What is needed to protect consumers is Comprehensive Healthcare Reform to place strict guidelines on the group insurance rate increases. Employers should look at their contracts very carefully for rate increase provisions. After all and for smaller companies, company owner's rates are also affected by this increase.

Health Insurance and How Companies are Sold Group Coverage's

Generally Health Insurance Companies sale insurance coverage (packages) to companies based on past insurance claims history; number of sick employees over the number of healthy employees and the types of claims. This is why there is group enrollment offered yearly. Group enrollment is the best time (if ill) to obtain insurance coverage otherwise if you are out or open enrollment and not a new employee of the company, your health history by be accessed in order to add you to the group.

'An Invasion of (corporate) Locust' by Darlene R. Miles
211

These health insurance systems (packages) offered to companies and their employees are generally sales driven and are created by software developers (humans), and in most cases developed and maintained by a team of incoming and outgoing systems developers. Enhancements and system changes are generally driven by Sales requirements, Legislative Changes (HIPAA, etc.), or defect resolution. Most systems development of automated Health Insurance Billing systems cross multiple infrastructures within the health insurance company, infrastructures such as Marketing, Sales, Medical Coding, and Invoicing amongst others. In some cases these infrastructures different software coding languages (use the technical terms here), aged hardware (legacy systems), and other issues.

Health Insurance 'Privately Insured' Employers (Employers Providing 'Private Insurance' to Employees) - What You Need To Know

What 'Employers – Privately Insured' - Private Insurance means is that your Employer literally pays your insurance claims. This also means your employer has access to your claims and medical records information as the provider of your insurance. Even though your medical information should be private we all sign authorizations to allow the insurance (company??) to have access to medical information in order for medical bills to be paid to the providers. So keep in mind what a 'Private Insurance' generally means when offered by your employer.

I do not think anyone wants your employer to have access to your medical records information 'at will'.

Chapter 13 - Wills and Power of Attorney – What You Should Know

Granting Power of Attorney for Healthcare and Living Wills – Why?

I have grown to understand the importance and power of a 'Will' and the 'Power of Attorney for Healthcare' documents. After watching both parents die without Wills and watching one parent become seriously ill, prior to dieing – I have realized just how important it is to allow someone to make healthcare decisions for you when you are unable.

It is stated that six out of ten individuals die without having a Will. For some reason I feel that number may be higher. There is no reason not to have a Will or Power of Attorney for Healthcare drafted to protect yourself and your love ones.

A 'Will' serves multiple purposes such as:

- Who should be the Executor of your Estate
- Who should receive your property upon your death
- Who should be the Guardian of your children
- Provides your estate the advantage of reducing taxes and costs to settle your estate
- Provides the detail of your personal and business assets

As for what can happen when there is no Will in place at your death. You can imagine. There may be bitter disputes amongst your family members for your asset's, and let me tell you, there are. Your state will step in and disperse your property as they see fit, which may not be your wishes. In addition, there are the additional taxes and cost. So stop procrastinating and have your Will drafted today. I have seen where individuals drafted there own Wills then have it reviewed by an Attorney, or have an Attorney draft the Will. There are also forms available in some office supply stores, so

'An Invasion of (corporate) Locust' by Darlene R. Miles

there is no reason not to have a Will.

In reference to 'Power of Attorney for Healthcare' forms. I found my form on the Internet, completed it and had it reviewed by my attorney. It was just that simple. I do not want to become ill and not provide someone with the legal right to make medical decisions or the deposition of my body or body parts any other way then how I would chose.

We have all seen where individuals became ill and the hospital made all the healthcare decisions. What is even worse is if someone that you marry, separate from and that person is the only person authorized to make medical decisions for you...now that is scary. Have your wishes for Healthcare drafted so your loved ones clearly know what your wishes are.

One important healthcare instruction could be, 'If I am deemed brain-dead, I do not want my life prolonged while connected to machines', or maybe you do. Another important healthcare instruction could be, 'As long as there is some form of brain activity, I want everything thing medically performed that will prolong my life'. There are ways to instruct your loved ones, so do it today. Do not leave your loved one in the position of not knowing your wishes. It is as simple as that. Let me tell you from experience, it is the most horrible position to be placed in when you do not know the wishes of your loved ones.

Everyone should have a legal "Will' and a 'Durable Power of Attorney for Healthcare'. I encountered this situation when my mother became ill. Initially she did not have a 'Durable Power of Attorney for Healthcare', which means that the medical facility would have to make all medical decisions for her care. Fortunately, my mother was (initially) mentally stable where she could designate me as the individual to act on her behalf. No one in your family is officially authorized to make healthcare decisions about you without your 'written authorization'. Please also take note that you must be legally (mentally) able to make the designation of that individual, so make the selection while you are not ill.

Now on a final note. For the individual who may become designated as the person to act on your behalf as the 'Durable Power of Attorney for Health Care'. If you are that person who may be designated, make sure you will be mentally able to make the hard medical decisions when asked.

I have inserted a sample 'Durable Power of Attorney for Health Care' form on the next page for your reference (only). Please understand that each state can have different guideline regarding this form so please check with your state for additional requirements. You can also search the internet and locate forms by each requirement online.

Durable Power of Attorney for Health Care –
(Sample Form)

Power of Attorney for Health Care

Information is provided for general information and is not intended to serve as legal advice. Any legal advice needed for a particular situation should be obtained from an attorney. Permission is granted to reproduce this document.

Medical Power of Attorney Form

Designation of Health Care Agent

I, (insert your name) _____
Appoint Name: _____
Address: _____
_____
Phone: _____
as my agent to make any and all health care decisions for me, except to the extent I state otherwise in this document. This Medical Power of Attorney takes effect if I become unable to make my own health care decisions and my physician certifies this fact in writing.
LIMITATIONS ON THE DECISION MAKING AUTHORITY OF MY AGENT ARE AS FOLLOWS:
_____

Designation of Alternate Agent
(You are not required to designate an alternate agent but you may do so. An alternate agent may make the same health care decisions as the designated agent if the designated agent is unable or unwilling to act as your agent. If the agent designated is your spouse, the designation is automatically revoked by law if your marriage is dissolved.)
If the person designated as my agent is unable or unwilling to make health care decisions for me, I designate the following persons to serve as my agent to make health care decisions for me as authorized by this document, who serve in the following order:

First Alternate Agent
Name: _____
Address: _____
Phone: _____
Second Alternate Agent
Name: _____
Address: _____
Phone: _____
The original of this document is kept at _____

Duration
I understand that this power of attorney exists indefinitely from the date I execute this document unless I establish a shorter time or revoke the power of attorney. If I am unable to make health care decisions for myself when this power of attorney expires, the authority I have granted my agent continues to exist until the time I become able to make health care decisions for myself.
(IF APPLICABLE) This power of attorney ends on

'An Invasion of (corporate) Locust' by Darlene R. Miles

the following date: _____

Prior Designations Revoked

I revoke any prior Medical Power of Attorney.

Acknowledgment of Disclosure Statement

I have been provided with a disclosure statement explaining the effect of this document. I have read and understand that information contained in the disclosure statement.

(YOU MUST DATE AND SIGN THIS POWER OF ATTORNEY)

I sign my name to this Medical Power of Attorney on

_____ Day of _____ month _____ year

At _____.

(City and State)

_____

(Signature)

_____

(Print Name)

Statement of Witness

I am not the person appointed an agent by this document. I am not related to the principal by blood or marriage. I would not be entitled to any portion of the principal's estate on the principal's death. I am not the attending physician of the principal or an employee of the attending physician. I have no claim against any portion of the principal's estate on the principal's death. Furthermore, if I am an employee of a health care facility in which the principal is a patient, I am not involved in providing direct patient care to the principal and am not an officer, director, partner, or business office employee of the health care facility or of any parent organization of the health care facility.

Signature: _____

Print Name: _____

Address: _____

Date: _____

Signature: _____

Print Name: _____

Address: _____

Date: _____

'An Invasion of (corporate) Locust' by Darlene R. Miles

217

Chapter 14 – Medical Bill Payment Service - Service Available to Help Pay Medical Bills For Consumers and Medical Providers

Throughout my book I have addressed several methods of corporate invasions and intrusions into the personal, financial and medical information of consumers. In this chapter, I address a company that is making a positive impact into the lives of consumers by assisting consumers in obtaining services to pay medical expenses.

On the side of excellent consumer systems and corporate services, in the State of Ohio, *and accessible to most state,* there is a company that will assist consumers in obtaining financial assistance to pay medical expenses. This company will assist consumers whether you are employed or un-employed, insured or under-insured in paying medical expenses.

The assistance in paying medical expenses is based on several factors such as current insurance status, income, assets, and a number of other factors, and please don't allow my reference to 'income and assets' to stop you from seeking assistance. I have seen where consumers who are homeowners and employed have received assistance in paying 'enormous' medical expenses. Medical illness can happen to anyone at anytime and these costs can force consumers into financial hardship.

The name of the company is HumanArc ™ and located in Cleveland, Ohio. Again, assistance from this company does not require that you are unemployed and the company will generally conduct the initial review assessment within 24 hours of contact.

I will not attempt to provide how these factors are combined in determining consumer eligibility for this assistance. However, it is important that you contact this company if assistance is needed. The company has a website and a toll free number, and a great customer service team of representatives that will assist you in qualifying. Again, the assistance is based on several factors that will be presented to you during your phone review and assessment.

The assistance is not only available to consumers. The service is provided to medical providers as well. In the area of medical providers, this company will match services and programs in assisting providers and their patients in obtaining payments for their medical expenses. This becomes a win-win situation for both, the provider of the medical service and the patient who has been burdened with a huge medical hardship.

This service is also available to companies seeking employee health insurance benefit programs for their employees.

There are various programs that can be designed to insure employees of large and small companies. This company also specializes in assisting hospitals and doctors in obtain payment for unpaid consumer medical bills by matching the appropriate consumer programs in order to obtain payment for consumer unpaid medical expenses.

Chapter 15 - Computer Based Patient Records Systems (What You Should Know)

While working on the development of a computer based patient medical records and billing systems, for one of the largest hospitals in the United States I had one of my most intriguing experiences ever. My exposure to the creation of this automated patient medical records system was phenomenal. This experience also left me scratching my head with questions and concerns about the development of these types of system and how they seriously affect all of our lives.

Did you know that 'medical knowledge' that is coded (added) into a computer based patient records system is not always provided by physicians, but instead is coded by software developers? The company creating this system did use physicians and nurses as 'subject matter experts' but some deficiencies still existed in the software coding phase of this project. In addition, I found that the coding of the application had several defects that in technical terms were 'Unmitigated Risks' (not addressed with any form of work-around), but yet deployed and made available to the client (hospital). Defects such as the 'patient demographics recommendations' feature would make incorrect recommendations, diagnosis were also incorrect, patient history of procedures were lost, and billing was not always correct.

At a 'high level', this system was designed to initially have the physician or nurse enter the patient's demographics; age, race, height, weight, sex, blood pressure, known illnesses, allergies, and any symptoms that the patient might be having. From that point, the system was to make the suggested diagnosis and recommended procedure then to prescribe the appropriate medication to treat the diagnosed symptoms. The system was also designed to make recommendation of necessary treatment procedures based on the patient's demographics for 'well care'. Recommendations such as, if the patient was a female - 30 years of age, the system would recommend a breast mammogram. If the patient were a male of the age of 40, the system would recommend a prostate exam and colonoscopy. Did you notice I only made the recommendation of the colonoscopy for the male☺ , that procedure is also a recommendation for a woman at age 40? The correct matching of procedures, amongst other issues was not occurring with this system.

Where all systems are not developed in this manner, unfortunately some are. Where some clients require that systems are developed with accuracy the ownership of that accuracy is initially on the company that is engaged to develop the system. Unfortunately and in most cases the company developing the system is only concern with the revenue from the client and not the quality of the product delivered.

With the appropriate staffing of IT staff and the appropriate amount of time allowed to code and test this application, I knew that this medical application (system) would have been one of the best medical systems ever, but it was not.

Since my involvement with the development of this patient system, I have since seen an even worse computer based patient records systems. Recent systems that I have seen did not retain patient history correctly, if any history was retained at all, and made no patient recommendations. This is even more serious since this system is being used everyday. How can a physician practice medicine utilizing a computerized patient system that is not retaining patient history correctly? Nevertheless, it is being used.

In the old days, doctors wrote everything down and in a patients chart, now some doctors are relying on faulty computer based patient system. I feel every consumer and physician should challenge these systems by selecting a couple of records (manually) and following the progress over a six month period of time (for a really ill patient) and at least one year for a relatively health patient. This is called (SQA) Software Quality Assurance, so you will not kill anyone by accident...hummmm.

A final note on this topic. Why again was this software application not successful? Hummmm, I would say - unreasonable timelines given to develop this application correctly and without defects was first. In addition, there were poor requirements, poor budgeting, and a lack of resources. These are some of the most common problems why software applications are not successful developed and, sometimes put consumers at risk.

Consumers Medical Information (History) – Now Being Sold

Did you know that your medical information could now be purchased without your permission? One of the largest background checking companies in the United States is now selling consumer medical information. This is extremely disturbing to me as a consumer, a professional and former Director of Operations of a Consumer Reporting Agency. I do not feel that there is ever a reason to sell or access a consumers' medical information without authorization from the consumer. The company that is now selling this information also sells 'private and unlisted' phone numbers to its clients. This company has also created a database that allows companies to discriminate against consumers based on their 'consumer-risk-analysis' and 'consumer-rankings'. Yes, 'consumer risk-based analysis' data- ranking. When I use the word discrimination, I am not directly stating because of race or demographics (inclusive), but based on several other factors. Factors such as credit, medical condition, demographics, background information, and several other factors. Medical records should never be bought and sold by anyone. There are consumer privacy laws that protect consumer's medical information and other personal (non-public) information. I personally feel that violations will be imposed on these corporate invasions when these companies and violators are caught.

One way to stop this practice is to force those privacy laws down the throats of the insurance companies who sell this information and any other automated entity that is also an abuser of consumer's rights and information.

Be aware that this practice exists.

Chapter 16 - How to 'Scam Proof' Your Life and Protect Your Personal Information

Disposing of Information

What is most challenging is the process of Scam Proofing our Lives. If we just look around the corner or log on to the Internet, write a check or use our Debit or Credit Cards anywhere, from Retail Stores to our own banks - we are receiving identity theft notifications that corporate systems have been hacked.

It is surprising how many notices I have received over the last year regarding my personal, checking, driver's license or bankcard information has been stolen. These companies are not taking consumer privacy very seriously. I recently received another 'theft of my personal information' notice from another vendor who provides check approval for 'large' upscale national retail stores. They informed me that one of their employees had stolen and sold consumer information, which included my checking account information and driver's license information. Now who wants to carry cash all the time – I don't. This (corporate) consumer identity theft has become an epidemic and the bad business practice of storing and resell consumer information continues.

Throughout my book, I have addressed several topics and privacy issues that affects a consumer privacy, and at times places us all in a position for possible Identity Theft or the next Scam. Topics such as, Protecting Your Credit, your Background Information, your Medical Information, and your Financial Information. Therefore, with that being said I will take a little different approach in this chapter.

There are several ways that scammers can gain access to our personal information. One simple form of access is a consumers simple sharing of what I consider to be critical information. Use of your Debit Card and Pin number instead of using your Credit Card, or Bankcard as a Credit Card.

Sharing of your personal information is not just limited to conversations over the phone with strangers - but also includes what we all through away in the trash. I have outlined a couple of areas that I consider to be quite critical and quite simple to immediately secure your privacy and information.

Those areas are:

- *Do not give personal information such as your Date of Birth and Social Security number over the phone or to anyone.* Understand that any business accounts that you have already established already have your personal information so why provide it at all. If you are asked to provide an account number or social security number for verification, go find the account number; do not give your social security number.
- *Have your Social Security number removed from your Drivers License.* Do you know how many people ask for your driver's license as proof of identification?
- *Don't provide Credit Card Information over the phone*
- *Do not purchases online at Unsecured Websites that are Unknown Websites.* Look for the letters https:// in the website address. The letter's' in https indicates that the website is secured.
- *Do not purchases online or by phone using your Bank Debit Cards.* A BIG no! No! Your Debit Card provides access to your bank account. If you need to use a credit card, limit your transactions to a Credit Card.
- *Do not register your Mobile Phone numbers with random sites.* Use Caller ID to block your cell phone and home phone numbers.
- *Do Stop Marketing Calls.* Since most companies can perform comprehensive background checks with just your name, do not allow marketing companies to call you. 'Opt

out' of their lists and place your number on the 'Do Not Call List', which is a national registry.

- *Do not open random unknown Text Messages or Emails on your Computer or Hand-Held Devices such as Palm, Treo, and Blackberry, etc...* Since there are known Computer Viruses and Spy ware available that can be planted on your device to monitor your activity and calls, it is best to delete any unknown text messages or emails.
- *Always delete your Temporary Folder and Cookies on your computer,* they store important information about you, your purchases, your userid/passwords, and the websites that you visit.
- *Do not just discard billing statements by throwing them in the trash,* Shred the documents instead. This included Bank Card statements, Pre-Approved Credit Card statements, Phone Statements, and Cellular Statements.
- *Consider the use of a Chipping-Shredder rather then to use a strip Shredder.* A Chipping-Shredder cuts your material into small chips of paper rather then the simple strips of paper that continues to contain your personal information.

Do not throw away bank or credit card statements, ever. These are those 'Pre-Approved' credit card statements and your monthly billing statements, this also includes your utility billing statements. Your personal information is stored on those 'pre-approved' and utility statements. If you detest paper statements, then use electronic statements from your financial and billing institutions. Save the documents electronically on your computer. I advise that you password-protect any important documents to prevent random access by others if your computer is ever hacked.

To dispose of any documents I advise that you shred your information using a *'chipper shredder'* rather then just a 'strip shredder'. Strip shredders leave important information on those strips while a *chipper* shredder not only cut across, it also cuts up and down only leaving a very small chip of paper rather then an

ENTIRE long strip of your personal information.

Be careful when providing personal information of any kind over the phone.

Make sure your social security number is removed from your driver's license.

Be careful where you right checks since all financial institutions and retail stores requires your drivers' license information in order to approve your check. This information is then transferred, and stored in a database by the 'check approval' company who is generally not the retail store that you shop. Most if not all of these 'check approval' sources have had their systems hacked or have had employees misusing of consumer information. In most cases, the use of cash is better.

Request your credit bureau report yearly to make sure that no one has accessed your credit information without your approval or has applied for credit in your name. Look for accounts that are not your accounts or inquiries by companies that you did not apply for credit with. Report any discrepancies quickly, and in writing, to the credit-reporting agency. You may also need to file a complaint with the (FTC) Fair Trade Commission if someone has illegally accessed your credit file. You can generally fax these inquires to most of the credit reporting agencies. When filing a complaint against a company, you can access the Fair Trade Commissions website and complete the complaint form online.

What Is Known About Your Address

I also recommendation that consumers obtain a post office box if keeping your address private is of concern. Every address that you are registered at, or receive mail - for whatever the reason is reported and stored in a database. Information such as magazine subscriptions mailed to your home (information is sold to a data broker). Utilities in your name and billed to your address, cable TV billing, and usage, including your cable movies purchased – all sold to data brokers. Your phone billing, and do not forget your employers information which includes your address that is reported to the credit reporting agencies (all information that is resold to data brokers). In addition to your information, anyone living at your address and receiving or registering anything where the address and name is stored in a database is also being attached to your address, and this information is purchased and sold to data brokers.

Even your credit report detail, yes credit report detail is sold to the highest bidder. Your purchase habits, credit card usage information is sold to subsidiaries of that 'parent' company that is why you get all that ridiculous marketing junk mail, or credit card offers.

Privacy Statement Forms Received from Service Providers – 'Opt-Out'

Remember to complete, sign, and return all privacy 'opt-out' statement forms that you receive to have your name and information kept as private as possible.

Have you noticed that companies send these Opt-Out Privacy Statements to you yearly? Why you wonder - so you will forget to return the request to keep your information private. As if, you would change your mind about keeping your privacy from year-to-year??? *Yeah, okay – So this year sell everything about me that you can, place my name on your entire friends list and by the way, allow your servers to be hacked while you're at it??? ...hummmm?*

Why can't these privacy statements, which are stated to be 'privacy' statements, remain on record for as long as that service provider; bank, credit card company, insurance company, etc., is doing business with you? I would say, because it is revenue. When we consumers forget to return those 'Opt-Out' requests to keep our information private companies quickly sell our information to whomever they chose. After all, we do not get a second request stating, 'Are you sure we can really sell your information?' Now do we?

Chapter 17 - Other Important Consumer Privacy Information to Know – About Your Office Computer, Email and Wireless Connections

New Law Enacted That Permits Companies to Read Your 'Company Email'

Did you know that your company can legally access and read your email? This includes your deleted email and any email stored on the company's computer. Be aware of this ability when you are exchanging personal information via your company email. The law below, and in summary was enacted several years ago. However, due to the continued possibilities of additional terrorism companies are now reading employees deleted emails. The Wiretap Act was recently revised and the scope of surveillance was broadened. The former written Act reads as follows:

General Statement of the Law

The law regards each of these situations as distinct.

1. Interception of e-mail during transmission is prohibited by federal wiretap statute, 18 U.S.C. § 2510-2521, and also some state wiretap statutes. The federal statutes were amended in 1986 by Title I of the Electronic Communications Privacy Act (ECPA) to include e-mail.
2. Reading e-mail during storage on a computer system is prohibited by federal statute, 18 U.S.C. § 2701-2711, Title II of the Electronic Communications Privacy Act (ECPA), provided that the system is "providing an electronic communication service to the public." This means, among other things, that your e-mail messages are confidential when stored on a computer owned by an ISP that offers to any member of the public the ability to send e-mail and you pay for the account yourself. But there is *no protection* in

18 U.S.C. § 2702 for e-mail stored on a computer system operated by a corporation primarily for its own business communications. Therefore, if you send e-mail to a company (e.g., `jdoe@ibm.com`) and the e-mail is stored on that company's computer, you have no privacy rights under this statute.

3. The recipient of e-mail is generally free to share the information in the e-mail with anyone, subject to legal obligations that are mentioned later in this paper.

Reading e-mail that is stored on a computer is *not* an "interception" under 18 U.S.C. § 2510, et seq., because an interception must be contemporaneous with the transmission of the message between different locations. *Steve Jackson Games v. U.S. Secret Service*, 816 F.Supp. 432, 442 (W.D.Tex. 1993), *aff'd*, 36 F.3d 457, 460 (5thCir. 1994). This holding has been accepted in several subsequent cases, including *Wesley College v. Pitts*, 974 F.Supp. 375, 384-390 (D.Del. 1997); *U.S. v. Moriarty*, 962 F.Supp. 217, 221 (D.Mass. 1997); *Bohach v. City of Reno*, 932 F.Supp. 1232, 1235-36 (D.Nev. 1996).

One court noted that there is a loophole in Title II of the ECPA, where an unknown person can make a copy of e-mail and give it away, and then other people who do not provide an electronic communication service can lawfully make a further distribution of copies of that private e-mail. *Wesley College v. Pitts*, 974 F.Supp. 375, 389 (D.Del. 1997).

Please refer to the Wiretap Act for complete details of this Act.

I would first recommend that you not use company email for your personal business, and of course not for those crazy 'chain-mail' emails. If you have a need to correspond via your company email, and for personal business, I would recommend that you create a document that is password protected. With your document password protected, you can at least then email the document as an attachment rather then emailing personal information within the body of the email. And please do not type the password in the

'An Invasion of (corporate) Locust' by Darlene R. Miles

231

body of the same email when sending the attachment. Send password in a text message, via your hand-held device, or call the individual or at least sent it in a separate email.

Besides, there are hosts of PC tools that can also be utilized to retrieve and undelete email. So what exactly is private about your deleted email?

How to create a password protected document in MS Word (For Office Privacy when Emailing)

If you have to create, store or email personal information, I advise that you 'password-protect' your document. This includes the emailing of personal or business documents that you do not want anyone else to 'open'. The instructions are as follows when 'password-protecting' a document in MSWord;

Click File, then Click Save As, Click Tools to display the drop-down list of options, then click on Security Options. A dialog box will immediately open for you to type a password to Open the document. You will be required to Re-enter the password again to complete the process.

Office Computer Privacy for the more 'Technically Savvy' – Protecting Personal Email and Documents While at Work

For those of you who are a little more technically savvy you can attach an external hard-drive to your office computer or laptop then create a path from your 'Outlook Archive' folder, in your office Outlook that is mapped to your external drive. The external hard-drive will allow you to archive manually or to set the archive frequency that will be forwarded to your external 'personal' hard-drive. These steps can also be utilized to save those 'personal' emails that you want to save in addition.

So begin by purchasing an external hard-drive from your

neighborhood office supply store. You can purchase an external hard-drive with a minimum of 150G, in a hard-case, with the necessary USB cables and installation software for approximately $100 to $150 dollars. You will not need to install any operating system such as Windows XP, or Windows Vista. You will not need to install any desktop applications such as Word, or Excel. This drive will be used as a 'backup' drive and you will be able to store your files, access those files, and edit them is needed. You should use this drive for any personal information that you may need to have access to while you are at work. In addition, stop using your work computers for your personal business, and it goes without saying - exposing your personal business and information to your company IT staff. Believe me they do scan for information.

What Can Be Seen On Your Desktop Computer at Work

Everything. From the accessing of the Internet, and even more. You are using the companies 'Local Area Network' and that Network access is monitored by your companies IT department. Be aware of that fact.

Most corporate systems administrators will designate themselves and 'you the user' of that desktop computer as an Administrator, the User and part of a Group of Users. However, they may designate themselves as the owner. What this mean is laymen's terms is, what you can do, they can also do. What you can access, they can also access. Last, some corporate system administrators will give themselves 'inherit' ownership of everything on your desktop dependent upon their level of craziness, they may also add themselves as a 'named-user' on your desktop. Now in the case of an administrator being named as a user on your desktop – I personally would delete them. Being added as an additional user of your work computer is a little much, but I have seen such crazed behavior. Just be careful and keep personal information, personal.

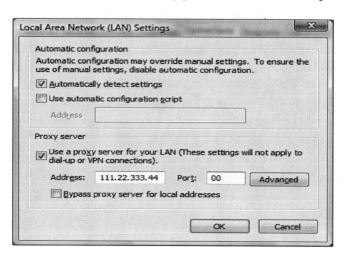

Also, be aware that your 'System Volume' folder, generally on your 'C' drive also contains a trail of every document and website that you create and or access. I find this folder to be somewhat interesting. Why would Microsoft create such a folder and name it 'System Volume', AAhhhh…..No! More like your 'Audit Trail' instead, just a little humor here! It is stated that this folder would be utilized as a system restore point in the event of a system crash? In all my years as an IT Consultant, I have never heard that anyone has utilized this folder to restore a system. However, you are now aware that this 'information storing' folder exist on your computer.

Make sure that you regularly clear your Temporary Folder and Cookies from your company computer, especially if you are using your company computer to purchase anything from the web or to access personal websites such as your personal bank with user ids and passwords. When you access various websites, in nearly all cases the website will place a 'Cookie' on your computer, which will identify you, your computer, and your userid, or passwords the next time you return to that site. It is not necessary to leave this type of information on your company's computer so delete your Temporary Folders and Cookies.

What Can Be Seen On Your Personal Laptop Computer at Work When Using a Wireless Network

Everything again, especially if you do not have your own firewalls installed on your Wireless connection on your personal laptop - and using the companies (LAN) Local Area Network Server. The Firewalls will only block other users' Wireless connections but not the ability of your 'snooping' Systems Administrator from seeing what sites you access.

You also want to modify your 'Share' as defined in your Network Connection. This can be viewed by clicking on the Network icon generally appearing in the right corner of your laptop. Also address your Password-Share, block other users from assessing your personal laptop. Sometimes the default is set to share passwords access to your laptop as a default in various Microsoft Operating Systems...hummmm?

Again, change your login passwords often and save any personal documents with passwords when necessary, or to an external 'personal' hard-drive. This includes documents that you save on your desktop. Adding passwords can be done by clicking 'File' then the 'Save As' option, from your document 'view', click the 'Tools' drop down option to display the 'Security' option. Click the 'Security Option' and add a password to 'Open' the document. And do not forget your password.

Wireless Laptop Devices and Hackers

Did you know that your Wireless connection can be randomly shared and hacked without your knowledge? Be careful when using wireless connections. Some hackers can search for accessible 'unsecured' wireless connections and execute spam or viruses from your wireless connection via your computer or laptop.

'An Invasion of (corporate) Locust' by Darlene R. Miles

235

Secure your wireless connections and do not use unsecured coffee shop wireless services.

Recently the FBI issued a warning regarding hackers and their ability to access wireless connection by breaching security protocols. Check the Internet for instructions on securing your wireless connection or consult with a technical consultant. You do not want your important information stolen or your hardware used as a portal to release viruses to other computers, this issue is critically important for shared Networks.

Securing Your Wireless Laptops for the more 'Technically Savvy'

For the more technically savvy you will want to consider creating a 'virtual' environment on your laptop. What I am stating here is, that there is currently 'free' software application that will allow you to install and create a secured 'working-space' wireless environment on your laptop. This tool (application) would be installed on your laptop and utilized when in any 'unsecured' wireless environments such as libraries, coffee shops and hotels which are all 'hot-spots' for hackers or just noisy people who want to know what you are doing on your laptop.

When you install an application such as VMWare this application allows you to create a working environment that is isolated on your laptop. This tool allows you to run the applications that you need, access the internet and save your emails on your computer without negatively affecting your laptop as a whole. When you create a 'virtual' environment on your laptop, you will be required to have a minimum amount of space available on your computer for the installation of the virtual software. Your will also need to install the applications that you plan to execute or use and that include the virus detection application that you may be running on your desktop, all in this new isolated 'virtual' environment.

What is great is that this is a separate environment running on your laptop. If any virus are detected you can delete this 'virtual' environment without any ill effects to any other areas of your laptop, its applications, or your files saved. This is a great environment for developers when testing new applications. The use of virtual environments also reduces the requirements for additional hardware or servers.

Ok, that's enough of the *techie* stuff. Visit VMWare on the internet for detail on system requirements and installation details. And remember, there is always some crazed person looking for ways to breach security. This is currently a safe way to search the internet and use wireless sources...for now.

Change Your Computer Passwords Often

MS Vista currently captures all of your computer and personal information via their automatic update process. The update process does not only provide updates to a specific operating system, but the update process also captures the software signature (who owns the applications installed on your personal computer), it also captures passwords and data (information that you have added to all applications; banking, documents, etc.) that you stored on your computer. Unfortunately, you are unable to turn off the automatic updates and as soon as you log on to the Internet the operating system is designed to turn the auto updates back on, immediately send files, and transfer information back to Microsoft.

There is no way to effectively turn off the Microsoft updates to your system when using the Vista operating system. What I also find to be quite ridiculous is that Microsoft insists on capturing everything including software, software keys, and our data on our computers. This occurs immediately upon accessing the Internet and continues each time you access the Internet. When I turned off the auto update feature and deleted the 'forced' updates my MS

Word was disabled and a message appeared on my desktop that required that I log on to the Microsoft website to obtain the necessary programs in order to use my MS Word. Are you kidding? Thank goodness, that I always back up my computer files, so I chose to clear my hard drive and re-install all of my software to its original settings. Now obviously you know I must have been quite pissed off to have taken this route to resolve this issue. This is my laptop, it did not come free neither did the software that I purchased and installed. I do not want my personal information saved on any company's server other then my own.

It seems as though it is a game with Microsoft, embedding these updates even after I deleted the updates and turned the feature off. I have also found that most consumers are avoiding updating their computers with the Vista operating system. In the new operating system, Microsoft has also disabled the ability for owners of their computers or laptops to maintain Administrator Rights, on your own computer equipment in the Vista Operating System??? What a joke and enough of the technical stuff.

Chapter 18 - Other Consumer Billing Systems to Watch For

Cable, Cellular and Phone Billing Systems

As a Consultant, I do advise that consumers pay close attention to these billing statements. I strongly advise that you save and review your Cable Billing statements for a period of time. Maybe even up to a year of longer, to review the detail of your charges and any changes that appear on your statement. I would also look very closely at billing statements with billing format changes, which generally means that there has been some form of computer software or system automation change or upgrade occurs (or for consumers – *a downgrade*).

Why - you ask would I make this recommendation? I recently experienced a situation where my cable billing statement changed and the amounts billed - in most cases doubled. These errors appeared for over six months and kept changing, never the same amounts. Being like most professionals, I would just pay the bill and keep moving, but one day I set down to look more closely at the detail. I started with the review of a couple of months and the level of errors pissed me off. I then began to look through old files and went back to review a sampling of invoices over a series of years (yes, years), I did not realize that I had filed so many cable invoices, but I did. I found that I had been over charged for nearly four years with the worse of the over-charging occurring in the last year and a half.

Cable billing was regulated in the past couple of years where cable companies were required to provide the detail of the bill without bungling all charges into one charge. This requirement produced the *visual* of their billing irregularities and billing errors that I did not catch with the statement changed. These irregularities included charges for remote devices, cable boxes, services and miscellaneous charges that I did not have or received.

It took the cable company nearly four months to correct my billing statement after speaking to nearly ten cable customer service personnel then giving up on the 'really smart' (what a joke) customer service representatives - and going straight to the president of the cable company. *One note here, there were two 'kind' customer service representatives that I did speak with; they just could not help...now to move on.* Yes, the president of the cable company. I sent both the President of the cable company and the Area District Manager the same letters that requested that my billing be corrected and a credit be granted (amongst other things). The President kindly assigned the District Manager, who assigned the Area Customer Service Manager-who ultimately resolved my billing issue.

The end result was that I was given approximately $600.00 dollars in credits to my cable bill along with three months of free cable and Internet service. I do not think the amount completely covered all of the overcharges but I was glad to get the problem resolved. What this says is… watch your cable billing closely. This includes your Phone and Cellular Billing since there are some levels of errors that appear quarterly on those billing invoices also.

As consumers, we have to take charge and not give up when we are being taken advantage of. Can you imagine how many other consumers that may have also been overcharged? Probably millions, or at least thousands, and for years? This is crazy and it is our (my) money. Watch your billing statements carefully. After all, these billing systems are also developed by some team of IT systems 'people' and people do make errors. What is most interesting is someone should perform some form of quality assurance in validating these systems and there clearly was none --- or was there?

Cellular Wireless Sync Systems – What to watch for

Okay, I guess this section gets even better on the 'kill my personal system' side of the world. I recently had the experience of having my wireless company accidentally delete my entire two-year appointment calendar and email, including email folders on my handheld device, which happened to be a Treo 650. Yes, Treo 650 not the Windows based 700. I think I have had enough of Microsoft for now.

What occurred was the deleting of what I considered to be my most important information, my complete calendar of information and schedules along with all email including established folders. What was most ridiculous was that I had not backed up my calendar or email since I thought it was also saved on the Wireless Sync website. Well, so much for that farce. Not only was my information deleted, my account was completely deleted as though it never existed on the Wireless Sync server and there was no way, believe me I tried, to recover all my lost information, and what was I offered – three month of free wireless service of nearly two years of lost information. What a joke. I guess if it could have happen to anyone, in this case – it was my turn...again.

Therefore, my recommendation to everyone who uses a wireless device is to back up your device on your computer or laptop, and back up your information regularly. When sending email from your handheld device, forward a (BC) Blind copy to yourself at an alternate email address if the information is important. This will become your backup copy saved at your *true* email providers site, be it a corporate site, gmail, AOL or whatever.

Do not rely on a Wirelesssync's website security or safety as I did. I lost my entire calendar, which consisted of nearly two years of information, schedules, billable notes, etc, and the cellular company was not able to retrieve or restore my information. This included my email and email folders created on my handheld. Do not make the same mistake. I now backup regularly, almost daily. What is sad, is once bitten, I no longer have any confidence in my cellular companies ability to secure my handheld data so what does that say, and what the heck am I paying for – just a phone?

'An Invasion of (corporate) Locust' by Darlene R. Miles

Chapter 19 - College Students – Protecting Your Credit and Background Information - Some Items of Importance

The following topics are (to me) some of the most important survival topics that any college student should know. The first item of importance would be to do your very best to graduate as fast as you can from college. Second, would be to protect yourself from harm while attending college and preparing for life after college, this includes your credit and background information. You will find after graduation that your GPA won't hold as much importance as your 'good background' or 'good credit record' information. Now, for any parent who may object to this statement I would share this bit of information. If a student can successfully graduate from college, they will be granted their degree. Most companies are not interested in your GPA. As a former Director of Operations, or as an Independent IT Consultant, both hiring college students, I was only interested in an individuals experience or ability to adapt and learn.

Your success after college starts while you are attending college. You do not want to graduate and not be able to obtain a good paying job due to a crazy arrest record, DUI offense, or bad credit? Most top paying jobs do require that your credit is in good standing or at least manageable without any delinquent accounts. One important reason for this requirement is that you can not focus on being the best employee for your new company if you are drowning in debt and have pending law suits due to delinquent accounts. In addition, most large companies where Sales and Marketing positions, or travel is required will issue company credit cards. You may not qualify if you have delinquent accounts on your credit report.

Protect Your Credit

Every student, when arriving to college has good credit (in most cases). In some cases, this may be your only time to maintain your good credit standing until college loans and normal living expenses invade your wallet.

The number one challenge for some new college students is just learning how to say *No*. No, to the barrage of credit card offers, offered to new college students once you arrive on campus. On most college campuses, credit card companies swarm like bees to honey after college students with offers of 'free' credit. *Really, free credit?* Don't do it, just say No! Do not begin to accept those campus credit cards just to obtain a funny looking T-Shirt... hummmm??? You know those crazy offers, being offered to get students to complete a credit card application. Do not give your personal financial information to strangers who invade your college campus or mailboxes. Do not put yourself in the position to have to work several part-time jobs while already challenged with heavy study hours, college financing, and in some cases already with one part-time job.

Do not put your family in the position of not being able to support you because you have accumulated more debt then they have, when you are not employed. Whatever allowance or monthly assistance you receive from your parents, make it work. Learn to budget, this is a good time to start. Anticipate those unforeseen class expenses for books and labs, etc. Don't get yourself caught up in a slue of campus parking tickets which are extremely costly. Purchase the quarterly parking permit and park where it is authorized, otherwise, the number of parking tickets will quickly out number what you could have simply paid for the quarterly or annual parking permit. And please, if you are ticketed for illegal parking – pay the ticket or ask the court for payment arrangements to pay over a period of time. Just do not walk away from even a parking ticket since most courts now issue warrants for any unpaid citations.

'An Invasion of (corporate) Locust' by Darlene R. Miles

Last, request a combined copy of your 'free' credit report from the top three credit reporting agencies yearly. As a student, you want to be clear about what is on your three credit reports.

If you have already began applying for credit cards you have now been placed on various credit card marketing lists as a college student. Some credit card companies will automatically start sending you (especially if you pay on time) pre-approved credit card offers, some credit card companies may go even further and send you the credit card without applying for it. Watch your credit report since those cards can be intercepted by other students and used, thus negatively affecting your credit. If errors exist or you recognize credit fraud, (accounts that are not yours), immediately contact the credit reporting agency to begin an investigation, and request the correction to your report. In a situation such as this, you may also want to place a 'Fraud Alert' on your credit report, which will require multiple forms of identification validation before credit can be issued. Based on the FCRA (Fair Credit Report Act) the credit-reporting agency has a limited about of time to correct their errors. Make sure you quote the act when dealing with the bureaus when they are uncooperative. Please refer to chapter 4 of my book for additional information of protecting your credit information.

Be Very Careful When Transferring Your College Loans

Following college graduation, college students are bombarded with college loan refinancing and loan consolidation offers. Be very careful when refinancing your school loans. Some college loan refinancing companies are legitimate companies, offering a reduction in your college loan interest rates and loan consolidations, but several of these companies are not. Some companies are what you would consider to be *Predatory Lending Companies.*

College Loans and Predatory Lenders

You may wonder how the Predatory Lending companies obtain college student information. What these 'Predatory Lending' companies do is what data brokers of consumer information would call 'fishing'. 'Fishing', by pulling your college loan information from your credit report, yes- your credit report. As I previously stated in Chapter 4, 'Protecting Your Credit Report', when discussing the levels of information that is being resold by data brokers and credit reporting agencies. I explained that the credit reporting companies will sell your financial information to companies and this information is not limited to just what the credit reporting agencies call 'header' information. They will sell your entire report if their client request access to it.

These credit reporting agencies will also group the type of consumer data. Grouping by age, demographics, and include your account transaction detail from your credit report. Transactions such as, college loan sources, car loans financing companies, credit cards types and company names, high interest rated loans, and so on. This is why consumers receive the types of offers that they do. If you have high interest rated credit cards from smaller financial or high-risk companies, then your information is sold to those types of companies. If you have excellent credit with low interest rate loans and credit cards, then you receive those types of credit offers, interesting isn't it?

When exposed to a 'predatory lender', you may also find yourself in a situation where your college loans are not completely transferred to the new company, or at all - as the new financing company may indicate.

Situations occur where companies partially (or not at all), assumes your college loans, and will leave balances with the existing 'funding' source. This situation has even occurred with government-funded loans where a student attempts to refinance their government loans but encounter a predatory lending source that takes your payment money but never transfers, or pays off your existing loans.

Always verify that a loan consolidation and or transfer have successfully occurred before paying any new loan financing company. Stay on top of your loan balances and the agreed interest rates or you may find yourself paying for a loan that you have not obtained, or an interest rate that you have not agreed to.

Make sure that you clearly understand the interest rates and that the rates are not 'introductory' rates or adjustable (increasing or decreasing over time). And last, pay as agreed. You do not want your college loans to affect your ability to gain financing in the future, or to *negatively* affect your future employment hire-ability since credit is sometimes a factor for employment.

Protect Your Driving Record

Do not allow yourself to be put in a position to have your license suspended for driving without auto insurance. In most states, the law requires that every licensed driver have auto insurance, so have insurance. This means that you must obtain insurance at the time that you are issued a drivers license, not when you purchase a vehicle. This includes your motorcycles. Do not drive a friend's auto just because they ask you to if you do not have auto insurance.

Driving without insurance, if caught, can results in a license suspension and heavy fines. And let's take this one a little further… if you don't pay the fines imposed, that are imposed for driving without insurance, and since you don't have the income as a student to pay the fines - you think you can just avoid the courts all together – not smart at all. On the date that your fine is due to be paid, and no payment is received in the court an additional license suspension is generally applied to your driving privileges, your fines are increased, and a warrant is issued for your arrest, an generally issued into a NATIONAL database. So do not drive without insurance, and if you are caught driving without insurance please pay your fines.

You can always request a payment plan with the court and request driving privileges to and from school, work, church or even to the doctor. Make sure if you request driving privileges that it covers the necessary times and days per week that you need. Do not drive outside of the court-approved times that will be documented on your driving privileges document.

Protect Your Background Information

Do not allow yourself to be arrested for some crazy offense such as 'fighting', assault, or for 'Failure to Pay' a Traffic or Parking Ticket, etc. Warrants can be issued for failure to pay court fines including Parking Tickets. Protecting your personal information includes not giving or sharing your social security number, driver's license, or any other personal information with strangers. Students are prime subjects for identification thieves especially since you do not 'generally' have bad credit or any negative information in your backgrounds, at least upon arrival to college.

College Students and Expungements

In my years as a Court Systems Consultant, I found that the courts surrounding most colleges had the highest number of college student arrests and criminal cases. College students, please have those court records expunged and or sealed before you leave college, or as soon as these types of records occur. An Arrest record alone can affect your ability to be employed, rent an apartment, or obtain a government job. Do not leave those records out there.

Most Background checks are performed in the cities that you attend or attended college along with the cities that are stated as residences, unless a Nationwide Background Check is preformed, and I have in previous chapters discussed the quality of Nationwide Background Checks – maybe they will pick up the information and maybe not. Do not take a chance.

It is important to have all 'associated' court case records removed in addition to the actual charge record or case. Associated records are any associated Jail, Arrest, or Civil records that may exist and reference the original conviction. Believe me these records will appear later if not removed, expunged, or sealed by the court of conviction. Keep in mind that passing the initial background check is not the only guarantee that you need.

As a former Director of Operations of the consumer reporting agency and background checking company, some companies that utilized our background checking system ran background check yearly on their employees looking for any new convictions or negative driving records. Do not allow information that can be expunged to remain in your background.

Watch what you place on your Web Pages

College students, be aware that some companies are also 'Goggling' prospective employees and or visiting the so-called 'friends networking' sites in order to view any Web pages that you have created. This information will be used against you in determining your hire ability and your character. Do not put information on your web page that you do not want a prospective employer to see because they will.

Students – Purchasing Books at a Discount

My daughter would recommend the website Half.com, and so would I as an excellent resource for purchasing textbooks cheap. Also, utilize the campus website as a source to locate students that are selling books. The college websites will always have students who are reselling previously used books.

Initially, as a parent of a 'new' college student, I did not want my daughter to purchase used books. What a joke. By my daughters sophomore year I hoped she could find those costly books at a discount. Why not purchase an already highlighted book, with important notes (in some cases), where you can save at times ¾ the cost? Not only did my daughter purchase books at a discount when she could, she also resold her un-needed books each year. Why not?

Pre-Paid Credit Cards and College Students

Pre-paid credit cards are best for College Students and Parents. Again, college students have the best credit when they arrive at college...then, the adventure begin. You start applying for credit cards all over the place, then your in financial trouble, your grades suffer and your parents are upset.

A pre-paid re-loadable credit card requires your cash deposits in order to reload the card. With a pre-paid, re-loadable credit card, only the cash amount on the card can be used. No credit is required and the card is re-usable and re-loadable. What a great idea and you will be in control of your spending. When the money runs out, so does the spending☺

When researching pre-paid credit cards you want to clearly understand the requirements surrounding any re-loadable pre-paid credit card that you purchase. Most pre-paid cards do not have any fees and are associated with the larger banks. I would advise

'An Invasion of (corporate) Locust' by Darlene R. Miles

consumers to purchase a pre-paid credit or re-loadable credit card directly from a bank. When purchasing from a bank you will then have the support of that financial institution behind your re-loadable credit card.

'Near College Campuses' Students Are Pulled Over More Often By the Police – What To Do

While working for years as a Court System Consultant, for the courts surrounding colleges I found that college students were pulled over or stopped most often by police. These stops always seemed to result in some type of minor citations.

When you are pulled over by the police, you should immediately call someone to let them know that you were just pulled over, where you are located, and the time that you were pulled over. You should stay on the phone with that person until the incident is over, as long as the police officer does not object. I know this is a huge commitment for someone to provide this type of support to you but it will save you from further harassment especially if you have not committed any offense that resulted in you being pulled over.

The best resource for this type of support is a parent, and that parent should reassure you that you would not be yelled-at for making the call, at whatever hour your stop occurs. Your resource should be ready to contact the superior of the officer at anytime if you are being harassed. Another note, in most states it is illegal for any officer to pull you over without cause and search your auto. In addition, believe me, if they see anything in your auto such as an open container, drugs, and any other illegal activity they do then have cause to search your auto. Be smart about the law and create a network of adults that can support and assist you when needed, at any hour of the day or night.

If you are stopped without cause, use your cell phone to record your surroundings quickly. Take photos of your surrounding area with your cell phone or video tape on your cell phone, if you have that feature. If photos or video of your surrounding area are taken – email them to yourself or to a friend at the time of occurrence. Do not allow yourself to be a victim. Always immediately, inform someone when you are being pulled over and of your location, immediately.

And a final note. I am not an attorney, nor am I attempting to give legal advice – only to share legal 'public' information. If you are ever in doubt, contact an attorney. Do not put yourself in harms way if a police is persistent and searches your vehicle without cause.

Checklist for College Students When Job Hunting

Just a couple of items to share that make good business sense:

- Have a one or two page resume.
- Have a professionally stated email address, not 'hotmama', or 'bigdaddy'.
- Have a professionally sounding outgoing voice message on the phone number that you will use to provide to employers. No employer wants to hear hard rock, rap, or anything else coming across a phone answering machine, only a pleasant sounding voice. Remember this is the 'first impression', and the first image that you are presenting to a prospective employer.
- Do not show up for an interview looking as though you are on your way to a club to dance, Ahhhh..No! Conservative is always good unless *extreme* casual is the environment?

Chapter 20 – Buying That First Home – A Consumer Story of 'Locusts'

I have chosen to include my experiences on this subject as a consumer and based on my (now) years of experience processing mortgages that followed this nightmare. I felt it was important to share what became a nightmare when building my first home. This information includes the contract process, the building process, and the mortgage process. As a then inexperienced consumer I made a series of mistakes and was taken advantage of financially. I felt this was an extremely important experience to share with my readers and I hope my story will help others to avoid some of the pitfalls that I encountered.

My, if I had known then what I know now - I would have saved myself thousand of dollars, and years of heartache.

The approach that I have taken in my life is to learn as much as I can about everything that affects my life. I decided after such a bad experience purchasing and building my home, I would include my experiences in my book, experiences both positive and negative to help other consumers through this process.

The Contract Process

My experience begins here. I thought I was doing all the right things; saving for the down payment for my home, ultimately acquiring an excellent interest rate on the mortgage and so on. But, Noooo! I did not realize how little I knew about the home building and mortgage process, and my - was I taken advantage of by the lender and builder.

When starting this mortgage process, I was only looking to purchase what I thought would be my dream home after saving for years. I had sacrifices going on vacations for nearly eight years just to put that additional money aside for a home for my daughter and myself. I was very thankful for my brother and his wife for including my daughter in their summer vacations for years, so the sacrifice became my own sacrifice.

Since that horrible experience years ago, I have learned so much. Unfortunately being a little green at that time in all that surrounded the purchasing a home there was much to learn before taking on that adventure and I had no idea.

I understood that an important factor was to obtain an excellent mortgage rate. I was not looking to build. As any consumer would be, I became excited when presented with the opportunity of building my first home on my own.

My mortgage loan was written and I was given my 'Good Faith' offer with an excellent interest rate. My mortgage officer was also the president of his (then) mortgage company and had also begun to build new homes in the area (hummmm?). This was my first mistake – allowing a mortgage company (broker) to build my home who clearly did not have years of experience in residential construction.

Following the securing of the mortgage loan approval this individual offered to build a home for me. Since I was referred to this individual by friends, I felt somewhat confident in the business referral. I was presented with the proposal (preliminary contract) to build my home. He also presented to me several home designs (models in blue print) for me to review and to select my home design from. I went further to ask where his current projects were being built, and asked to view those homes. This builder was building several homes around the city but one of those homes was a home for a friend of the referring couple. I went to view the construction of that home and was very pleased with the quality of the construction and the style of the home. The house was beautiful and he was offering a lot of square footage for not a lot of money (again, beware of what you think may be free).

Since I was not happy with the blueprint designs presented to me, the builder offered to allow me to redesign the blue prints of my home for a mere fee and offered an available lot of land that I could build on, that he currently owned. I went to view the lot of land with the mortgage officer/builder, walked the land to verify the lot size and borders. After viewing the lot and his parcel document, I gave him the signed approval to move forward.

I completed my design changes and the final blue prints were drawn, and benchmarked. I approved the final blueprints, signed the contract, and paid the down payment. Sounds simple enough? Well at the mortgage closing, and nearly 2 hours into the closing, since I chose to read all the documents - I found that the interest rate had increased on the mortgage loan. He had also gained approval for a Construction Loan that I did not request, for the building of my home. The construction loan would be in place for six months, which was the estimated amount of time to build my home. The construction loan would then automatically roll into the mortgage loan after a six-month period of time.

I was quite upset about the increase in the mortgage rate at closing and the need for a construction loan to build. Today, and with experience now processing mortgages - I understand why he increased the rate and why the construction loan. The increase in the rate was so that he could take the yield spread offered by the lender. The yield spread appeared on my mortgage closing documents but I did not understand what it actually meant to me during this closing process, and of course, it was not explained. A yield spread are funds offered to a mortgage company by the lender and can add thousand to the lenders profits and to the mortgage brokers fees, and of course increases the interest rate which can cost the consumer thousands over the life of your mortgage loan.

The increase in the mortgage rate was a half percentage point higher, which over the years has cost me a lot of money. The construction loan was to his advantage since he had no funds to build my home, I would be ultimately financially responsible, –

and this was mistake number two. Of course, he had an excellent explanation for every aspect of these changes. The rate had increased from the lender within the last two weeks he stated, Ahhh...No! The other statement for the construction loan was to protect me if he defaulted on building my home; this statement may have had some truth to it – but not fully. After nearly four hours, I went ahead and closed on the mortgage... *Yes I did?*

I clearly did not understand the dangers of allowing an inexperienced builder (and lack of project management skills) to utilizing a construction loan to build my home, especially a construction loan that was tied to my mortgage loan. An additional mistake was not seeking additional legal advice, and I should have. The construction loan was designed to be utilized for the cost to build my home. The construction loan was approved and made available by the same lender who would hold my mortgage loan.

How the construction loan was to work - was as my home was being completed a percentage of funds, equal to the phased building completion would be drawn from the construction loan balance. I would be billed the interest on the funds drawn from the construction loan only and during the building process. The total of the construction loan was equal to the purchase price of my home. As the house was being completed the banks building inspector was to verify the completion of each phase and authorized the amount to be drawn from my construction loan. I was the only authorized signer on these draws, so there would be a final validation point – my signature and work performed. While not trusting this individual, I began to look closely and the percentage of work completed against the construction loan funds drawn. What I found was, work stated as completed - by both the builder and bank inspector was not correct. More funds were being drawn then work completed, and I was paying the interest on these funds monthly. I had been put in a position of being 'flipped upside down' in funds to completed construction (more work remaining, with no funds to pay sub-contractors).

At the point that I realized that the construction loan was

overdrawn, it was overdrawn by approximately $50,000 dollars. The building project that was to take six months now had taken nearly nine months with only 60 percent of construction completion. I was now living in a hotel since the home that I was living in was sold. Now for a visual…. My home was not complete, contractors were not being paid by the builder from the funds that were previously drawn, I'm paying nearly $150 per day for my daughter and I to live a hotel, I'm paying a monthly construction loan interest payment and NOW the mortgage payments are also now due?? I thought I would lose my mind.

I hired an attorney and had the remaining construction loan funds frozen. I contacted my city for help and received it. I filed a lawsuit against the builder, which really did not make much of a difference. I was informed, through my attorney that I was one of the lucky consumers. Lucky, are you kidding? There were approximately 30 or so other consumers and contractors now suing this builder. My city building department became more involved and pulled this individual into court for the many violations, ultimately issuing warrants for this contractor and threatened jail. My attorney assisted me in protecting the remaining funds of my construction loan and I was forces to use my remaining savings and to borrow to complete my home. It took me nearly 2 ½ years to complete my home on my own and hiring my own contractors. The builder ultimately filed bankruptcy and walked away from everything as though it never happened. Do you wonder what I got in the lawsuit…nothing, due to his bankruptcy?

With all that I endured, I was one of the lucky consumers that encountered this individual since some consumers were left with only a frame of a home and land. Yes, I did say the frame and the land only. Unfortunately, most of their construction loans were diminished to zero. Was this an education in residential building or what?

'An Invasion of (corporate) Locust' by Darlene R. Miles

Always Verify Public Records When Purchasing Property

During the land excavating phase of the building of my home, I visited the lot of land. I noticed that the trees were not marked correctly for removal and this was in important process since the existing trees were nearly four to five stories high and if not removed during excavating they would be quite costly to uproot later. While on the lot, I phoned the builder and his project manager to discuss my concern. Instead, I was informed by the excavator, and the neighbors, who bordered the lot, that my lot was not the actual size that I thought. In addition, I was informed that the additional trees that I wanted removed belonged to my neighbors. The builder had lied about the lot size, and walked the land that actually was owned by my neighbors. I lost my mind.

Now understand that in a normal home building contract process, you should not have to check on every step that a builder is performing – but I felt that I did. Years back, and while married, I had a partner in the process and an excellent builder. A consumer should be able to obtain a mortgage and select a reputable builder who will fund the building of the home that you are purchasing, manage their own budget, absorb any cost overruns and complete your home on time. The builder that I had could not perform any of these tasks.

The lot size was only half the actual size that was presented to me prior to the close of my mortgage loan. After crying for years, I now laugh at myself, at this one. How did this happen you ask? I allowed the contractor to walk the land with me. I allowed him to visually show me the land boundaries without my following up with the city to verify the actual parcel, and square footage of the land. It was not until my mortgage loan closed and the building process had began that I found that the lot size was not what was originally stated or presented to me by the builder/mortgage loan officer. Sadly, it took the neighbors and the excavators to point out

'An Invasion of (corporate) Locust' by Darlene R. Miles

257

my true property boundaries. In other words, my neighbors informed me that the additional trees that I wanted marked for removal were theirs. You can imagine how I felt.

This incident was the last piece of pooh in the pile for me. I immediately contacted the bank to find out what I my options were, if any, in reversing this mortgage close. My objective was to find a way to get out of this very bad business deal. And of course, why would I think the answer would be to contact the bank? It was their loan. Again, I thought I was doing the right thing. I was told by the bank that it would be extremely costly to reverse the mortgage close in order to get out of the entire deal – mortgage loan and building contract. I quickly attempted to find an attorney for assistance me. With no immediate luck in finding an attorney fast - I was stuck, so I allowed this nightmare of a process to proceed. I should have known better and immediately stopped everything until I obtained an attorney but I allowed the bank to miss-inform me. It would have saved me nearly 100 thousand dollars if I would have had the nerve to stop this dishonest process right then.

I must also say that the building process should not be as complex or full of such dishonesty. I was building a custom home, and purchased the lot from this, 'builder-mortgage' person. When my last home was built years ago, my former spouse handled nearly all aspects of the building and mortgage process. All aspects were handled professionally and conducted in a timely manner and without incident. The difference was building with a reputable building contractor, with a successful history of residential construction under his built.

Where I failed was, everywhere. I should have verified with the city the actual land and lot dimensions, and I did not. At the time that I purchased the lot from the builder I didn't expect that he would go to the extent to actually walk someone else's land then sell it to me? Nevertheless, how ignorant could I have been to the process? I lost track of this incident after he increased the interest rate at the close of my loan. I was buried and overwhelmed – and truly needed to have legal advice. Little did I know that more incidents were to come?

I was troubled that my interest rate was changed in the closing process, and began to want to validate everything else. The project did not start on time; the sub-contractors were not being paid, even though draws were being drawn from my construction loan. Original designs were being severally altered or not included at all. The building project was to have taken six months. Ten months later it was now winter and the builder was in financial trouble and folding. The builder's sub-contractors stopped working and I was now living in a hotel. My home was 70 percent complete, and the contractors refused to work free, obviously. Several consumers were in a worse condition then I, resulting from their contracts with this builder. Most consumers were left with only the frames of their homes and nothing else.

You should always know your property measurements and boundaries. You should contact your city to verify and view the actual parcel/land documentation on your own. You should check to see if there are any impeding issues with the neighbors such as fences crossing property lines. Shrubs? Neighbors landscaping, joint landscaping, who will maintain, etc.? Most importantly, when in doubt contact an attorney for help.

Now understand that in a normal home building contract process, you should not have to check on every step that a builder is performing – but I felt that I did.

What You Need To Know About the 'Construction Loan' Building Process

The building contract was broken. Work was never on schedule; draws for funds off my construction loan were falsified and overdrawn when I checked the percent of completion to the money drawn from the bank. Meaning I started the building process using a construction loan that would roll into the mortgage on a stated date which was six months for the builder to build the home. The builder has the consumer sign bank drafts forms for bank draws against the total amount of the cost to build the home, which must equal a 'percent of completion' as work is preformed. What bothered me is there should have been a bank inspector correctly verifying all draws and the percent of completion, and that person failed me. As a consumer, I could not see nor validate under ground water and sewer lines or electrical now covered in drywall. These were two of the major areas charged to me as completed.

Some how blank bank drafts were being sent to the bank and funds where being released to the builder without my signature and work being performed. This is was a serious issue in itself and the bank should not have allowed that to happen. These behaviors went on for nearly nine months. Ultimately the builder files bankruptcy and several consumers are left without a home or finished property. The bank officials eventually leave this small bank, and the bank is eventually sold - several times over the years? Yes, sold. Unfortunately, several other consumers who were also taken advantage of were left with a mortgage to pay and no homes to live in. I feel I fared better them most other consumers who chose to do business with this builder - but experienced hell while entangled in his mess.

Protecting Yourself during the Home Building Process

I should have walked out of that office at the first sign of deception, which was the increasing of my mortgage rate interest at the mortgage close. Little did I realize that this was the beginning of the hell to come? What I did not understand was that this individual had done nothing for me that I could not have done for myself, including finding a lender. I ultimately became my own general contractor and project manager, hiring sub-contractors, negotiating contracts, and assuring proper permits were obtained to complete the construction of my home. It to two additional years, but I did it.

There are laws in place that were not in place during my home building experience that can protect consumers. One important law is the 'Construction Contracts Act 2002' (in force on April 1, 2003). This law now provides added protection for both the homeowner who contracts with a builder and the sub-contractors that are paid by the contractor.

The following is a summary of suggested validation points that I missed or should have implemented prior to and during the construction of my home:

- The Construction contract should have had a provision where the builder paid (me) the buyer a financial penalty either daily or weekly for the delay in completing my home. This penalty would have to be included in the building contract and paid directly to me, daily or weekly and not be applied to the cost of construction of the home.
- Make sure your builder is a licensed Master Builder and is insured.
- You should request a contracted quote and not an estimate. You should request quotes from several builders not just one.
- Make sure that your contract is specifically for the building of your home and not a standard contract.
- Make sure that your contract complies with Building codes.
- Make sure that your contract, plans, and building specifications include dates in which each phase of the building project is to be completed and where penalties can be added for delays.
- Make sure that you include a home warranty and maintenance clause in your contract. The maintenance contract can be from one to 5 years. I did have a

maintenance contract but once the building filed bankruptcy I was on my own. This is where the builder's insurance policy could have stepped in.

My sharing of this information is to help consumers understand what and where the validation points are in the mortgage and home building process, and how to recognize issues before you close on a mortgage loan. I hope that my sharing of my experience will help consumers in the future if challenged with any of these dilemmas. And again, if every in doubt – seek legal advice.

With such a horrible experience I decided to become a mortgage loan processor to learn as much as I could about the mortgage business, also while working as a consultant. In later chapters, I will share with consumers what you need to know and understand about the Mortgage Loan Process.

Chapter 21 - Investment Property Purchasing

For first time property investors, purchasing rental or investment property for the first time, be very careful how you expose yourself financially for this investment.

Understand that if you are financing investment property, your interest rate will be a little higher for rental property then it would be for your 'primary home' mortgage loan. Do not take on an additional mortgage loan that might hurt you financially. Make sure you can afford the additional payment if the renters move out or if you are unable to resell the property quickly, and are left paying both mortgages, and sometimes paying both mortgages for an indefinite period of time.

Make sure you know what repairs, if any, have to be performed on your new property and ask yourself can you afford to make these repairs. Get several good estimates and eventually a 'solid' signed contract for the repairs. Make sure you are working with a contractor's final (solid) contract and not an 'open-ended' estimate for repairs or construction. Make sure you have some type of cash reserve for these repairs and not your credit cards, which will get you into serious financial trouble once the credit cards are maxed out from repairs.

Beware that there may be cost overruns for repairs and additional repairs may be found after you have dove into walls, attics, plumbing and electric. Make sure you know what your city code requirements are before you purchase the investment property since those requirements may affect you financially. Last, if you plan to rent or lease the property - make sure you have a signed lease and security deposits from someone and if possible, and as soon as possible.

Put together a Project Plan and Schedule with Estimates for cost of repairs. Tie the project plan, schedule, and cost to the contract and contractor who will be performing the repairs. I would personally add some form of incentives in the contract, where if the work is not performed within a certain period of time, the cost will of the project will be reduce (in writing). You should try to obtain a signed contract from a reputable contractor and not from your Uncle Freddy who fixes *things* on the side, on the weekends☻. That 'On-The-Side' *stuff* can force you into financial ruin. You will become quite angry - very quickly.

Investment Property (Flipping)

Hummmm. This activity is not looked at favorable by lenders especially if you have obtained a mortgage loan for the property that you plan to 'Flip' or resale. Most mortgage companies have pre-payment penalties attached to your mortgage loans so you will be paying for your 'flipped' property for a specified period of time. In addition, you need to know that if you are not truthful with a lender and state that the property will be your primary residence, to avoid a higher interest rate for investment property, or to try to avoid pre-payment penalties, you are wrong. Your loan appears on your credit report, the date, the term, the amount and lender name all appears. Other lenders will see that information and require documentation before the property can be sold to another consumer, especially if that consumer plans to obtain a mortgage for the purchase of that property from you.

Keep in mind the information will appear on your credit report for 7 years so if you think no lender will know that you are 'slightly' dishonest about the type of mortgage loans that you are acquiring, you are wrong. So do not think you will (always) get away with that incorrect piece of information for long.

If you do not have the cash reserve, and investing in property for quick resale you may want to take an equity loan on your primary property and pay cash for the investment property purchase. Make sure you know what you are purchasing, i.e., what is the true state of the property, is there any equity in the property where you will make money on the resale, what are the level of repairs and can you afford to perform the repairs? Last, how long can you financially expose yourself to the additional debt that can occur when 'Flipping' property? Be careful and be prepared for the worse situations but plan for the best☺

Chapter 22 - Mortgage Financing and Home Buying

Steps to Perform Before You Apply For a Mortgage Loan

To save you time, aggravation, and unwanted surprises you should have a clear financial picture of your credit history and budget. I recommend that you do the following:

- Draft a budget and be honest about your monthly expenses; Insurance costs for auto and life, food, clothing, current utilities, credit cards and loan payments, money to family members, etc. and don't forget any monthly entertainment, be honest with yourself. Now let's see what you have left for this new house?
- Request your free credit reports from the top three credit bureaus
- Consider your current income to debt ration. Your debt ration should not be higher the 70 percent of your income. (Monthly payments on loans and revolving debt such as credit cards, and a total of those monthly payments.) If your credit score is high, at least 650 or greater you should be able to obtain a good mortgage interest rate (based on current year statistics)…but can you afford the mortgage payment alone with your current monthly debt ratio, be honest with yourself.
- Consider the price range of the home that you can afford and any 'idle' expenses for that home such as:
  - Homeowners insurance monthly cost (get an estimate for your insurance company)
  - PMI – Private Mortgage Insurance added to your mortgage payment if your down payment is less 20 percent.
  - Inspections and appraisal costs

- Any estimated home improvement cost; landscaping, appliances, painting, carpet, etc.
- Once you have determined how much house you can afford, obtain a Pre-qualification (pre-approval) from a mortgage lender. Note: a 'solid' pre-approval will consist of submitting all of your documentation; recent pay-stubs, tax returns or W-2, mortgage history, employment verification, etc.
- Have your Pre-Approval Rate Locked for at least 30 or 60 days. An additional note here, *get the pre-approved rate then request the 'Lock'.* Some finance companies will increase the rate based on the 'Locked – In' quoted rate, so get the 'Lock' in writing and begin to house hunt. *It would be best to have found your house in advance, if possible.*
- Do not waste time, it can cost you a possible rate increase if the rate goes up and your 'locked' period expires.

How to Improve Your Credit before Applying for a Mortgage Loan

In order to obtain a good or excellent mortgage interest rate you must first get your credit report and credit score in shape, and of course before applying for a mortgage loan. If you believe your credit is in poor shape then it probably is.

You will want to quickly begin the 'clean-up' process by first requesting your credit reports from the top three credit reporting agencies to view the contents of your credit report. You want to make sure that the information appearing on your credit reports are correct. If the information is incorrect, immediately notify the credit reporting agencies and request the corrections. I have written a section in my book on 'Repairing Your Credit', reference that information as a good guide to begin the process.

For any accounts that may be behind, immediately get those

accounts caught up to begin to establish payment reliability. Good payment history, for lenders to view is generally over a period of at least one to two years of good payment history and before starting your loan paperwork. Another smart idea is to eliminate your overall debt potential. If you have multiple credit cards, try to pay them down or off. If your pocket is overrun with a crazy amount of credit cards, then I would personally recommend that you pay off and close some of your unneeded credit cards. Lenders do review your credit file for any available credit cards or lines of credit as an amount of available credit. Lenders view revolving accounts as accounts that can be utilized by the consumer at any time, and can affect the calculation of debt to income ratio. These accounts will also affect the amount of your qualifying mortgage loan amount. By closing a couple of unneeded or unused credit cards, this can improve your credit rating by showing you have less potential debt waiting to happen. If you close any accounts, make sure that the credit reporting agency reports on your credit report for those accounts as, 'Closed by Consumer'.

Most consumers think that paying on time is all that is needed to maintain a good credit score and rating, but it is not all that is needed. Creditors will also consider too many revolving accounts with high balances as negative credit information. You must also pay off credit cards or what are considered as revolving debt. Too many credit cards with high balances, even if the credit cards are being paid on time, then reused are looked at negatively by some creditors. The mortgage loan process hinges on a good credit report. If you have erroneous items on your credit report, have them corrected by challenging them in writing with the credit reporting agencies. Be sure to get resolution and a corrected credit report before you begin work on the mortgage loan. You may need several months to clear up contested entries on your credit report—its best to begin the contesting process early. Another important point regarding credit report correction, if you find that there are a great number of incorrect accounts and other information on your credit report, you may want to obtain your credit score *before* the correction process begins. You may wonder why I would make this statement. After the corrections are made to your credit report, your credit score should increase. As it exists today, most lenders will calculate the mortgage loan interest rates based on the credit score of the consumer. In some cases, it may be necessary to request a 'rescoring' by the credit-reporting agency.

In addition, remember the (FCRA) Fair Credit Report Act requires that all credit-reporting agencies report accurate information. If you dispute information, the credit-reporting agency has a limited amount of time to validate that the information is correct or incorrect. In addition, credit-reporting agencies cannot report credit information that is over 7 years old, with no activity unless it is a bankruptcy Chapter 7, which is reported on your credit report for 10 years from date of discharge.

In reference to accounts that were not paid and still appear on your credit report, they must be paid in order to be considered for a mortgage loan. Most lenders will not write a mortgage for a consumer with any 'charged off' or bad debt accounts appearing on your credit report. The issue of 'no account' activity would reference any account that is or was in bad standing (uncollected but charged off) as example and there has been no activity or contact with you the consumer. When you contact that company or they make actual contact with you, the clock starts ticking for another 7 years. That means that the account can remain on your credit report for another 7 years from the date of creditor contact with you. Keep in mind that if an account is due to fall off your credit report within months; do you really want the account reported as a delinquent account, that was charged off, for another 7 years? Would you prefer to allow the account to reach its limitations of already being reported for the seven-year period, which is now approaching its reporting end?

Protecting Your Credit Score

Do not shop for anything that requires credit approval during the financing of a mortgage. Especially for auto financing during the financing of a mortgage, the 'credit inquires' do negatively affect your credit score. Most Auto Finance companies will shop your credit around and most times will not care about the number of companies who generate new credit reports on you when they forward your credit application to them for consideration.

Some times consumers will request that the auto finance company hunt for the lowest auto interest rate and the results are the negative impacts to your credit score. Too many credit inquires within short amount of time reduces your credit score. The same situation occurs when you mortgage shop. How to stop this madness, request that one credit report be sent to any potential financing companies and request that they do not request a new credit report without your written approval. Get this in writing if necessary. You can do the same when shopping for competitive rates for a mortgage. In this case, you may want to request your combined credit report with the credit score and provide copies to the respective lenders or mortgage brokers. Also request from your mortgage lender, in writing that they do not generate additional credit reports until needed. The lender will need to obtain *their own* combined report for your mortgage close.

You should know what your credit score is before you begin the process. In addition, do not apply for new credit during the financing of a home or refinancing of a mortgage. This behavior is not looked at favorable since your mortgage application is a snap shot of your financial picture and that picture will be used to determine your interest rate of financing. Be careful.

Home Purchasing and those Miscellaneous Enhancement Costs

Be aware, not only are you acquiring a new mortgage, but you may also be taking on additional miscellaneous costs that will be added to your monthly expenses. Some expenses are short term and some are long term. Some examples of those expenses are outlined as follows:

- Moving expense
- Painting (interior and exterior)
- New carpet
- Remodeling (carpentry, electrical, kitchen counter upgrades)
- Appliances
- Furnace
- Hot Water Tank
- Air conditioning
- Roofing
- Landscaping enhancements
- Home Owners Insurance (long term expense)
- Property Taxes (long term expense)

Just some possible home expenses when purchasing a home.

Some Items to Watch for When House Hunting:

The following items are some of the items that should be watched for or considered carefully when 'house hunting'.

- Smell of water or dampness is generally a sign of water damage of moisture; upstairs indicates potential roof issues.
- Smell of water in the basement generally indicates the need of a dehumidifier or water damage.
- Foundation cracks
- Fresh drywall repairs
- Neighbors and how they maintain their property; it does affect yours.
- Turn on all lights to be assured that there are no electrical

problems when all lights are turned on at once.

- Roof age of existing homes
- Furnace and Hot Water Tank condition, status (leaks?) and age
- Status and age of appliances in the purchase home or the cost of new
- Is the house insurable? Has there been insurance damages reported that may cause your insurance company not to insure this home?
- Cost of property taxes and home owners insurance

Some Items to Consider When Purchasing Your Home

The Home Inspection Process

One very important item to consider is a Home Inspection prior to purchasing your new home. When making an offer to purchase a home, you should always have a contingency clause that would be based on the outcome of a home inspection.

A Home Inspection can generally be conducted by the city Building Department for which you are purchasing your home. If a Home Inspection is not available by the city, I would hire a Licensed Home Inspection company on your own. You do not want to rely on an inspection that is conducted only by the Seller or seller Agent.

Some items that your Home Inspection should include:

- Foundation (stability and any cracks)
- Exterior Brick (cracks, spacing and overall condition)
- Driveways and Sidewalks (stability and any cracks, is it up to code in depth)
- Doors and Windows

- Siding
- Roof (condition, age, possible leaks)
- Ceilings, Moldings and Walls (cracks and overall condition)
- Plumbing (Inside and Outside)
- Electrical (up to code, outlets, etc.)
- Water Heater (condition, leakage, age, etc.)
- Air conditioning (condition, code, age, etc.)
- Insulation (up to code, in appropriate locations, etc.)
- Furnace (condition, leakage, age, etc.)
- Garage
- Basement (cracks, water damage, overall condition, etc.)
- Attic (insulation, etc.)
- Appliances (condition, code, electrical and gas connections, etc.)
- Septic Tanks (conditions, code, etc.)

Upon completion of the inspection, the Home Inspector will compile an inspection report. The report will typically include any major problems that were found. As the Buyer you should address these issues with the Seller and either re-negotiate the selling price or determine how these issues will be resolved.

Some items to consider about your Home Inspector:

- Make sure that the Inspector is (ASHI) American Society of Home Inspectors certified. This would indicate that this individual has performed at least 250 inspections and have passed the written exam.
- Do not use a Home Inspector that may be *buddies* with the Selling Agent, since this individual may be encouraged to push the inspection through.
- Make sure the inspector is licensed

Property Claims History

Most consumers are not aware that the claims history of the property you want to purchase can affect your ability to insure the property after your purchase. Insurance companies retain claims history for all claims and will shun away from properties with a history of at least one claim of water or mold damage and or a high volume of property claims. Obtain an estimate from your insurance company and allow them to run a claims history report on the property, be assured they will and this will be to your benefit.

Most insurance companies that collects and stores claims information, collect both insurance claims and damage reports history. Now if you are the seller of damaged property all that I can say is ...hummmm.

Chapter 23 - Mortgage Application Process - Identifying Predatory Lending and Avoiding Foreclosure

What is a 'Good Faith Offer and Why It's Important?'

When applying for a mortgage loan, you should be presented with a 'Good Faith' offer from your mortgage representative. The 'Good Faith' offer will contain your personal information, name, address, employment, loan amount (new mortgage or equity loan), purchase or refinancing amount, the proposed interest rate, and terms (months) of your loan. This proposed rate should be presented after you have signed the authorization for the mortgage company to request a copy of your credit report from a credit-reporting agency. The most effective credit report would be a combined report from the top three credit reporting agencies, which will list your lowest and highest credit scores. Strangely, and in most cases your credit score is reported differently by all three credit-reporting agencies. Credit scores can be different between the three credit reporting agencies because they don't all report on the same information, they retain information differently and sometimes the reports have errors.

The credit scores will initially help to determine your proposed mortgage loan interest rate and which lenders that can be utilized to write your loan. You should always know the status and content of your credit report by obtaining a free credit report yearly from all three top credit-reporting bureaus. A good mortgage company will provide you with a good proposed rate that should not vary to far from your 'final' interest rate at the mortgage close. What this mean is, the official rate is not offered until all of your documentation is presented to the lender and the lender agrees to a 'Locked In' rate for a specified period of time. Documents that are generally required are, two years of Income Statements or W2's, your last two recent pay stubs, mortgage or rent history for your current residence, proof of other income, signed statement from your employer (if used), and if purchasing a new property, the Purchase Agreement and Appraisal (if applicable). Once all documents are presented to the lender, the mortgage company will provide you with an interest rate 'Lock' in for a period of time.

Where I went wrong, as an uninformed consumer was that I was not aware that your 'locked in' rate should not change if you close within the 'locked in' specified dates. I was working with quite a scrupulous mortgage broker. Even though I was told that, my mortgage rate was a 'locked' rate it changed. In addition, I was not aware that by law the lender was to provide me with the HUD statement, which details the total fees that the mortgage broker and bank will receive. These fees should not have increased as they did without any change (negative or other) in my finances or credit.

Even though my challenges were great when financing my home years ago, I have learned over the years is that, there are some advantages in utilizing a mortgage broker. Mortgage brokers have access to several lenders and more flexibility in obtaining you a lower rate, while banks are limited to the mortgage loan programs within their respective banks. Mortgage brokers can also find mortgage lenders when you have had financial problems. However, the other side is a mortgage broker can also rake you over the hot-coals with high fees if you are not an educated consumer, as I was not when writing my mortgage loan years ago. Unfortunately, the same situations can occur with the use of traditional banks to write your loan. With a bank, you can qualify for a prime (low) interest rate, but is charged several percentage points higher, and/or higher closing cost fees for your mortgage loan.

You must protect yourself by allowing both the bank and a good reputable mortgage broker to work for you and compete for your business. After all, you do not close on a loan until you sign on that dotted line.

Mortgage Fees

Although some mortgage fees are not negotiable and out of the control of the bank or mortgage company, some fees and closing costs are negotiable and within the mortgage company or banks control. An explanation of some of the mortgage fees are shown in this section.

There are currently no standards for mortgage fees so a scrupulous loan officer will try to make as much money as possible from the consumer with these fees, (and please note...scrupulous). After being in the mortgage business for several years and experiencing the negative results as a consumer years ago, I have seen how some loan officers, banks, and mortgage companies - gouge their clients every day. It is a rampant common occurrence.

Mortgage brokers are generally paid through commissions from every loan that closes. While some traditional bank loan officers are sometimes only paid just above the minimum wage, this lack of income sometimes puts the pressure on the bank loan officer to make as much money as possible, wherever possible. Since there is generally no salary for a mortgage broker, they will typically split the profits of the closing cost, usually 50/50 for each loan closed with their mortgage office.

Mortgage brokers do tend to work harder on obtaining the mortgage loan for a consumer since they have to match your credit score and overall percentage of debt-to-income with a lender. A disadvantage of working with a bank is that they do have limitations on loan products available at their respective bank branches. Traditional banks can only offer the various loans that are available with their specific bank. While you may worry about excessive fees from a mortgage broker, a traditional bank may rack you over the coals with a higher mortgage interest rate that will affect you for the life of your mortgage loan thus costing you hundreds of thousands of dollars. I will provide some advice on avoiding both situations later in this section.

- Origination or Application Fees: These are fees for processing the mortgage application and may be a flat fee or a percentage of the mortgage. They usually are equal to one percentage point.
- Points: A point is equal to 1% of the amount borrowed. For example, one point on a loan amount of $50,000.00 is $500.00 dollars. Points can be payable when the loan is approved (before closing) or at closing. For FHA and VA mortgages, the seller-not the buyer-must pay the points. Even if you are not using an FHA or VA mortgage, you may want to negotiate points in the purchase offer. Some lenders will let you finance points, adding this cost to the mortgage, which will increase your interest costs. If you pay the points up front, they are deductible from your income taxes in the year they are paid. Different deductibility rules apply to second homes.
- Application Fees: Application fees are non-refundable and 100% pure profit for the mortgage broker or bank if charged. I would walk out if they ask for an application fee up front. The only exception to this rule is if you have tough credit. In this case, the loan officer will have to do a lot of work before he or she can tell if your loan will go through. Time is money, and they will want to be paid for this effort. If your loan is denied without an application fee up front, the loan officer has put in many hours for nothing.

Why Is the HUD Statement Important To You

The HUD Statement is provided to you as a consumer and should disclose all of the fees and the cost of your mortgage loan. This HUD Statement should also display the total amount that the lender will receive as their fee for the loan; this includes your broker fee and profits. The HUD Statement should be either mailed to you by the lender or presented to you by the broker or bank loan officer, before you close your loan.

'An Invasion of (corporate) Locust' by Darlene R. Miles

What Is a Mortgage Point

These are fees and commissions earned by the mortgage broker or bank for processing your mortgage loan.

The "normal fees" in the industry are an origination fee (1 "point") plus one additional point. Some brokers and banks have a limit on how much a loan officer can charge in fees-the loan application fee, the origination fee, and the points, but not all. However, there are no absolute hard and fast rules across the mortgage industry.

Getting Points on the Back

'Points on the Back', also known as "yield-spread fees", points on the back are one of the ways a loan officer makes more funds available to the total loan. Yield Spread fees are essentially an incentive to the broker provided by the lender to the loan officer. This incentive is earned by selling a customer a loan at an interest rate that is above the going rate but can still be lower then what a bank may offer direct.

In order for the mortgage officer to get the yield spread, they have to increase the rate. Each day, loan officers receive rates from lenders for all of the lenders loan programs. Any 'points on the back' will be credited to the loan proceeds at closing and must be disclosed to the consumer on the 'good-faith' offer and final HUD disclosure.

How do you know if the Lender is increasing Your Interest Rate?

It bears repeating that it is the loan officer (bank or mortgage broker) who picks the interest rate that is sold to you and, consequently, the commissions they will earn on the loan. If the loan officer is competing with another loan company to get your loan, they may not be greedy and not increase the rate.

'An Invasion of (corporate) Locust' by Darlene R. Miles
279

Nevertheless, if you do not shop around, do not trust them to be honest, unless you have a personal relationship. Some loan officers are completely up-front with you, but some are not. Always shop around, especially if you have "A", good credit. Some loan officers will charge you less if they know your loan will be an easy mortgage loan to process.

Take extra caution if you have had some credit problems and must get a non-conforming or sub-prime loan, as these are typically the biggest targets of shady loan officers. Desperate consumers have been known to have paid higher interest rates and 5 points in fees. This definitely is wrong.

No-cost Loans – Do They Really Exist?

You have heard of those no-cost refinance loans. Forget it. There is no such thing. A broker must make money on every loan, and so does a traditional bank. Many well-intentioned loan officers honestly believe they are giving you a loan free, but this simply is not the case.

In the example above, I showed you how you could get a loan at an interest rate above the par rate and get points on the back. The points on the back translate to extra funds available to pay the cost of the loan and pay the loan officer a commission. So what is wrong with this? Nothing, but you are financing the "free cost" of the loan over the term of the loan (usually 30 years), which can double or triple the closing costs (by way of additional interest) as compared to paying the closing costs up front and in cash.

Fixed Rate Mortgage verses Adjustable Rate Mortgage Loans

These are the two primary mortgage types of loans. A Fixed Rate Mortgage has a rate of interest that does not change throughout the life of the loan and is based on the terms (number of years) financed. An Adjustable Rate Mortgage (ARM) rate of interest and principle payments will vary over the life of the mortgage.

The advantage of a Fixed Rate Mortgage loan is that the rate of interest will not change and your payments will remain the same during the life of the loan. The Fixed Rate Mortgage generally has payment terms of 30, 20, or 15 years. The longer the payment term for a fixed rate mortgage, the higher the interest rate. The shorter the term of a fixed rate mortgage, the small the interest rate but has a higher monthly payment.

With an Adjustable Rate Mortgage, your payments and interest will vary based on the pre-arranged loan frequency. What I mean here is your loan document will state the number of years or months that your interest rate will remain the same, generally 3, or 6 years. At the time, your Adjustable Rate loan reaches the 'adjustment frequency period' your rate will change and lately - most likely increase.

What is most complicated about the Adjustable Rate mortgages is that there are several factors that may be used to determine how much your mortgage payment (principal and interest) may increase or decrease – and lately there have only been increases to Adjustable Rate Mortgage loans. The following are some factors to consider about Adjustable Rate loans. These factors generally affect your ARMs.'

- Your Interest Rate *Ceiling* – This is the highest rate that your Adjustable Rate loan can go during the life of your loan. This is important and should appear on your loan documents.
- Your *Adjustment Loan Frequency* – This is the amount of time, (months, or years) between adjustments to your loan.
- Your *Loan Caps* – This is the maximum that your loan interest rate can increase during each adjustment period.
- What is *your Margin* – When you write your loan you

agree to pay a rate that is a stated percent higher then the adjustment index? An example could be; Prime plus 3% points, or what ever stated. The 3% points are your Margin.

- What is the *Adjustment Index* – The interest rate are all tied to an index. Which index is our loan tied to? Treasury Bills, Certificate of Deposits, or something else. This is important, so is the frequency of change for this 'adjustment index'.

So with all of this being said, you need to look closely at the type of loan that best fits your life. Most consumers chose the Fixed Rate Mortgage over the unknown market factors of an Adjustable Rate Mortgage.

On a personal note, I feel Adjustable Rate Mortgages fit the lives of Corporate Relocation personnel, or consumers that may not plan to live in their home for a long period of time. What I mean here is, if your corporation constantly relocates you, generally 3 to 5 years – then an Adjustable Rate Mortgage would be a good loan for you. Adjustable Rate loans are generally designed to have lower (attractive) payments during the first 'adjustment frequency' of the loan – the first 3 to 6 years before becoming higher.

What is an '80 / 20' Mortgage Loan – What You Should Know

The 80/20 Mortgage Loan is generally considered as a 'No Down Payment without PMI' loan, even though the buyer generally pays the closing cost for their new home. The 80/20 Mortgage loan consists of 80 percent of the home purchase price with the second 20 percent as a second mortgage. This is a way for consumers to get into a new home without the normal 20 percent down payment, and to avoid paying PMI (Private Mortgage Insurance) for the 'no down payment' mortgage loan.

Where I caution consumers is to make sure that you can afford both loan payments. Generally, the 80 percent mortgage loan is your fixed rate for the term of 30 years. The 20 percent (equity loan) is generally at a higher rated loan since equity loans, generally are for a short term – but are paid simultaneously. Having two loans can sometimes get consumer into financial trouble.

Now for those consumers who can afford the 80/20 Mortgage Loans this is a great way to get into a new home with no money down and only your closing costs, with no PMI required on the loan. Some consumers may also pay of the 20 percent loan sooner then the term set. I do advise that you understand what pre-payment penalties may apply to your loan early termination.

One last note here is, compare closing costs for these types of loans – not to be hit with huge costs for both loans. You may also want to *not* mix a fixed rate 80 percent loan with an Adjustable Rate 20 percent loan. Set your monthly budgets and watch your closing documents. Make sure you are clear on all terms before you close on a mortgage deal.

Predatory Lending – What Can Be Considered 'Predatory Mortgage Lending'

If you were to compile all of the negative statements made throughout this 'Home Buying and Financing' chapter, they could strongly be considered as 'Predatory Mortgage Lending'. Just to be a little more precise the following examples are items to guard against when financing your mortgage, be it refinancing a mortgage or the financing or a new home.

What to watch for when financing a mortgage:

- *Watch for over inflated appraisals on a home that you plan to purchase.* Check public records to view what the home was appraised for on the last selling transaction. If a home was appraised at, $80,000.00 in 2003 and in 2007 it is now appraised at $150,000.00 that is a $70,000.00 dollar increase. Have the seller show you what work has been performed between 2003 and 2007. Be aware that some lenders or mortgage brokers will chose the Appraiser, which can result in an inflated (incorrect) appraisal on the property you are to purchase. Sometimes it may not hurt for you, the consumer and purchaser, to contact an Appraisal company on your own that has 'proven' years of accurate appraisal assessments and has not been pulled from any lenders list. The 'pulling from lenders list' results when a lender has *identified irregular or inaccurate high numbers of appraisers* from an appraisal company. An inflated appraisal can hurt you if the property is not truly valued at a particular price. This practice of inflating appraisals can cause you to be in a mortgage where your home has no equity or added value for years and may put you in a position to pay a higher monthly payment for a home that is not truly value at what you are paying.

- *I would look to finance with a lender that will not sell your loan and is a local lender.* You can find a local lender when financing with a mortgage broker or when financing with a bank for financing. In addition, keep in mind that some banks also sell mortgage loans. Review your 'Closing' loan documents to read whether your lender will or may sell your loan. Why is this important you ask? When mortgage loans are sold, some 'predatory' companies (sometimes) change the provisions of your loan. Some provisions can place you into immediate foreclosure when your payments are missed for whatever reason. In addition, as loans are sometimes sold from lender to lender, escrows are lost, lender don't bill you for your mortgage payment right away and more, then late hit you with a huge payment at one time. Try to obtain a mortgage loan that will not be sold and will remain supported locally if

'An Invasion of (corporate) Locust' by Darlene R. Miles

possible.

- Understand your credit score and how it affects the interest rate that you are given. Generally, and in this current year an average combined Credit Score of 650 should not result in a mortgage rate in double figures. Double figures of 10% and greater, this to me is predatory even if you had fallen behind a couple of months due to illness or loss of employment. With documented proof of your illness or loss of employment presented to your lender, you should be able to obtain a mortgage loan in the 7% to 8% (and possible lower) range with an average 650 credit score. Now if your credit score is 700 or greater your interest rate based on the year 2007 should be around 5% to 6% and even lower with some lenders when you have no delinquencies or negative information on your credit report. Challenge lenders or mortgage brokers by always comparing offers from other financial institutions or other mortgage brokers. Remember to have your own copy of your top three credit bureaus so that these competing lenders or brokers do not continue to generate new credit reports each time you contact one. Get a statement in writing that they will not generate a new credit report on you or your combined buyer without your permission. Too many inquires on your credit report appearing in a short amount of time can affect and lower your credit score. There is nothing wrong with you presenting your own credit report for mortgage consideration and providing a copy to each lender or broker that you contact. Keep in mind that you will need to have your credit score on that report since the credit score will be the consideration factor.

- Make sure you receive your HUD Statement since this document will list the true profit (fees) to the broker or lender for your mortgage loan. What would be considered 'Predatory' to me is if these fees are much greater then what was shown on your 'Good Faith' offer and were not previously disclosed to you.

(PMI) Private Mortgage Insurance – What You Should Know

'PMI' or Private Mortgage Insurance is the extra insurance that a lender requires when your loan amount is less then 80% percent of your home value and you put less then 20% down on your home. The financial institution has a right to insurance the mortgage loan for a period of time in order for the property to retain equity, generally 20% equity of the loan balance.

Where most consumers go wrong is they forget to monitor the value of their home as equity increases and will continue to pay the PMI along with your mortgage loan. Generally, your home value will increase yearly and in most cases within two to five years, you may have more then 20% loan-to-value with over 20% equity in your home. The PMI (Private Mortgage Insurance) can sometimes be one hundred dollars ($100.00), or more per month added to your monthly mortgage loan payment.

Are There Any Benefits of Private Mortgage Insurance

I feel only for the lender. PMI protects the lender against any loss if a borrower does not pay or defaults on their mortgage loan. PMI also helps consumers with little cash for a down payment to qualify for a mortgage loan. PMI provides the ability for consumers with small down payment to gain homeownership sooner and without having to save a large down payment, generally that 20 percent down, and to get into a home much sooner.

New Laws to Protect Consumers with PMI

The Homeowner's Protection Act (HPA) of 1998, now requires lenders or mortgage servicers to provide disclosures concerning consumer rights and PMI for all loans written on a consumers primary residence that was obtained on or after July 29, 1999. The Homeowners Protection Act also outlines provisions for loans written after July 29, 1999.

In most cases when a consumer contacted a lender, the lender would honor the request as long as the equity in the home had reached a high of 78 percent or a low of 80 percent. However, there were those other lenders who would not honor the consumers request or take their good old time to remove the PMI from the loan. The HPA Act now protects consumers and assures compliance of this act.

In the past consumers had to keep track of the equity and loan payments made in order to be assured that PMI would be removed in a timely manner by the lender. Even though the Act now protect consumers, I would still keep track of the equity percentages, after all your PMI payment can range from $100 to $1300 yearly, that's a lot of money that can be placed back into your household.

Loans with Limitations under the HPA ACT

The HPA Act does not cover FHA or VA government loans. There are also additional requirements for consumer loans that are classified as 'high-risk' loans. Even though there are limitations for high-risk loans, the Act does provide provisions for Freddie Mac and Fannie Mae funded loans. Freddie Mac and Fannie Mae are government-funded corporations that are chartered by congress that create continuous flow of funds to mortgage lenders in support of consumer home ownership. Loans that are considered as 'Conforming' loans are loans of $252,700 or less are considered as conforming loans.

What Is Considered a 'Primary' Residential Mortgage Transaction?

The four key requirements for a mortgage to be considered a Residential Mortgage Transaction are as follows:

1) Must be a Primary Residence of the Borrower and
2) The consumers purpose must be to finance the property, initial construction or refinance of the property
3) You must create or retain a mortgage deed or trust
4) Your property must be a single-family dwelling

How to Cancel Your (PMI) Private Mortgage Insurance

The HPA Act provides the consumer the right to request cancellation of your PMI when you pay down your mortgage to 80 percent of the original purchase price or appraised value of your home increases to 80 percent of your mortgage loan balance. This value must be calculated from the original loan amount to your current or appraised home value, or whichever is less.

In addition to having an increased equity in your home value, some lenders also require that you are current on your mortgage loan payments at the time you request that your PMI be cancelled. If you are not current on your loan, your lender may require that your loan is current before the PMI can be cancelled. An additional requirement from your lender can be that you have not been delinquent on your mortgage within the last 12 months from your cancellation request and that no second mortgage exists on your property.

If you feel your property value has greatly increased, contact your lender for their PMI requirements. You can stop the PMI payments by having your property appraised and if you now have the 20% equity in your home, contact your lender to have the PMI payment stopped. They have to stop the payments by law.

Automatic Termination of (PMI) Private Mortgage Insurance

The Homeowners Protection Act also states that the mortgage lender or mortgage servicer must automatically cancel your PMI coverage on most consumer loans once you have reached a 78 percent loan to value. Again, your loan payments may have to be current. The Act also provided a provision that states that the premium must be returned to you within 45 days of your cancellation or termination, so keep this in mind if you are currently paying PMI and you have not been contacted by your lender – you may be due a refund of your overpaid PMI.

For a consumers mortgage loans that are considered 'high-risk' the value must be at least 77 percent of the loan value. If the loan is delinquent, the automatic termination will not kick in until the loan is current. The lender has 30 days from the date that the 77 percent is reached and cannot add the premium back to your loan for the history of your loan.

What HPA considers Final Termination of PMI (even if Equity is not reached)

Generally, a loan with 360 months of monthly payments, when the loan reached the midpoint of 180 payments is generally the amortization period. The consumer must be current on their mortgage loan payments. The final termination must occur within 30 days of the date of amortization. *(Amortization; paying back, paying off.)*

(HPA) Homeowner Protection Act Required Disclosures

For Loans Obtained on or after July 29, 1999

If you obtained your loan on or after July 29, 1999 the HPA, established three periods when your lender or mortgage servicer must inform you of your rights, those times are as follows:

1) First, at your loan Closing
2) Annually and generally on your annual mortgage statement
3) When you cancel or terminate your Private Mortgage Insurance

Be aware that the disclosure varies depending on whether:

1) PMI is borrower paid or lender paid
2) The loan is classified as a fixed-rate mortgage or adjustable-rate mortgage
3) The loan is designated as high-risk

If Your Loan was obtained prior to July 29, 1999

The Act provides that an annual statement be sent to consumers with mortgages that were obtained before July 29, 1999. The statement content should outline the under which circumstances PMI can or may be cancelled along with the lender or servicers contact information.

Please be aware that the 'Automatic Termination' provision does not apply to mortgage loans prior to July 29, 1999, so stay on top of your loan to value amounts equity values.

'An Invasion of (corporate) Locust' by Darlene R. Miles

Escrowing Taxes and Insurance- What You Should Know

What is a Mortgage Escrow Accounts

This is an amount of money paid by the borrower but maintained with and by the lending institution, in order to pay the annual taxes and insurance on mortgaged property. Approximately one-twelfth of the estimated annual cost of taxes and insurance is paid into the Escrow account each month from the borrower's monthly mortgage payment. The lending institution pays the taxes and insurance from this account when they are due. An escrow account is required by many lending institutions in order to insure that the taxes and insurance premiums are paid on time.

It is, in a sense, a budgeting device which requires borrowers to set aside enough money to pay their taxes when due. If there is not enough money in the customer's escrow account at the time of tax payment, sometimes lenders will advance the funds at no charge, and allow the customer to pay back the advance through higher escrow payments.

Do Consumers Have a Choice Whether to Maintain an Escrow Account on Not

The lender usually decides whether you must maintain an escrow account, but sometimes government regulations leave the lender no choice. The Federal Housing Administration (FHA), for example, requires that lenders making FHA insured loans establish escrow accounts on those loans. The Veterans Administration (VA) does not require that escrow accounts be maintained on all VA-guaranteed home mortgages, but most lenders do.

Mortgage loans other than FHA and VA loans are generally known as conventional mortgages. Conventional mortgage loans are

'An Invasion of (corporate) Locust' by Darlene R. Miles

made by mortgage companies, banks, savings banks, and some credit unions are of two types – prime, and sub-prime mortgages. For each type of conventional mortgage loan, the lender decides whether to require an escrow account. Most conventional loan contracts contain escrow clauses, especially those with very low down payments. The lender may also take into consideration the customer's previous payment history.

In addition, even if a lender does not require it, some borrowers may prefer to maintain escrow accounts because they view escrows as convenient budgeting devices.

Can Consumers Earn Interest on Escrow Accounts

Few, if any lending institutions pay interest on the money in an escrow account. Many borrowers feel that they are entitled to share the interest that the lender earns by investing these tax and insurance funds. If an escrow account were not required, a borrower could deposit tax and insurance money in an interest-bearing account until a payment was due.

What Can Happen If Your Lender Does Not Pay Taxes and Insurance On Time?

A lending institution must pay the taxes in full if the escrow account balance is enough to cover the payment due. If there is enough money in the account and the lender fails to pay the taxes when due, it is liable to the customer for all penalties or fees incurred because of the failure to pay. Borrowers generally can tell whether taxes have been paid on time because lenders are required to send escrow account statements listing deposits and disbursements. An institution must send these statements at least once a year, but may instead choose to include information about the escrow account balance in the monthly billing statement.

What if Your Taxes Increases

When taxes increase, an escrow account may run short unless the money payment is adjusted. When the tax increase is large, which might occur with a tax mill increase, a special assessment for street improvements, or a new home assessment, a borrower may not be able to meet the added expense right away. Lending institutions generally recognize this and usually notify the borrower of the date and the amount of the increase. The borrower then has the option of paying the increase all at once or paying it in installments after the next payment adjustment date.

What are the Limits on How and What the Lenders Can Collect for Escrow Accounts

Federal law allows institutions that include escrow provisions in their mortgage contracts to collect the amount needed to pay for taxes and insurance plus one-sixth over that amount. This is important because many lending institutions do not require the extra one sixth in deposits, while others require varying amounts up to the limit. The main purpose for this practice is to prevent a deficiency from occurring in an escrow account as taxes and insurance rise from year to year. The larger collection also helps to insure that the institution will be able to make each tax payment when it is due in the event that a borrower is unable to make a monthly payment on time.

Reverse Mortgage – What Is a Reverse Mortgage and It's Benefits for Seniors 62 and Older

A Reverse Mortgage is a Government Insured, special type of loan used to convert the equity in a home into cash. The money obtained through a reverse mortgage is usually used to provide seniors with financial security in their retirement years.

The reverse mortgage is appropriately named because the payment stream is reversed. Instead of the borrower making monthly payments to a lender, as with a regular mortgage, a lender makes payments to the borrower. While a reverse mortgage loan is outstanding, the borrower owns the home and holds title to it, without having to make any monthly mortgage payments.

If you own your own home and are at least 62 years of age, a reverse mortgage provides an opportunity to convert your home equity into cash. In the most basic terms, the reverse mortgage allows you to take out a loan against the equity in your home, but you do not have to repay the loan during your lifetime as long as you are living in the home and have not sold it. If you want to increase the amount of money available to fund your retirement, but do not like the idea of making payments on a loan, a reverse mortgage is an option worth considering.

How a Reverse Mortgage Works

Reverse Mortgages are Government Insured. With a reverse mortgage, a lender makes payments to you based on a percentage of the value in your home. When you no longer occupy the property, the lender sells it in order to recover the money that was paid out to you.

While there are several types of reverse mortgages, including those offered by private lenders, they generally share the following features:

Older homeowners are offered longer loan amounts than younger homeowners. Homes that are more expensive qualify for larger loans.

A reverse mortgage must be the primary debt against the house.

'An Invasion of (corporate) Locust' by Darlene R. Miles
294

Other lenders must be repaid or agree to subordinate their loans to the primary mortgage holder. (Subordinate: take secondary positions.)

The lender can request repayment in the event you fail to maintain the property, fail to keep the property insured, fail to pay your property taxes declare bankruptcy, abandon the property, or commit fraud. The lender may also request repayment if the home is condemned or if you add a new owner to the property's title, sublet all or part of the property, change the property's zoning classification, or take out additional loans against the property.

Revise your 'Living Will' when writing a Reverse Mortgage

Please read your contract carefully before signing a Reverse Mortgage contract agreement. Also be aware that you may have equity in your home which may far exceed the payments received from your lender over your remaining lifetime, so remember to revise your 'Will' and appoint a beneficiary. You would not want to sign over property that may be worth a half million and only receive one hundred thousand from a Reverse Mortgage. In other words, do not give your home away in a Reverse Mortgage deal.

Bridge Loans (Buying a New Home While Selling Your Existing)

A 'Bridge Loan' may be necessary for a consumer when a buyer needs to sell an existing property before buying the new residence. Some lenders say it may make better sense to get a home equity loan, since it's cheaper and faster then to obtain a 'Bridge Loan' to purchase a new home while still the owner of another property being sold.

A Bridge Loan is a temporary loan that bridges the gap between the sales price of a new home and the buyer's new mortgage. The type of loan is necessary when the buyers existing home have not yet sold but they have found the next home to purchase.

Again, you may want to consider a home equity loan rather then apply for a bridge loan. If you decide to apply for a home equity loan, for the down payment, you should do this before you put your home on the market, most lenders do not want to do the work of financing a loan that will be quickly closed, and some may.

Equity Loans and Equity Lines of Credit – How they work

A home equity loan or line of credit allows you to borrow money, using your home's equity as collateral. Collateral is property that you pledge as a guarantee that you will repay a debt. If you do not repay the debt, the lender can take your collateral and sell the property to get their money back.

With a home equity loan or line of credit, you pledge your home as collateral. You can lose the home and be forced to move out, if you do not repay the debt. Equity is the difference between how much the home is worth and how much you owe on the mortgage (or mortgages, if you have more than one on the property).

A home equity loan (or line of credit) is a second mortgage that lets you turn equity into cash, allowing you to spend it on home improvements, debt consolidation, college education or other expenses. There are two types of home equity debt: home equity loans and home equity lines of credit, also known as HELOCs. Both are sometimes referred to as second mortgages, because they are secured by your property, just like the original, or primary, mortgage.

Home equity loans and lines of credit usually are repaid in a shorter period than first mortgages. Most commonly, mortgages are set up to be repaid over 30 years. Equity loans and lines of credit often have a repayment period of 15 or 20 years, although it might be as short as five or and as long as 30 years.

Equity Loan Borrowers – Beware

Homeowners beware that your home is your greatest asset and you do not want to put that asset at Risk. As a mortgage representative, I have seen where some homeowners who are already in financial trouble seek to absorb equity (funds) out of their only asset, which is their home. Please don't do it. If you are unable to pay your current expenses, do you honestly think adding an additional monthly payment without added income will help you overall? It will not. Do not allow anyone to tell you otherwise, especially the elderly or consumers who are already suffering with poor credit. These higher rated interest rate loans will only cause you to lose your property if you are unable to pay an additional loan.

Which is exactly what an equity loan is?

Also, beware of equity loans with variable rates since those rates will change as the interest rates increase.

Beware of equity loans with hidden terms and fees. Some scrupulous lenders will hide terms that change or increase your payments just as you become comfortable with a set payment in your budget, the payment changes because you missed a statement in small print on your loan disclosure. Please be extremely careful and read all documents. Also, make sure that you have copies of all documents that you sign. *Go as far as to initial each page and obtain a copy of your initialed or signed pages so that the documents are not changed after your signing.*

Last, do not sign away all of your equity in your home by obtaining an equity loan that will absorb all of your equity – unless

'An Invasion of (corporate) Locust' by Darlene R. Miles

you really do not care about the equity in your home. What if you have to sell your property? Where can you negotiate on the selling price if you have stripped all of your equity out of your home? Keep these concerns in mind.

Do you own your home? If so, it is likely to be your greatest single asset. Unfortunately, if you agree to a loan that is based on the equity you have in your home; you may be putting your most valuable asset at risk.

Homeowners-particularly elderly, minority and those with low incomes or poor credit-should be careful when borrowing money based on their home equity. Why? Certain abusive or exploitative lenders target these borrowers, who unwittingly may be putting their home on the line.

Abusive lending practices range from equity stripping and loan flipping to hiding loan terms and packing a loan with extra charges. The Federal Trade Commission urges you to be aware of these loan practices to avoid losing your home. Beware of lenders who call to offer an increased equity loan since some of these lenders will change the terms and increase your closing cost and fees, this is called 'loan flipping'.

Last, do not ever sign over your title for a mortgage loan. If you are every asked to do so – either walk away or consult an attorney. There is never a reason to sign over the title of your home to any lender when obtaining a mortgage or equity loan.

Mortgage Troubles and Avoiding Foreclosure

Situations occur during our lives that can result in missed mortgage payments; loss of job, illness, or a reduction in income. First I would say always pay your mortgage on time. However, if some unforeseen situation occurs that results in falling behind on your mortgage do not fall into Foreclosure - you do have options. In most cases, you can contact your mortgage company and request a *Forbearance agreement* (paying an increased amount with your regular mortgage payment for a specified period of time until your are caught up. You may also qualify for a loan *Modification* (reduction or increase to cover the missed payments); or *Recalculation* of your terms (extending the number of months the repay your mortgage with missed payments being placed on the end of your loan).

What is important here is that the mortgage company will generally want to work with you to save your home. In late 2007, several financial institutions have agreed to work with consumers on avoiding foreclosure. You can find a list of these financial institutions on the HUD website. It is important that you check to see if your financial company is listed since help is available for consumers. Unfortunately, the difference here is working with a financial company or bank verses an investment group. Investment groups who may have written a high-risk sub-prime mortgage loan (note here the term for high interest mortgage loans) may not be as willing to assist you. In this case, contact another financial institution immediately. Do not allow time to pass without responding to the mortgage delinquency. Do not avoid opening your mail out of fear.

Some temporary solutions may be to re-assess your available assets; do you have assets that you can sell to meet your mortgage payments such as a second car or jewelry? You may consider taking on a second job temporarily. You may also need to establish a budget and reprioritize your spending on items such as cable, gym memberships, or dining out. This is a time sensitive situation so act fast.

Avoid Mortgage Foreclosure Scams

Avoid using mortgage foreclosure prevention companies or foreclosure recovery scams. You don't have to pay a fee for foreclosure prevention. There are supposedly non-profit companies contacting consumers to assist with foreclosure prevention everyday. Where these agencies differ is that they will charge consumers one to three months of your mortgage payments to assist you in avoiding a foreclosure, pay those payments to your mortgage company instead.

Some companies will also contact you and state that they can stop your foreclosure immediately if you sign over your title of your home to them, don't do it. Several consumers have lost their homes to these types of scams. There should never be a reason to sign your home title over to a company or agency for their assistance.

If possible, do not allow home to be taken in a Foreclosure.

A Message to My Readers,

Thank you for your support, and your purchase of my book. I extend an offer to book clubs or discussion groups, to participate in a conference call with me to discuss my book. I extend this offer from January 1, 2008 through December 31, 2008. One weekly conference call will be granted to one group.

Please email your request and contact information to my email address below.

Thank you again for your support. I look forward to our discussions.

Darlene R. Miles
www.DarleneRMiles.com
myreaders@DarleneRMiles.com

The Qualities of Our Lives are determined by The
Quality of Our Decisions.

Thank You for Your Support

Darlene

'An Invasion of (corporate) Locust' by Darlene R. Miles

Disclaimer

The book, articles, and other materials (collectively "Content") in this book are provided for informational purposes only. The Content is not intended to, and does not, constitute legal advice. Neither my providing nor your reviewing the Content creates a client relationship between you. You should not act on any Content without seeking legal counsel.

The Content is protected by copyrights, trademarks, service marks and, other rights and laws. Any duplication of any kind, without written authorization from the author of this book is prohibited.

The Content is not guaranteed to be correct, complete, or up-to-date. The book is provided "AS-IS' and AS-Available'.

'An Invasion of (corporate) Locust' by Darlene R. Miles

'This great book will become an essential tool for 21st Century living.'

Samuel E. Tidmore IV
President/CEO
The Village TV

'This book is very detailed on its subject matter, and should serve as a reference book in every home. The book is written to guide the layperson against corporate intrusion into their personal and financial information. Every consumer will find this book to be extremely beneficial as a reference guide for life. There is information for everyone. I heartily recommend *'An Invasion of (corporate) Locust'* to all. "

Kwaku Obosu-Mensa Ph.D.